The Rottweiler

The Rottweiler

Essential reading for owners, breeders and judges

Jim Pettengell

DAVID & CHARLES
Newton Abbot   London

British Library Cataloguing in Publication Data

Pettengell, Jim
  The rottweiler.
  1. Rottweiler dog
  I. Title
  636.7'3   SF429.R7

  ISBN 0-7153-8827-4

Typeset by Typesetters (Birmingham) Ltd,
Smethwick, West Midlands
and printed in Great Britain
by Butler & Tanner Limited,
Frome and London
for David & Charles Publishers plc
Brunel House Newton Abbot Devon

Contents

Head study of Ch Saarlund Quanabie Mist who is Australia's most consistent show winner of the 1980s, and who, in 1986, won under both Mary Macphail and Joan Klem. Owned by T. and J. O'Brien, Mist was bred by Mr M. Shnukal

1 Origin and Early History

Tracing the history of any breed of dog is almost impossible prior to the 1850s, as authentic records only became available with the advent of the breed societies at about this time. However, one can draw certain conclusions from the history of man's own evolution, campaigns, commercial ventures and fossil remains; from these, an intelligent synthesis can be made.

Most accounts of Rottweiler history start with the Roman invasion of Germany and the crossing of the Alps by the legions in the first century AD. Statements made to support or reject this source are difficult to prove or disprove, but conclusions can be drawn from premises which have a measure of acceptability. One may say, without fear of contradiction, that the term 'Rottweiler' *cannot* be applied to the herding-guarding dogs used by the Roman legionaries during the course of their stay in Germany. The Roman influence lasted not much longer than two hundred years, and the dogs they brought with them certainly influenced the breed, whilst the settlement they built, *das Rote Wil* (which later became Rotwil and still later Rottweil), gave the breed the name by which it is known today. The Romans returned to Rome in the third century AD, after their defeat by the Germanic tribe known as the Alemanni.

Bazille, an early Rottweiler authority, accepted the theory that the breed is a direct descendant of the Bavarois Bouvier, dating back to Roman times, supported by evidence that this herding breed is found in areas serviced by the roads built by early Romans. On the other hand, Hans Korn, author of the classic *Der Rottweiler*, is of the opinion that the breed descended partly from this early Roman dog and partly from a breed that already existed in Germany, or arrived there from the north after the Roman invasion.

A feature that emerges very clearly in the history of the dog's evolution is that no dog was confined to a particular country. When one refers to a British or a German breed, the reference is only valid if applied to a definite and limited time period. A dog may have originated in a particular country, but its ancestors most probably came from outside, whilst its descendants may have emigrated to create further breeds elsewhere. The term 'pure breed' cannot be applied to any breed except in the very limited sense demanded by the breed or canine societies, in the context of pedigrees.

In the study of the Rottweiler, it is useful to have some idea of its antecedents, how the dog developed and how its instincts and capacities were modified and adapted to carry out its working role. This knowledge will help us to appreciate the modern breed and see its mental and physical characteristics in true perspective. This is the basis for any interpretation of the standard, the correctness of which is necessary to every breeder, judge and student.

Development of Breeds

The timing and nature of the dog's transition from wild to domesticated animal was influenced by man and the pace of his own evolution. Certain features were cultivated by selective breeding which enabled the dog's rate of improvement to accelerate because it was no longer dependent on natural selection or gradual adaptation to the environment. Man quickly appreciated the usefulness of developing certain traits to improve the performance of certain functions, and these traits were then appreciated most in the physical structure that best suited the required duties. Thus, both the instincts and the bodily make-up of a pointer are those which are most conducive to the role of hunting or gundog. Likewise, shepherding breeds were developed to fit both the work and the environment in which that work was to be performed. The droving and guard breeds were also carefully developed, with utility as the prime consideration, and, ironically, it is the factors that made them successful in their roles then that are, today, the cause of some concern to diligent breeders.

The great danger in manipulating natural instincts is that when these are of an aggressive nature, they can produce patterns of behaviour not fully understood, and hence not controlled. The mixed-up dog is a twentieth-century phenomenon that has given rise to a new profession – the canine psychiatrist. The great dilemma confronting the owners and breeders of the old drover-guards, is how best they can be integrated into a modern society that, quite often, is totally removed from the conditions they were originally bred to work in. This will be discussed more fully in later chapters.

Before we study the situation obtaining in Rome immediately prior to the invasion of Germany, let us look briefly at the period that preceded it. One factor that emerges is the astonishing distances that people travelled in those days when there was a great interchange of people between northern Asia and eastern Europe, along the trade routes. Nomadic tribes migrated over vast areas, and, in addition, the whole era was punctuated by a series of military campaigns. Philip of Macedonia, and later his son, Alexander, conquered the area as far as the Indus;

King Porus extended the Persian empire far from its home base, whilst Hannibal made his celebrated crossing of the Alps after a long journey from Carthage. Where people went, dogs went too, travelling far and wide, and the 'breeds' that figured most prominently were of the mastiff type. These, often enormous, dogs were introduced first to Gaul and Greece by the Phoenicians and then to Britain by the Romans. Centuries later, Marco Polo reported their presence in Asia, and it is generally agreed that this was probably their place of origin. It is also quite probable that such dogs had arrived in both north and south Germany prior to the Roman invasion.

The Molossi, in western Greece, and the Hycranians, from the shores of the Caspian Sea, were shepherd peoples who used large and aggressive dogs to guard and herd their cattle. These dogs were probably descended from the Tibetan mastiff of Asia and dogs acquired from these peoples would have been taken to Rome at some point.

The Roman Influence

Dogs played a significant part in the life of the Roman citizen, as they were used to guard homes and farms from marauders, control cattle, help in hunting and, not least, to participate in many of the sadistic spectacles seen in the Colosseum where they would be pitted against either men or wild beasts, in fights to the death. For a time the Molossus was the most popular fighting dog (a large mastiff-type breed), but this was later replaced by an equally ferocious dog known as *Canus pugnaces* – which soon became a generic term for all fighting breeds. This breed was imported from Britain and, in AD 14, the defeated British chief, Cunobelinus, was obliged to accept a treaty with the Emperor Tiberius under which the British were required to supply to Rome, amongst other things, both hunting and fighting dogs.

It can therefore be seen that a gene pool of dogs existed in ancient Rome that would one day influence not only the Rottweiler, but many other drover-guarding breeds as well.

The Romans, and Julius Caesar in particular, influenced the character of herding dogs by the reforms introduced into military tactics. Rome raised the first-ever standing army and thus caused a great change in the traditional attitude to logistics, especially with regard to food. Caesar introduced fresh meat into his soldiers' rations and this was taken to campaigns 'on the hoof' rather than in limited, salted, form as in earlier times. Such rations could not be effectively moved without the controlling influence of dogs whose expertise, both in herding and guarding cattle, improved with each campaign. This development brought the dog's character into sharp focus, as was seen in later years in the long treks to the Rottweil cattle markets. The Romans required a· particular type of dog for this role and these had to be large and powerful, with the ability to work for long periods, with their masters, under arduous conditions. Needless to say, such dogs could also be decidedly unfriendly when the situation demanded.

One may therefore draw the conclusion that the basis for the breed's character and capacity was established indirectly by the reforms of Julius Caesar and directly by pressures placed on the dogs by both their environment and the work they were expected to perform. These qualities were refined over the years that followed; during the fifteenth century by cattle drovers and in later centuries by the Swabian butchers. It is said that, having sold cattle at the Rottweil market, the drovers made the long and perilous journey home with their gold in a purse tied around their dog's neck where it was perfectly safe. Such stories are wonderful testimony to the implicit faith of the owners on the one hand and the unshakable integrity of the dogs on the other.

The process of refinement and development was continued in the early part of this century by the codification of breeding principles, the final polish being applied by the breed clubs, of which the ADRK must be especially singled out for its influence after 1921.

Although pedigrees are a relatively recent innovation, this should not be taken to suggest that earlier breeders were any less able to recognise and use superior animals in developing the various breeds. Two factors assured steady progress, the first being the observation and selection of types of dogs most likely to be good at their job. This done, only those who actually proved capable had the opportunity of perpetuating their genes. The hard reality was that any dog or bitch that proved less than up to the work just did not survive. The most able animals would live longer, and their influence would therefore be more lasting than those who died younger. These two selective factors were the foundation of the character, integrity, aggression and stubbornness on which later generations of breeders were to add recognisable type, until we arrive at what we know today as the Rottweiler.

The Roman Invasion of Germany

A glance at the relief map of southern Europe shows the awesome mountain barrier that separates Italy from her northern neighbours. Crossing this monster, especially in those early days, was a formidable task. However, crossed it was, first by Hannibal with his elephants in 218 BC and later by the Roman legions. Hannibal crossed via the Little St Bernard Pass, whereas it is generally held that the Romans crossed via the more easterly St Gotthard Pass. Most Rottweiler authorities have

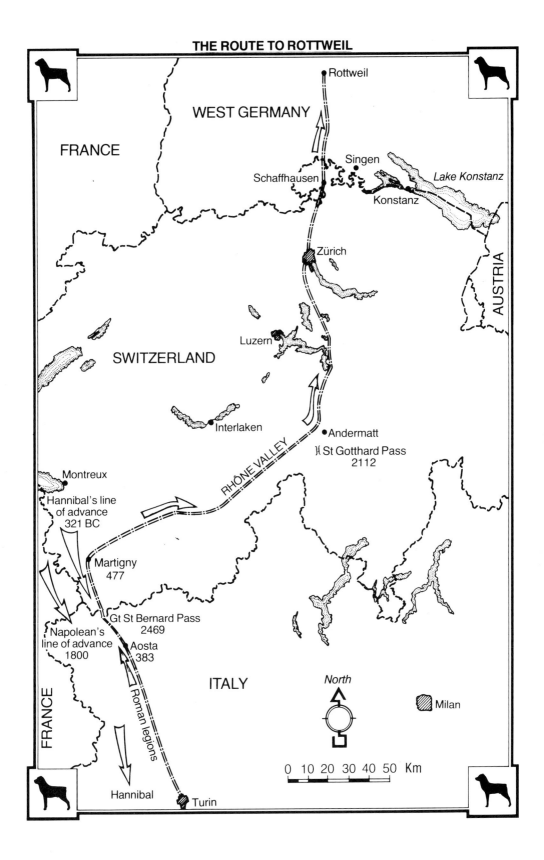

THE ROUTE TO ROTTWEIL

Rottweil

WEST GERMANY

FRANCE

Singen

Schaffhausen

Lake Konstanz

Konstanz

Zürich

AUSTRIA

SWITZERLAND

Luzern

Interlaken

Andermatt

)(St Gotthard Pass
2112

RHÔNE VALLEY

Montreux

Hannibal's line
of advance
321 BC

Martigny
477

Gt St Bernard Pass
2469

Napolean's
line of advance
1800

Aosta
383

FRANCE

ITALY

North

Milan

Roman legions

Hannibal

Turin

0 10 20 30 40 50 Km

always agreed with this notion – Schangle, in his thesis, and the ADRK, in *The Rottweiler in Word and Picture* and *The Regulations Regarding Breeding Matters of the Rottweiler*, are specific about this. Hans Korn, in *Der Rottweiler*, is noncommittal, merely stating the Alpine passes used by the legions.

The author, having viewed the St Gotthard, had doubts as to its use and these were confirmed, following correspondence with Mr Ballmer, of the Swiss embassy in Australia, and Dr Frei-Stolba, of Berne University, who provided information which clearly showed that the most likely route used was via the Great St Bernard Pass, lying somewhat to the east of the pass used by Hannibal. It is probable that the St Gotthard only became passable as late as the eleventh century.

Having broken through the mountain barrier, the initial thrust of the Roman legions was in a north-easterly direction, following the Rhône valley, before marching north. In AD 74 the Eleventh Legion, known as the *Claudia Pia Fedulus*, conquered the area later to be known as Rottweil. They built a *Kastellan*, or stronghold, on the left bank of the Neckar river, at its junction with the river Prim. Following custom, they set up altars, naming them after the Flavian Emperor Vespasian, and the area became known as the Arae Flavia.

En route to Germany, many dogs would have settled in the outposts established by the Romans in Switzerland; the descendants of these Roman mastiff-type dogs would acquire characteristics that differentiated them from the dogs of the neighbouring valleys, after which they were named. In 1908 the Swiss cynologist Prof A. Heim identified four such breeds, these being the Bernese, the Appenzell, the Entlebucker and the Sennehund. Could these breeds be near relatives of our Rottweiler?

These dogs now appear different in form, both from the present-day Rottweiler and their own ancestors of the first century. Some characteristics, however, are common to both, and the first Rottweiler standard did in fact serve as a blueprint for the Rottweiler *and* the Leonberger – a dog not unlike the Swiss mountain dogs. Portions of the Sennehund standard could equally be applied to the Rottweiler, whilst early pictures of the Entlebuckers, although the smallest of these breeds, may be mistaken for Rottweilers. In considering the relationship of the Swiss cattle dogs to the Rottweiler, one must remember that the division occurred in the first century. At that time all these breeds belonged to the same broad type. During the course of the next 1,900 years, travellers who visited Germany met what Korn describes as 'local herding dogs and broad-mouthed forms of British and Dutch bulldogs', and interbreeding obviously took place among the different types.

As the Roman conquest moved north, the area which had once been the limit of its influence became a centre of communication and the hub from which roads led in all directions. The geographical significance of the area, and its accessibility, is apparent. It was important, tactically, to the Romans in their administration of Germany. When, in about AD 260, Roman military influence waned, commercial application took over. It was a thriving area where cattle, sheep, goats and pigs were taken for sale in the many markets. Dogs, particularly those able to herd or guard, were at a premium. During the Middle Ages, many butchers were naturally attracted to this centre and their dogs were very much a necessity.

The fame of these dogs spread to neighbouring countries, such as Switzerland, France and Austria. No journey to or from a cattle market could be made, in safety, without both the companionship and assistance of the stalwart drover dogs. The emerging breed's versatility was adapted to many purposes too. The Black Forest area to the west abounded in game, and strong, fearless dogs were used in hunting bear and boar. Others were used to pull the carts of the various traders who plied their products (meat, milk, vegetables, bread) around outlying villages.

The City of Rottweil

No history of the breed would be complete without some reference to the city from which it derives its name and with which, to this day, it still retains strong associations.

Five hundred years after the departure of the Romans, new conquerors, in the shape of the Franks of the Holy Roman Empire, arrived and exerted considerable influence on the area. A Christian church was built and a new settlement grew up. The site, like earlier Roman ones, was called *wil* (from *villa*) and, to distinguish it from others, it was called *das Rote Wil* after the red colour of the tiles and bricks unearthed from earlier Roman buildings and reused.

The author is greatly indebted to Dr Hecht, the city archivist, for information about his city. He states that Rottweil and dogs are synonymous, pointing out that the dog featured in numerous early forms of art. These ranged from mosaics in Roman residences, created around AD 180, to stone carvings featured on a chapel tower.

Although dogs were not generally popular – beyond their utilitarian role – Rottweil held them in great esteem. In 1468, for example, two citizens from Schomberg seized a dog they believed to be the property of a fellow citizen. The dog lovers of Rottweil threw them into jail where they remained until the intervention of the Archduchess Mechtild. In 1661, a Rottweil councillor, Jakob Pfister, suspecting his dog had rabies, killed it, and was forced to resign his position. In 1695, Ignaz Maurer, having had an 'argument' with his barber's dog, foolishly killed it and was lucky to escape with only a severe fine of three gulden.

Rottweil had its dog problems too. In 1610, the local priest announced that the dog population was to be reduced and superfluous and biting dogs were to be destroyed. Biters, however, were allowed a respite for a first offence; dogs were branded each time they transgressed, and the capital penalty was not exacted until the fourth offence, although owners paid damages each time. In 1686, the law required all dogs to be kept indoors at night and each citizen was allowed only one dog – the public executioner, on the other hand, was allowed four, no doubt reflecting the alienating nature of his work!

Alas! The butchers who did so much for the Rottweiler were not always above criticism. A letter written by a lady resident in 1849 stated: 'the thing that is hardest to bear about these dogs is when the worst of them gather in packs and fight; invariably this happens in front of the town hall. To make matters worse the masters, apprentices and the servant boys show great delight when their dogs excel in street fighting'. This was against the law, enacted in 1841, that required all biting dogs to be muzzled.

It was during this period that the Rottweiler began to go into decline, largely because the changing world around it no longer had need of the very assets that had made it such a necessary working companion. Cattle droving became illegal; it became more efficient for carts to take larger loads, pulled by donkeys or horses; the dangers from bears, boars and wolves – as well as human predators – was rapidly receding. The importance of Rottweil also diminished, following its partial destruction by Napoleon, which delivered a mortal blow to its independence – it became part of Württemburg.

It was reported, sadly, that in 1905 only one Rottweiler bitch was registered in the city and this was to be the breed's lowest point of popularity. Happily, the situation then took an upward turn as a result of the efforts of interested devotees in other areas of Germany. By 1950, 420 dogs were registered in the city with a further 100 in the outskirts. The attitude of the Rottweil council and its affection for the breed was a great help. Today, the city endows each Rottweiler litter with a 400 DM payment to its breeder – rather different to the attitude of administrations in most other countries!

The ADRK, with its headquarters in Stuttgart, recognised the place that Rottweil occupies in the breed's history and the first Klub Sieger show was held in Rottweil in October 1971. The fourth show was also held at the same venue which is appropriate and brings much credit to the city, its inhabitants and to the officials of the ADRK.

In concluding this brief historical look at the Rottweiler, any attempt to appraise the relative contributions made at different points in time to the breed seems quite unfair and inappropriate. A superstructure is only as sound as the foundation on which it is built, and the metaphorical extension of this would be to conclude that the Romans selected the ground and cleared the way for the Renaissance drovers to lay the foundations; the Swabian butchers built the superstructure and the finish was applied by the German breed clubs.

2 The Rottweiler in Germany

Although Rottweilers made their first appearances in the show ring about the year 1882, it was not until 1899 that they were both bred and exhibited on a systematic basis. In 1901, in Stuttgart, Albert Kull formed the International Club for Leonberger and Rottweiler Dogs and also produced the first standard which was a joint one for both breeds. However, the club was short-lived and it was not until 1905 that the breed again attracted much attention. In that year, on the occasion of the Heidelberg Kennel Club Show, it was decided to give the club's president a gift of a dog which should be 'a fine dog of unusual breed and irreproachable character'. The cynologist Boppel was consulted and he suggested a Rottweiler, a choice agreed with by the club chairman, Albert Graf; indeed, so impressed was he with the breed that he became secretary of the *Deutscher Rottweiler Klub* (DRK) when it was formed at Heidelberg in January 1907.

The German Breed Clubs

Hardly had the DRK been created when a member was expelled and this led to the formation of a second club, in April of the same year, which was called the *International Rottweiler Klub* (IRK). This was not an ideal situation, as both clubs kept their own stud books which ran on the same lines with similar objectives – a sure way of guaranteeing confusion. To make matters worse a third club, the South German Rottweiler Club, was formed in 1919. Fortunately, good sense prevailed and negotiations between the DRK and the IRK resulted in a merger to create the *Allgemeiner Deutscher Rottweiler Klub* (ADRK). This major event took place in 1921, at Wurzburg, and the negotiators were E. Stiefel, chairman of the IRK, and O. Hell, chairman of the DRK. Stiefel was appointed chairman of the ADRK and, appropriately, when he resigned in 1926, Hell took his place. The unification of the Rottweiler clubs was finally completed when, in 1924, the third club capitulated and joined the ADRK.

The most important result of having a single club was that a single stud book was produced thereafter. However, the attitudes of the formerly separate club members were not easily reconciled. The DRK had placed greater emphasis on working qualities and the heads of its dogs were weak, being predominantly of the pointer type, called *Jagdhundköpf*. The IRK had eliminated this weakness in their dogs which were bred much more with uniform type and conformation as the prime objective. The influence of the IRK was soon felt, not only by the superior attitude to breeding, but also by the sheer weight of membership.

The IRK foundation dog was Leo v Cannstatt No 29. He was bred by Gottlieb Haug in the Plattenhardt kennels and was whelped in July 1908. Leo was owned by Huckele who led the breakaway group in 1919 that formed the South German Club, but he was later purchased by Heinrich Boppel. The superior head found in the IRK dogs was due to the influence of Sgr Lord vd Teck 413 whose broad skull and powerful lower jaw were passed on to his progeny – he was the first great producer, siring sixty-three litters. His sire, Lord Remo v Schifferstadt 130, was the subject of controversy due to his size of 72cm (28in), this being 6cm (2½in) over the then limit. However, Stiefel, his owner, was determined that his quality should be passed on and he was mated to Fanny vd Teck 270. From the resulting litter, Lord 413 and Minna 411 vd Teck were mated, the first brother-to-sister mating to take place, and they produced the Torfwerk 'A' litter, whelped in 1918.

In this litter was Arco Torfwerk 955, the breed's greatest producer until Bulli v Hungerbühl appeared in the early 1970s. Arco sired 100 litters and his almost unbelievable influence is seen throughout his line, especially in Fels v Stuttgart 7471, Alfons (Brendle) 12646, Arno v Zenthoff 18896, Odo v Gaisburg 20852, the Bexback 'G' litter, and the greatest of them all, Hackel v Köhlerwald 15691 – the first triple *Sieger*.

The DRK breeding was represented, essentially, by three dogs. Graf's Sgr Russ v Brückenbuckel 1, together with Ralph v Neckar 2 and Max vd Strahlenburg 48. Even here the IRK influence is shown through the remarkable Leo. Russ sired 20 per cent of the DRK breeding in Volume 1 of their stud book, but his only influence was through his son, Rhino v Kork 188. Rhino's grandfather, on his dam's side, was Leo. The Strahlenburg line made a large contribution to police dogs, although Max carried the typical pointer head. Ralph was lacking in substance. It is interesting that the IRK favoured close line-breeding and, in the case of Lord x Minna, this was taken to the optimum level of inbreeding. The result was predictable, but it must be stated that success was due as much to the quality of the dogs as to the principle. The Pfalzgau kennel also used this system, but with inferior dogs; the results were poor but, fortunately, not permanent.

The emergence of the German breed clubs coincided rather fortuitously with a new attitude to dogdom – or were they, instead, a

Important early German Rottweilers

Leo v Cannstatt

Lord Remo v Schifferstadt

Lord vd Teck

Odo v Gaisburg

product of it? The Rottweiler's historic usefulness had begun to diminish in a changing environment influenced by the industrial revolution; greater wealth, more leisure, growing technology and increasing urbanisation were eroding old values. The Rottweiler had now to fit into a world where *Siegers* and *Schutzhunds* replaced the intrepid cattle herder. It is difficult to say whether the philosophy of the day was deliberately developed by the breed's pioneers, or whether it was an extemporaneous measure of the times. One cannot underestimate the capacity of men like Korn, or fail to appreciate the greatness of their contribution, both to the breed's development and to its new relevancy in a changing world.

By the introduction of registers, the breed clubs left the first historical impression of the breed and, by virtue of the information they contained, enabled future breeders to maintain and improve the Rottweiler. That the clubs did not lose sight of the original Rottweiler type is evidenced by the words of one breeder, Julius Wallenstein, on the occasion of acquiring one of the 'new' dogs from the stud book lines of 1907. 'I was not a little surprised at seeing again the same breed that I kept thirty years ago for cattle driving and cart pulling.'

The majority of Rottweilers came from Swabia and whilst black and brown were the predominant colours, there were also others, such as tan, as well as many with white markings. The ADRK decided that black and brown should be the only permitted colours and applied themselves to the selection of only such dogs to be used in breeding. The club issued a standard which was applied wisely and brought about a gradual uniformity in the breed.

The programme of development preserved the criteria that had distinguished the breed over many years, but it also rounded off the rough edges, improving looks without sacrificing character. A common goal was defined and uniform methods of attaining it were accepted, because the breeders were bound by a common tie – a genuine love of the breed. This tie, as other countries later found, is always in need of reinforcing. The first stud book issued by the ADRK listed dogs and bitches separately; 500 were featured, dogs 1–286, and bitches 1–214. It is interesting to note that Leo v Schwarzwald 11, a consistent winner at international shows, had no recorded parents. By 1911, all registrations contained the names of both parents, but puppies were registered individually; the alphabetical system had not yet been introduced. More and more information began to appear on registrations about a dog's character, conformation and performance. The fact that it was all available in a single publication was of enormous benefit to breeders.

The breed warden system was introduced in 1924 and each regional club, of which there were forty, had a warden elected by its members.

The warden inspected potential brood bitches, was familiar with the performance and antecedents of sires, and examined each litter. Wardens attended all shows and met monthly to report their findings. This intelligence was collated and the total Rottweiler picture in Germany was presented to the wardens on a regular basis. From 1933, all registrations included details of sires and dams, the number of puppies alive and dead and performance of studs, with attention focused on the quality of all progeny. It is pertinent to note here that some other countries have flirted with the idea of installing a breed warden system. It must be borne in mind that the quality of wardens, related to their experience and knowledge of the breed, is imperative, and the success of the system will rest entirely on this factor. German breed wardens have an unrivalled opportunity, denied to people in other countries, as they are constantly exposed to the conditions that make the system work.

The ADRK slowly tightened its grip on breeding, but, very wisely, the emphasis was on tolerance, and the changes were gradual. In 1930 the working degree *Schutzhund* was introduced, although the classes 1, 2 and 3 were a later development. Mistakes in pedigrees were rectified and registrations became possible only where grandparents were also registered. Dogs had to be surveyed as 'suitable for breeding', *Zuchttauglich*, and then 'approved for breeding', *Angekört*. A list was published containing the names of dogs withdrawn from breeding, either because of a flaw that showed up in the dog, or because progeny failed to measure up to the stringent interpretation of the standard. Breeders producing inferior stock were warned and, if this was not heeded, their litters were refused registration. The Pfalzgau kennel, mentioned earlier, was deregistered after such a warning about temperament. Even in those early days the influence of environment and upbringing on temperament was recognised and attention drawn to this vital aspect.

Confusion still existed with names. Owners were allowed to add their suffix to the registered name of the kennel from which the dog came. This practice was later discontinued and it became mandatory to register puppies using the alphabetical system.

The direction of the club in the 1930s had strong political overtones. Korn wrote of 'a certain restlessness and uncertainty, our interests being tampered with from above according to the tendencies of the political regime' and 'Orders and obligations which were absolutely foreign and irrelevant to us dog fanciers were meant to limit and restrict to authority-guided paths the independence of our sport.' The implementation of these policies is evident in the events that followed. The direct influence of the ADRK was replaced by policy direction which came from the new National Association for Canine Matters, *Reichsverband für*

Hundewesen, controlled by a ministry; this had replaced the more benign authority of the German Cartel for Canine Matters, *Deutsche Kartell für Hundewesen*. Military requirements demanded a courier dog, into which role the Rottweiler was to be converted – rather like an overweight Dobermann or pointer! Opinion in northern Germany favoured this, but, fortunately, it foundered on hard-core opposition from the south, although not before some experimentation had taken place. It was found that the lighter dog suffered in character and self-confidence; moreover, the existing type, when trained and fit, proved its capability beyond doubt. In 1939 all Rottweiler registrations from Austria and Czechoslovakia were controlled by the new ministry!

Naturally, the breed suffered during the Second World War, as scarcity of food and the deployment of manpower influenced breeding. The position was, however, better than in other countries, as the registrations show: 1940 – 284, 1941 – 289 and 1942 – 350. In fact, the breed survived the ravages of war remarkably well and the spirit of the ADRK was undaunted. The level of quality remained consistent and, under the direction of the ADRK, which regained control in 1943, the breed was ready to face the challenge of post-war reconstruction.

The selection for breeding approval has always been rigorously applied and no animal is allowed to breed until it has been approved. The first test, for eligibility, is called the *Zuchttauglichkeitsprüfung* (ZTP). To enter the examination the dog must be at least eighteen months of age, free of disqualifying faults and its hip status must be acceptable (see page 26). During the examination the *Körmeister* completes a test sheet, filling in such details as date and place of test, his name, name of dog and date whelped, name of parents and breeder, and the address of owner. The dog's physical characteristics such as height, weight, length of back etc are measured, together with a general critique of the dog. The *Körmeister* completes a proforma test sheet in which a grading is given for the following thirteen characteristics: confidence, fearlessness, temperament, stamina, observation, trainability, suspiciousness, sharpness, courage, fighting instinct, protective instinct, hardness, excitability. The dog is also tested for gun sureness. The dog is judged to have passed or failed and the result is published in *Der Rottweiler* and the stud book. If it fails the first time it may return six months later. Prior to May 1984 the dog was allowed to return only once. After that date it may return as often as required to pass. This relaxation did not please some members and two of the senior *Körmeisters* resigned.

The next test, the *Körung*, is much more selective. The examination is held twice a year; the following qualifications are necessary: dogs must be three years old and have a Sch H3 degree; bitches must be two and a half years and have Sch H1. Animals must have been graded V (*vorzüglich*-excellent) in conformation, or SG (*sehr gut*–very good) under different judges and have no sign of hereditary faults. Dogs are weighed and measured. The same proforma test sheet as used for the ZTP is completed but the tests are more stringent. The object of the test is to select only the most suitable so that they may be used more extensively. When the dog qualifies, its pedigree is endorsed *gekört* for two years. These details are recorded in the pedigree and advertised. During these two years the dog's performance as a producer is studied by the warden. After two years the dog appears at another *Körung* to be re-evaluated. Dogs are required to produce progeny from three litters, a bitch only one. If it passes, the pedigree is endorsed *gekört bis EzA*; qualified for the period of his/her breeding life which is nine years for dogs and eight for bitches. This is the highest breeding qualification. If the dog fails, breeding approval is withdrawn.

Early German Figures of Note

We tend to think and speak of deeds performed by committees or clubs, often without giving due credit to the personalities whose imagination and energy made these deeds possible.

Hans Korn, one-time president of the ADRK and author of the classic work *Der Rottweiler*, stands out in this context. Others were to follow him, whilst contemporaries and those who preceded him, such as Stiefel, Paulli, Graf, Schraeder and Boppel, helped to make his contribution possible and ensured it would be lasting. Korn himself refers to 'Emil Stiefel, our late patriarch, accomplishing a heroic task.' Forty years of stud book recorded.

Paulli, who appears to have shouldered the entire IRK burden during the war years, and who died in 1920 before his plans could come to fruition, deserves special mention. His widow continued the Paulli breed association and the ADRK acknowledged her work in 1926 with an honorary membership. Two other personalities who shared the same honour were Albert Graf, prominent in the first Rottweiler club, and Richard Schraeder, the DRK secretary at the time of the IRK–DRK merger.

Franze Bazille was a tireless worker for the breed, until his death in 1952. He maintained the breed register, making corrections in early pedigrees, and ensured that existing records were accurate and in a form that would be usable. He was assisted in his work by Frau Josephine Rieble-Zeller, secretary of the ADRK for twenty-five years. Bazille's other great contribution was in preserving the character of the Rottweiler. The type of dog that was handed down was a working breed and it had only two essentials – soundness and character. Whilst Bazille realised that beauty shows, with the emphasis on form, would provide some place for the breed, he also recognised the need for strong action to preserve its character. His work, in establishing criteria for character-testing, and discovering and eliminating all weaknesses, has no greater testimony than the fact that the rules, formulated by him forty years ago, remain almost unchanged to this day. Bazille did not solve a problem – his anticipation and foresight prevented one from occurring. A great number of breeders today do not appreciate how working breeds are affected by the loss of employment and by the vast amount of money and time spent on beauty shows, or the steps that are necessary to preserve breed character in the shallowness of a climate that is, frankly, artificial.

In the 1930s, type was endangered by the attempts of northern breeders, such as Cornell, Grohse and Passick, who were anxious to transform the breed into a sporting form, and the firm hand of people like Korn and Köpf, and the breeding talents of Weber, were needed to retain the sturdy robustness and unshakable character of the Rottweiler.

I am sure that these personalities will stand whatever test history cares to make, and names like Berger, Nagelschmidt, Glow and Bruns will find a place in the Rottweiller Hall of Fame.

Perhaps special mention should be made here of Miss Marieanne Bruns's contribution, particularly to the breed in Britain after the Second World War. The early Mallion dogs, imported by Mrs Joanna Chadwick, were raised in the Eulenspiegel kennel of Miss Bruns and, together with Captain Roy-Smith's Ajax v Fuhrenkamp, formed the nucleus of British breeding. Miss Bruns held the high office of Chief Breed Warden. She devoted fifty years of her life to the breed, and it was the author's great privilege to correspond with her for many years. To this day she remains an active breeder.

It is to be hoped that people witnessing the spectacle of a dozen Rottweilers going through their paces in the ring, savouring the play of the sun on rippling muscles and the rapport between dog and handler in a trial, will spare a moment to consider the part played by the people mentioned above. Most of them have now departed from the scene, but the faint echo of their footsteps may still be heard if one has the time and is disposed to listen.

ADRK Stud Books and Pedigrees

All German Rottweiler owners are presented with complete information on every dog and bitch in their country, and this information is then applied to their own breeding programmes. The system is not unique to

Rottweilers, it also applies to some other breeds; it enables the Germans to have a far greater insight into their breed than is the case in most other countries. The information is presented on a regular basis in three ways:

1 Stud books (*Zucht-Kör* und *Leistungsbuch*). These are issued annually.
2 Pedigrees (*Ahnentafel*). These, like the stud books, are issued by the ADRK.
3 A magazine called *Der Rottweiler* issued monthly by the ADRK.

The stud book is the bible of Rottweiler owners and is in constant use. The format changes from time to time but it is divided into a number of sections which, collectively, carry a wealth of data.

The following is a description of the current book which applies to 1984, Band number LXVIII. Band LXVIII shows the numbers of all dogs registered in 1984 starting with the numbers 63006 to 65053. The stud book for 1935, Band XIX, has the numbers 20928–21725. A simple calculation gives the number of pups registered between 1935–84. A description of the contents of the 1984 book is as follows: Pages 1–8 list kennels registering pups in alphabetical order. Pages 9–70 have all litter details listed numerically. Each entry includes numbers born, culled, and registered, kennel prefix and address of owners, names of parents and grandparents, and also hip status. Pages 71–140 have the *Körung* details of all dogs examined. Each dog has two pages in which the following details are recorded. Place, date, *Körmeister*, names of dog, parents and grandparents with HD status, date when the period of breeding approval expires, addresses of breeder and owner, and the weight, height, and other physical details of the dog.

The same proforma sheet used for the ZTP is completed but in a much stricter fashion. Pages 148–464 show the details of all dogs appearing for the ZTP. Pages 466–468 publish the names of dogs deferred from tests. Page 469 names the dogs that have been withdrawn from breeding and gives the reasons. Pages 471–510 list names and evaluations of all dogs X-rayed showing whether breeding approval has been granted or withheld. Pages 511–519 contain names of new kennel owners showing prefix and address. Pages 520–614 have the complete details of all *Schutzhund* trials.

Pedigrees
Pedigrees are issued on sheets measuring 38 × 28cm (15 × 11in). The sheet is divided into two parts. The top half is confined to administrative details whilst the bottom has the actual pedigree. The top half has ten sections. The first has the name of the dog and the owner's address. The second the number of pups born, died, culled and registered and

the registered number of the dog. The third confirms these details by the secretary of the ADRK. The fourth has the name and address of the owner of the pup and date of transfer; the fifth has provision for the future transfer of the dog. The sixth the date of X-ray and the tattoo number; tattooing is done by the breed warden before the pup is eight weeks old. The seventh has the hip evaluation details confirmed by the ADRK secretary and signed by him. The eighth has a record of ZTP details and whether the dog passed or failed. The ninth has details of the *Körung* and the tenth details of the second *Körung* when the dog is endorsed or, in the case of failure, when breeding approval is withdrawn.

The lower half of the sheet shows a four generation pedigree with a critique of parents and grandparents, the working qualifications, show wins and the hip evaluation of every animal on the sheet.

There are pink and white pedigrees. Colour of the pedigree form depends on the qualifications of breeding partners. Categories are:

Kör und Leistungszucht (Pink pedigree) Both parents are qualified (*gekört*) and all grandparents have working degrees.
Leistungszucht (Pink pedigree) Parents and grandparents have working degrees.
Körzucht (Pink pedigree) Both parents are qualified for breeding (*gekört*)
Gebrauchundzucht (White pedigree) Both parents have working degrees.
Einfache Zucht (White pedigree) Only one parent has a working degree.

Der Rottweiler

Der Rottweiler, with a coloured photograph of a Rottweiler on the cover, contains the following information. Reports of shows usually held in Germany, but sometimes in places such as Mexico, USA, Canada etc, reports from all wardens by district, names of all new members, non-German members are shown under the heading of *Ausland*, results of shows, trials, tests, HD evaluations, details of forthcoming shows, dates and places of all matings and articles which are of interest, issued monthly.

Hip Dysplasia (HD)

The Germans were one of the first nations to embark on a programme to control hip dysplasia; the decision was taken at a conference in Frankfurt in 1968. The programme was introduced, very sensibly, in stages starting in 1972. The Dutch Kennel Club implemented a control programme in the same year. Pedigrees were issued only to pups whose parents were HD free. This had the effect of removing some of their top dogs from breeding and many litters were not registered. Four years later the rule was relaxed to allow dogs with mild HD to breed. The German attitude to gradual control is reflected in the comments made by the Chief Breed Warden, Mr Willi Hedtke, in 1984. 'This was the only way to gain *some* control. Even with close HD selection one must not forget the correct mental characteristics and other hereditary faults. It is not always easy to consider all aspects of breeding'.

There are five grades of HD.

1 HD – Normal hips free of HD. *Zucht und Körfähig*
2 HD +/– Minor changes. *Zucht und Körfähig*
3 HD+ HD is present but not severe. *Zuchttauglich*. Breeding restricted to particular partners. Not eligible for *Körung*
4 HD ++ Breeding forbidden
5 HD+++ Breeding forbidden

Dogs graded in category 3 (HD+) are eligible for the ZTP but not for the *Körung*.

The ADRK has a panel of approved veterinarians who take X-rays in a manner prescribed by the ADRK. Veterinarians who do not comply with regulations are removed from the approved list. X-rays are sent to the University of Göttingen for scrutiny. Each dog is identified by the tattoo number inside its ear. When the letters HD° appear they indicate that the hip status is unknown. This may apply to very old dogs or to pups whose hip evaluation has not been completed.

One may see from the foregoing details why the Germans are so well informed about their dogs. Many people in other nations are of the opinion that our KCs could do well to adopt the German method. However, it is not practical in an all-breed organisation, although it would be of immense value if it were.

The Great Producers

The influence of IRK bloodlines at the beginning of recorded Rottweiler history has been stated earlier, as has the importance of Leo v Cannstatt, whose title of Father of the Breed is unchallenged. Leo's influence is shown by viewing Chart 1. Also mentioned in the early part of this chapter is Arco Torfwerk 955 whose influence was carried on through his famous grandson, Fels v Stuttgart 7471. The line is continued through two important dogs, Alfons (Brendle) 12646 and Arno v Zenthoff 18896. Alfons sired twenty-six litters, producing 130 puppies.

The most important Alfons son was Hackel v Köhlerwald who is regarded as the first of the 'modern' dogs and the first triple *Sieger*. Hackel was bred by Weber and owned by Jakob Köpf, head breeding supervisor of the ADRK, and one of the most successful and knowledgeable breeders of all time. His comments on the dog at the fiftieth

Chart 1: the influence of Leo v Cannstatt

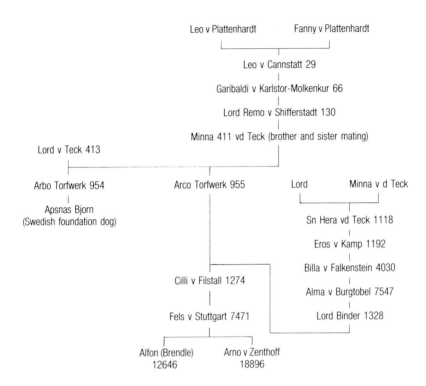

Leo v Plattenhardt   Fanny v Plattenhardt

Leo v Cannstatt 29

Garibaldi v Karlstor-Molkenkur 66

Lord Remo v Shifferstadt 130

Minna 411 vd Teck (brother and sister mating)

Lord v Teck 413

Arbo Torfwerk 954   Arco Torfwerk 955   Lord   Minna v d Teck

Apsnas Bjorn
(Swedish foundation dog)

Sn Hera vd Teck 1118

Eros v Kamp 1192

Billa v Falkenstein 4030

Cilli v Filstall 1274

Alma v Burgtobel 7547

Fels v Stuttgart 7471

Lord Binder 1328

Alfon (Brendle)   Arno v Zenthoff
12646   18896

Chart 2: the influence of Fels v Stuttgart

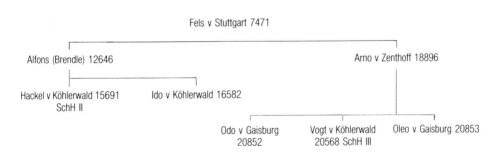

Fels v Stuttgart 7471

Alfons (Brendle) 12646   Arno v Zenthoff 18896

Hackel v Köhlerwald 15691   Ido v Köhlerwald 16582
SchH II

Odo v Gaisburg   Vogt v Köhlerwald   Oleo v Gaisburg 20853
20852   20568 SchH III

Doldi vd Helenenhöhe, a rare photograph of this influential bitch (Photo: courtesy M. Bruns)

The great triple Sieger *Hackel v Köhlerwald passed on both looks and character to his progeny, making him, possibly, the breed's greatest sire* (courtesy M. Bruns)

anniversary of the ADRK are revealing, not only of the dog, but also of the man who, unfortunately, was killed in a motor car accident at the age of seventy-five.

I must mention one [dog] in particular, Hackel v Köhlerwald. He was the best Rottweiler that I have ever known. Unfortunately I was not his breeder, but I did have the good luck to own him for ten years. Hackel was smarter than any dog I ever had. His nerves were of steel, he had his total freedom, did everything right, was frightened by nothing and yet was very good-natured so that anyone could touch him. If necessary he attacked immediately, but never seriously hurt anyone. He sired the greatest number of Rottweilers, and did so to the breed's great benefit. My wish; another Hackel in my life. He does not have to be so handsome as the Köhlerwald dog, but he would have to bring a Rottweiler's character like Hackel's. It is possible that other working breeds are better in this or that characteristic, but in steadiness, courage and aggressiveness, none is superior to the Rottweiler.

1 June 1957

Hackel sired eighty-two litters, with 375 puppies being registered. He produced over 100 champions and the greatest number of dogs graded 'excellent'.

Chart 3: the influence of Hackel v Köhlerwald

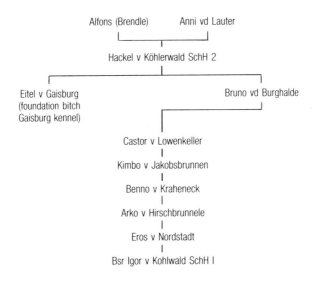

His influence through Igor v Kohlwald 32149 SchH I provided the main breeding lines in Britain, the USA and Scandinavia. Igor was bred by Eugen Schertel (Saar region) and owned by Ewald Kuhlman. He was whelped on 17 May 1951 and was the *Bundessieger* of 1954. His breeder

Chart 4: the influence of Igor v Kohlwald

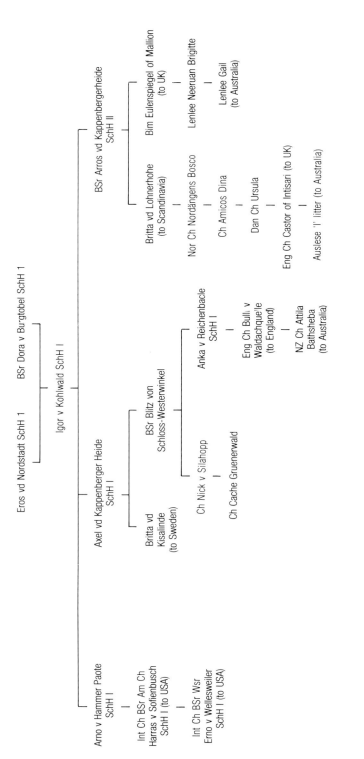

Eros vd Nordstadt SchH 1   BSr Dora v Burgtobel SchH 1

Igor v Kohlwald SchH I

Axel vd Kappenberger Heide SchH I

BSr Arros vd Kappenbergerheide SchH II

Arno v Hammer Paote SchH I

Int Ch BSr Am Ch Harras v Sofienbusch SchH I (to USA)

Int Ch BSr Wsr Erno v Wellesweiler SchH I (to USA)

BSr Blitz von Schloss-Westerwinkel

Britta vd Kisalinde (to Sweden)

Ch Nick v Silahopp

Ch Cache Gruenerwald

Anka v Reichenbacle SchH I

Eng Ch Bull. v Waldachquelle (to England)

NZ Ch Attila Bathsheba (to Australia)

Britta vd Lohnerhohe (to Scandinavia)

Nor Ch Nordängens Bosco

Ch Amicos Dina

Dan Ch Ursula

Eng Ch Castor of Intisari (to UK)

Auslese 'I' litter (to Australia)

Bim Eulenspiegel of Mallion (to UK)

Lenlee Neeruan Brigitte

Lenlee Gail (to Australia)

Chart 5: the influence of Arno v Zenthoff

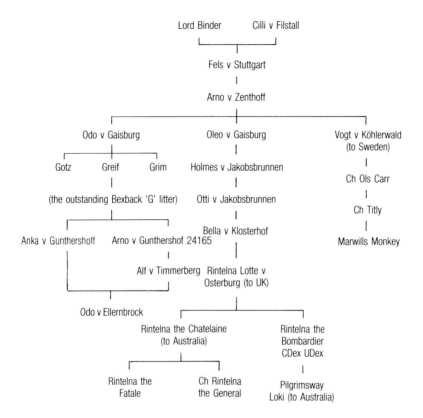

had the distinction of producing five successive *Bundessiegers* from
1951–5. Igor's main lines are shown in Chart 4. The influence of Arno v
Zenthoff 18896, another Fels son, may be seen in Chart 5. Fels
continued his influence through the Alfons line by the great producer
WSr Ido v Köhlerwald 16582, a half-brother of Hackel. Ido's mother,
Alma vd Burghalde 17445, was a Fels grand-daughter, so the strong line
breeding was continued. In the seventh and eighth generations, Ido
produced Dieter v Kohlwald 30654 SchH I and Jarro v Kohlwald 33168
SchH I, the *Bundessiegers* for 1952 and 1955.

Chart 6: the influence of Ido v Köhlerwald

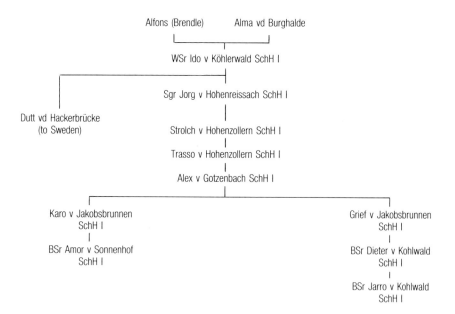

The dogs mentioned up to this point have all been German and their
influence, in the main, has been restricted to their homeland. My final
'great producer' does not quite fit into this category as he was exported
to the USA where his indelible stamp was to be clearly seen; indeed,
Harras v Sofienbusch 36474 SchH I has probably influenced the breed,
since the Second World War, more than any other dog, and this
influence has been extended, in depth, to five continents. He was
whelped on 13 December 1957 in Theodore Busch's vom Sofienbusch
kennel in Dortmund. Harras was tested by Hermann Diehl who gave
him a faultless critique. He was a dog that never refused a fight, a point
not always appreciated in the USA, but loved in Germany. His
American handlers must have been relieved when he qualified as

Britta della Riva Petrosa (whelped 1983), owned and bred by Frederico Lensi (courtesy Dr Lensi)

Ives della Riva Petrosa (whelped 1978), owned and bred by Frederico Lensi (courtesy Dr Lensi)

Asso della Riva Petrosa, bred by Frederico Lensi, owned by C. Nascardi (courtesy Dr Lensi)

Condor della Riva Petrosa, bred by Frederico Lensi, owned by M. Castoldi (courtesy Dr Lensi)

Hexe v Märchenwald, bred by Arthur Gallas, was a top German winner who, sadly, never produced a litter (courtesy F. Berger)

champion! He was almost 66cm (26in) tall and of superb proportions. His outstanding quality was his ability to pass on his characteristics to his progeny – which he did with several litters whilst still in Germany. He was the third, and last, dog to gain the title *Bundessieger* on three successive occasions, 1960–2. His influence on the American scene was twofold; firstly, directly through his American-born offspring, and, secondly, via his German-born children who were later imported into the USA. He is discussed further in the chapter on the Rottweiler in America.

The great producers are those who put their stamp on whole generations; they are not merely the product of a breeder's talent and industry, but are, as Korn stated, 'an extra gift from heaven which does not come to a breeder every day'. Beyond those cited there are, of course, many others, but space precludes all being discussed and the author has therefore selected the special few which he feels are worthy of being singled out.

The omission of bitches from this section is open to criticism in an age of sex equality so might I add that I have never believed in canine sex equality, maintaining that in many ways bitches are far superior and their influence far greater. It is not by chance that the fighting bulls of the Carmargue are produced only from cows tested for their bravery whilst

Droll vd Brötzingergrasse, Sch H2 3 May 1957 by Emile Fränkle. His progeny influenced the breed in three continents (Photo: courtesy Mrs Rademacher)

they were heifers. No breeder of consequence will fail to acknowledge that the excellence of his stock is determined by the quality of his bitches. We have found in our kennel that the bitch has a considerable influence on the acquired characteristics of a litter – something the sire is invariably denied. Moreover, her genetic contribution is exactly one half. There have been outstanding bitches in such kennels as Gaisburg, Brötzingergasse, Burgtobel, Jakobsbrunnen, Eulenspiegel, Köhlerwald, Kohlwald and others in Germany. In Holland, bitches have had a lasting effect in such kennels as Brantsberg, Brabantpark and Triomfator to name but three, whilst in Scandinavia vom Heidenmoor, Fandangos and Nordängens are household names. However, the dogs have far greater scope to influence; dogs like Arco Torfwerk and Bulli v Hungerbühl, who were mated something like 250 times between them, have had far greater impact, quantitatively, than any ten bitches.

The title of *Bundessieger* is competed for annually at an all-breeds show comparable to Crufts or Westminster.

Table 1: German National Champions, *Bundessiegers* (BSr) 1947–85

Year	Sieger (Sr)	Siegerin (Sn)
1947	Xerxes v Jakobsbrunnen	Freia Jakobsbrunnen
1948	Odo v Ellernbrock	(no title)
1949	Odo v Ellernbrock	(no title)
1950	Bruno v Hohen-Ybach	(no title)
1951	Dieter v Kohlwald	Dora v Burgtobel
1952	Dieter v Kohlwald	Vroni v Gaisburg
1953	Dieter v Kohlwald	(no title)

Year	Sieger (Sr)	Siegerin (Sn)
1954	Igor v Kohlwald	Blanka v Eppendorfer-Baum
1955	Jarro v Kohlwald	Anka vd Wolfsbusch
1956	(no title)	Carin vd Braukkante
1957	Arros vd Kappenbergerheide	No *Siegerin*. Jubilee Sgr Asta v Alt-Sickingen
1958	Arno v Ries	(no title)
1959	Bengo vd Kappenbergerheide	(no title)
1960	Harras v Sofienbusch	(no title)
1961	Harras v Sofienbusch	Andra Ruhrstrom
1962	Harras v Sofienbusch	Jenni v Goldenen Ritter
1963	Blitz v Schloss Westerwinkel	Assy v Ziffelbach
1964	Alex v Ludwigshafen/See	Cora v Lindeck
1965	Erno v Wellesweiler	Ina v Schifferstadt
1966	Emir v Freienhagen	Flora v Kursaal
1967	Emir v Freienhagen	Carin vd Bonninghardt
1968	Igor v Hause Henseler	(no title)
1969	Igor v Hause Henseler	(no title)
1970	Falco v Grunsfeld	Anka v Reichenbachle
1971	Falco v Grunsfeld	Dolli v Schloss Ickern
1972	Ferro vd Löwenau	Dolli v Schloss Ickern
1973	Karol v Wellesweiler	Dolli vd Meierei

Diva vd Meierei, an excellent bitch from a litter that was most influential and included Dolli the first Klub Siegerin *in 1971* (Photo: courtesy M. Bruns)

Year	Sieger (Sr)	Siegerin (Sn)
1974	Grief v Fleisher	(no title)
1975	Ari v Walduck	Anka v Lohauserholz
1976	Max v Emstal	Asta v Lohauserholz
1977	Ari v Walduck	(no title)
1978	Benno v Allgäuer Tor	Olfa v Hennekamp
1979	Ero v Karlshof	Dina v Schwaiger Wappen
1980	Dingo v Schwaiger Wappen	Alfa v Schwarzwasser
1981	Dingo v Schwaiger Wappen	Britta v Hause Schneider
1982	Nero v Schloss Reitheim	Anja v Herzberger See
1983	Falko vd Tente	Cendy v Siedlerpfad
1984	Nero v Schloss Rietheim	Falka v Herbernerland
1985	Morris v Rauchfang	Olga v Echterdingen

The title of *Klubsieger* is awarded annually at the major specialist show. It was introduced in 1971 by the Chief Breed Warden, Friederich Berger.

Table 2: German Club Champions, *Klubsiegers* (KSr) 1971–85

Year	Venue	Sieger (Sr)	Siegerin (Sn)
1971	Rottweil	Bulli v Hungerbühl	Dolli vd Meierei
1972	Koln	Bulli v Hungerbühl	Edda v Schloss Ickern
1973	Porta Westfalica	Greif v Fleischer	Afra v Haus Schöttroy
1974	Rottweil	Karol v Wellesweiler	Anka v Lohauserholz
1975	Niefern-Öschelbronn	Axel v Fuse der Eifel	Bienne v Geiselstein
1976	Aachen	Ari v Walduck	Asta v Lohauserholz
1977	Niefern-Öschelbronn	Carlo v Fuse der Eifel	Asta v Lohauserholz
1978	Borken-Burio	Aias	Assy v Haugenfeld
1979	Rottweil	Condor zur Klamm	Assy v Haugenfeld
1980	Bad Eilsen	Dingo v Schwaiger Wappen	Babette v Mägdeberg
1981	Bensheim/ Bergstrabe	Nero v Schloss Rietheim	Carmen v Old Germany
1982	Stadhagen	Bronco v Räuberfeld	Itta v Zimmerplatz
1983	Blatzheim	Mirko v Steinkopf	Hulda v Königsgarten
1984	Niefern	Falko vd Tente	Hulda v Königsgarten
1985	Coesfeld	Hassan v Königsgarten	Yvonne v Margräflerland

The competition for the title of *Leistungssieger* is held annually in the autumn. Dogs with SchH3 degree must obtain a qualifying score at regional trials. There is only one *Leistungssieger* each year.

Table 3: German Working Champions, *Leistungssiegers* (LSr) 1949–85

Year	Venue	Sieger (Sr)
1949	Munich	Pluto v Jakobsbrunnen
1950		(no title)
1951	Dortmund	Blanca v Cilabrunnen (the only bitch to win the title)
1952	Nurnberg	Marko v Filstalstrand
1953	Bremen	Barry v Rheintor
1954		(no title)
1955	Frankfurt	Barry v Rheintor
1956		(no title)
1957	Dusseldorf	Castor vd Bokermühle
1958	Stuttgart	Arko v Hipplerhof
1959	Oberhausen	Axel v Spiekerhof
1960	Niefern	Bob v Haus Hader
1961	Nurnberg	Arco v Fichtenschlag
1962		(no title)
1963	Ober-Castrop	Dolf vd Schmechting
1964	Idar-Oberstein	Arras v Moritzberg
1965	Bayreuth	Droll v Baumbusch
1966	Stuttgart	Quick vd Solitude
1967	Oberhausen	Ajax v Asenburg
1968	Heppenheim	Cäsar vd Lüneburger Heide
1969	Nurnberg	Alc Zerberus
1970	Hannover	Armin v Königshardt
1971	Castrop-Rauxel	Armin v Königshardt
1972	Aalen	Axel vd Wegscheide
1973	Troisdorf-Spich	Cralo v Mischa
1974	Ilvesheim	Felix v Sonnenberg
1975	Oberhausen	Astor v Hause Pfarr
1976	Bayreuth	Barry v Walduck
1977	Neuwied	Barry v Walduck
1978	Goslar	Etzel v Amselhof
1979	Blatzheim	Osko v Klösterschen
1980	Idar-Oberstein	Axel v Rhein-Elbe-Park
1981	Gladbeck	Bengo v Bengo v Klösterchen
1982	Stadthagen	Axel v Rhein-Elbe-Park
1983	Trossingen	Axel v Rhein-Elbe-Park
1984	Coesfeld	Enzor v Rauchfang
1985	Rehburg	Erasmus v Mägdeberg

3 The Rottweiler in Britain

The Early Years

The first authentic report of the Rottweiler in Great Britain is that made by Miss Isobel Morrison, then living in Campeltown, Argyll. She recalls her association with a beautiful black and brown dog when she was twelve, just after the First World War. Together with her friends, she met the dog regularly and one day the dog's owner offered a shilling to any child who could identify the breed. Miss Morrison, overcoming her shyness, said, 'I think it is a Rottweiler.' The account was detailed in the Rottweiler Club's newsletter No 9 of 1961. It is interesting to note that the dog had a long tail. Miss Morrison was to become a founder member of the Rottweiler Club, so her account is quite clearly authoritative. No doubt the dog had been brought back by a returning serviceman.

The breed pioneer was Mrs Thelma Gray, then Miss Evans, an all-breeds judge of international repute. Her kennel prefix, Rozavel, is known throughout the world and closely associated with Corgis and German Shepherd dogs. Mrs Gray now lives in South Australia and has the honour, shared with only two others, of being a Life Member of the English Rottweiler Club. She first admired the breed whilst visiting Germany and, in 1936, imported a bitch, Diana vd Amalienburg, who was sired by the great German dog BSr Hackel v Köhlerwald SchH2. The dam was Alma v Hartmanshofen, bred by Herr Heim in Munich. Diana was sold to Mrs Simmons of the Crowsteps kennel, who embarked her on a show and obedience career which saw her obtain Companion (CD) and Utility Dog (UD) qualifications. Mrs Simmons imported a dog herself from Germany, Arbo v Gaisburg (he came out of quarantine on 1 March 1938) but, sadly, further information on these dogs is no longer available.

Mrs Gray later acquired another bitch, Enne v Pfalzgau, who had been shown in Germany and graded 'V'. Enne was mated to an Alfons (Brendle) son, WSr Ido v Köhlerwald SchH2 – Enne was described by Mrs Gray as being a lovely bitch behind the collar, but, unfortunately, with the *Jagdhundköpf* pointer-type head, a weakness to which the Pfalzgau kennel was subject – along with suspect temperament, although Mrs Gray reports that Enne had a wonderful disposition. Enne was sold to Mrs Paton and her litter, born in quarantine, was struck by

Int Ch Ives Eulenspiegel SchH3. An outstanding sire who was not used as much as his quality suggested. Bred by M. Bruns (courtesy M. Bruns)

distemper. All the puppies died except one which was nursed to health by Mrs Gray, and was called Anna from Rozavel. Anna was trained by Mr Montgomery and performed brilliantly in trials; she qualified CDex, winning on thirty-six occasions, both in trials and the show ring – including Best of Breed at Crufts in 1939 under Sid Simpson. When war was declared in 1939 Anna 'joined up' and served with the RAF. She survived the Second World War but was by then too old for breeding. She was devoted to her handler with whom she remained until she died at the ripe old age of sixteen.

Mrs Gray, with the help of the ADRK, imported another pair of Rottweilers in 1936. One was a dog, Arnolf vd Eichner Ruine, bred by Simon Oldermatt, and the other was a bitch, Asta v Norden, bred by Karl Rohm. Arnolf was a splendid specimen and arrived in the UK at five months of age. He was Best of Breed at Crufts in 1937 under Mr Croxton Smith, and won a further five similar awards at other shows. He did well in the obedience ring too, and put his stamp on early progeny. Sadly, his temperament was to fail him, and eventually he was destroyed. Asta had been mated to Hackel v Köhlerwald before leaving Germany and one of the puppies, Hedda from Rozavel, was sold to Miss D. Homan who owned the Rigi kennels in Croydon.

Mrs Gray's final import was her best. She was a lovely bitch, bred by Herr Weber, called Vefa v Köhlerwald, sired by Arno v Gunthershof out of Aga v Lederberg. Arno sired some fine dogs in Scandinavia and his blood was reintroduced into the UK after the Second World War, by Mrs Chadwick when she imported Rudi Eulenspiegel. However, Vefa left no mark on the British scene. Early in 1939, Miss Homan imported a handsome dog called Benno v Köhlerwald, but war was declared shortly afterwards and Benno was called to duty and never heard of again.

Rottweilers had made a considerable impression on the British dog world and one fancier attracted to the breed was Mrs Maud Wait. She purchased two dogs from Mrs Gray, but both died. Undaunted, a third pup was acquired, called Kurt from Rozavel. Mrs Wait, together with her children and Kurt, were to spend the war years in Canada, but, on her return, she again took up her interest in the Rottweiler.

But what of the other pre-war efforts to establish the breed? The blood that had cascaded in such full body and promised so much for the future was, alas, to struggle to a miserable close in the sluggish delta of the war years. Mrs Gray's home was requisitioned by the army and her dogs scattered around the country, with the Rottweilers going to Ireland where they vanished forever. Mrs Simmons died and Miss Paton married and lost interest in the breed.

The Rottweiler Starts Again

Captain Roy-Smith, a young veterinary officer serving with the occupation forces in Germany, was attracted to the breed which he met in the course of his duties – the closeness of this contact could be proved by a scar on his knee! He was helping to test some Rottweilers for the army when a canny dog, disregarding the sleeve, took a firm hold on something he was more able to sink his teeth into. Roy-Smith was so impressed that he decided to take one back to England.

He was unfamiliar with the ADRK and contacted Carl Voigt who was the secretary of the German Kennel Club. Through him, Roy-Smith purchased a bitch called Berny v Weyher which was whelped on 11 June 1952. Berny proved to be longhaired and was not registered with the ADRK; indeed, that body was not at all pleased about the transaction when they found out. Roy-Smith then wrote to The Kennel Club to obtain information on the number of Rottweilers registered in the UK – the answer was short and to the point – none! Eventually Roy-Smith contacted the ADRK and the club secured for him a dog, Ajax v Fuhrenkamp, who was to be the first stud dog in the UK and whose name still appears in pedigrees if they are traced back far enough.

Ajax was bred by Wilhelm Drevenstedt and was whelped on 20 April 1952. Amongst his famous ancestors were such names as Ido v

Ajax v Fuhrenkamp, the first stud dog to come to the UK after the Second World War, imported by Captain Roy-Smith

Köhlerwald, Arno v Zenthoff, Odo v Gaisberg and Holmes Jakobsbrunnen. His pedigree is shown in Pedigree 1. Ajax and Berny went to Britain in March 1953 and Ajax was shown in the same year, gaining a third on his first outing. However, his show career was restricted as Rottweilers were classed under Any Other Variety (AOV) and very few judges were familiar with them. He was shown at Crufts in 1955 and gained a third under May Pacey. His stud career was also restricted because of the scarcity of bitches. He was mated to Berny a total of six times, producing four pups on two different occasions. All of these died except one which was sold as a pet. In view of its phenotype and ancestry of the mother it is fortunate that the puppy was never heard of again. Berny was destroyed in 1956.

It is of interest to note the number of times that bitches 'missed' during the early post-war period. Ajax was mated to another of Roy-Smith's imports, Rintelna Lotte v Osterburg, on no less than seven occasions. She whelped a litter in February 1957, but all the puppies were born dead. Of another litter, whelped in July 1958, five of the seven survived, one of which was the illustrious Rintelna the Bombardier, owned and trained by Mary Macphail of the famous Blackforest kennel. Only one bitch from a litter of six puppies was to survive Lotte's last mating and this was Rintelna the Chatelaine. (Lotte's pedigree is shown in Pedigree 2.) Ajax was mated to Anne of Mallion without result. He

Pedigree 1

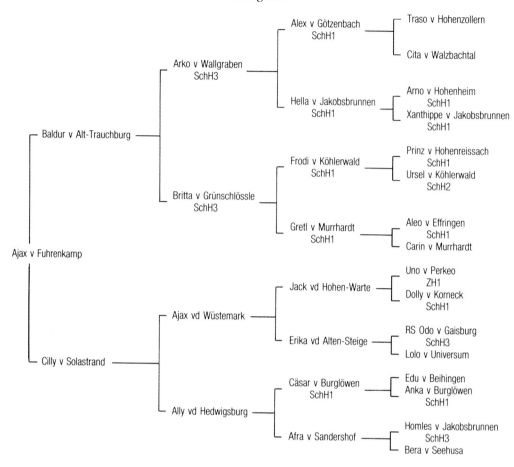

Pedigree 2

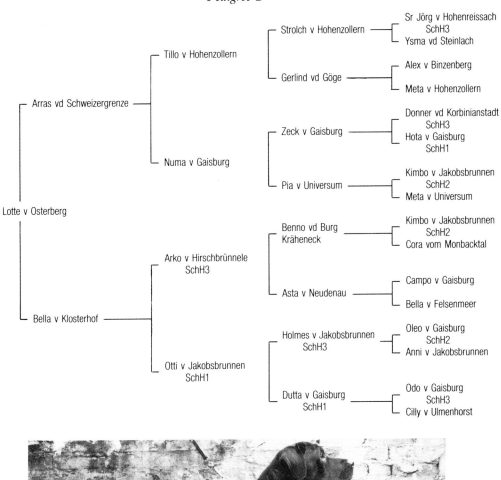

```
                                                              ┌─ Sr Jörg v Hohenreissach
                                    ┌─ Strolch v Hohenzollern ┤     SchH3
                                    │                         └─ Ysma vd Steinlach
             ┌─ Tillo v Hohenzollern┤
             │                      │                         ┌─ Alex v Binzenberg
             │                      └─ Gerlind vd Göge ───────┤
             │                                                └─ Meta v Hohenzollern
 Arras vd Schweizergrenze ──┤
             │                                                ┌─ Donner vd Korbinianstadt
             │                      ┌─ Zeck v Gaisburg ───────┤     SchH3
             │                      │                         └─ Hota v Gaisburg
             └─ Numa v Gaisburg ────┤                               SchH1
                                    │                         ┌─ Kimbo v Jakobsbrunnen
                                    └─ Pia v Universum ───────┤     SchH2
                                                              └─ Meta v Universum
 Lotte v Osterberg ─┤
                                                              ┌─ Kimbo v Jakobsbrunnen
             ┌─ Arko v Hirschbrünnele┌─ Benno vd Burg          │     SchH2
             │     SchH3            │   Kräheneck ────────────┤
             │                      │                         └─ Cora vom Monbacktal
             │                      ┤
             │                      │                         ┌─ Campo v Gaisburg
             │                      └─ Asta v Neudenau ───────┤
 Bella v Klosterhof ──┤                                       └─ Bella v Felsenmeer
             │
             │                      ┌─ Holmes v Jakobsbrunnen ┌─ Oleo v Gaisburg
             │                      │   SchH3                 │     SchH2
             └─ Otti v Jakobsbrunnen┤                         └─ Anni v Jakobsbrunnen
                   SchH1            │
                                    │                         ┌─ Odo v Gaisburg
                                    └─ Dutta v Gaisburg ──────┤     SchH3
                                        SchH1                 └─ Cilly v Ulmenhorst
```

Rintelna Lotte v Osterberg w 1952, imported 1955 by Captain Roy-Smith

Pedigree 3

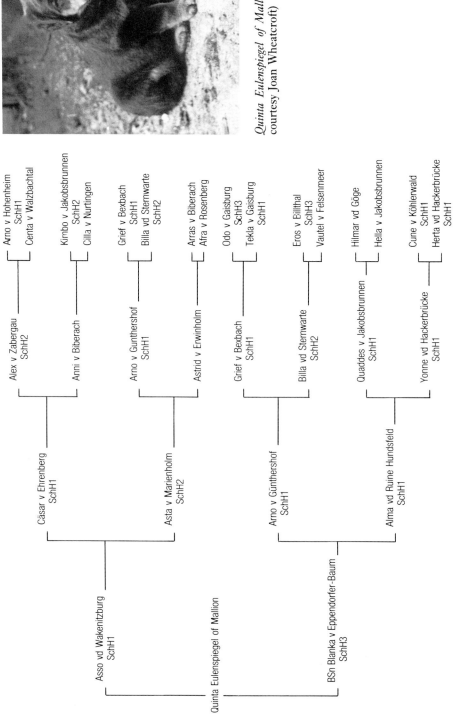

Quinta Eulenspiegel of Mallion (Photo: courtesy Joan Wheatcroft)

Quinta Eulenspiegel of Mallion

Asso vd Wakenitzburg
SchH1

Cäsar v Ehrenberg
SchH1

Alex v Zabergau
SchH2

Arno v Hohenheim
SchH1

Centa v Walzbachtal

Anni v Biberach

Kimbo v Jakobsbrunnen
SchH2

Cilla v Nürtingen

Asta v Marienholm
SchH2

Arno v Günthershof
SchH1

Grief v Bexbach
SchH1

Billa vd Sternwarte
SchH2

Astrid v Erwinholm

Arras v Biberach

Afra v Rosenberg

BSn Blanka v Eppendorfer-Baum
SchH3

Arno v Günthershof
SchH1

Grief v Bexbach
SchH1

Odo v Gaisburg
SchH3

Tekla v Gaisburg
SchH1

Billa vd Sternwarte
SchH2

Eros v Eillthal
SchH3

Vautel v Felsenmeer

Alma vd Ruine Hundsfeld
SchH1

Quaddes v Jakobsbrunnen
SchH1

Hilmar vd Göge

Hella v Jakobsbrunnen

Yonne vd Hackerbrücke
SchH1

Cune v Köhlerwald
SchH1

Herta vd Hackerbrücke
SchH1

Pedigree 4

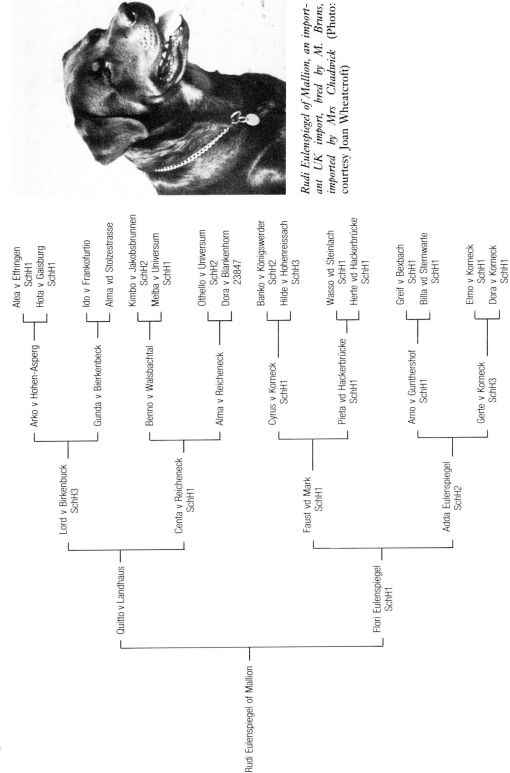

Rudi Eulenspiegel of Mallion, an import-ant UK import, bred by M. Bruns, imported by Mrs Chadwick (Photo: courtesy Joan Wheatcroft)

Rudi Eulenspiegel of Mallion

Quitto v Landhaus

Flori Eulenspiegel
SchH1

Lord v Birkenbuck
SchH3

Centa v Reicheneck
SchH1

Faust vd Mark
SchH1

Adda Eulenspiegel
SchH2

Arko v Hohen-Asperg

Gunda v Bierkenbeck

Benno v Walsbachtal

Alma v Reicheneck

Cyrus v Korneck
SchH1

Pieta vd Hackerbrücke
SchH1

Arno v Gunthershof
SchH1

Gerte v Korneck
SchH3

Alea v Effringen
SchH1
Hota v Gaisburg
SchH1

Ido v Frankofurtio
Alma vd Stolzestrasse

Kimbo v Jakobsbrunnen
SchH2
Melba v Universum
SchH1

Othello v Universum
SchH2
Dora v Blankenhorn
23847

Banko v Königswerder
SchH2
Hilde v Hohenreissach
SchH3

Wasso vd Steinlach
SchH1
Herte vd Hackerbrücke
SchH1

Greif v Bexbach
SchH1
Billa vd Sternwarte
SchH1

Elmo v Korneck
SchH1
Dora v Korneck
SchH1

had better luck with the bitch Quinta Eulenspiegel, imported by Mrs Chadwick, producing nine puppies in 1958. In spite of these setbacks, Ajax left his mark in Britain and one of his grandsons, Pilgrimsway Loki, was exported to Australia where he was used extensively in Mr Mummery's Heatherglen kennel.

The third English import after the Second World War was Quinta, mentioned above. She was bred by Marieanne Bruns and whelped on 28 February 1954. She had a considerable influence on the breed in England and her grand-daughter, Lenlee Gail, was exported to Australia, again to Mr Mummery. Her sire, Asso vd Wakenitzburg, carried the gene for entropion which was seen in Scandinavia, Britain and Australia, but is happily no longer such a major worry in the breed. (Quinta's pedigree is shown in Pedigree 3.)

Quinta was imported by Mrs Joanna Chadwick, with help and encouragement from her mother, the famous novelist Denise Robins. Mrs Chadwick soon imported another dog – the fourth import – called Rudi Eulenspiegel. Rudi was one of the best Rottweilers to go to Britain. He was bred by Miss Bruns, and whelped on 21 May 1954. His pedigree is seen in Pedigree 4. Although his brothers made no impact in Germany, Rudi left a very definite impression in Britain. The next British import was the bitch Lotte v Osterburg, whelped in February 1952. She had been mated before leaving Germany, to Droll v Kocher

Sgn Blanka v Eppendorfer-Baum 1954 Sgrn, the dam of Quinta of Mallion (Photo: courtesy M. Bruns)

Bruin of Mallion CD UDex TDex, bred by Mrs Chadwick, owned by Mrs Wait, an outstanding Rottweiler of the late 1950s and the first to gain Working Trial Champion status (Photo: courtesy Joan Wheatcroft)

SchH3 (sire Lord v Birkenbuck SchH3 out of Betty v Kocher), and produced six dogs and four bitches of which only one dog, Rintelna the Adjutant, survived, and was exported to the USA.

Mrs Chadwick mated Rudi to Quinta to produce the second litter born in Britain after the war – the Mallion 'A' litter. Adonis went to that redoubtable Rottweiler character, Maud Wait. Abelard, a longhaired pup, went to the Metropolitan police where he was handled by Roy Hunter. He had a distinguished career and was retired after many years of useful service. Alberich went to Miss Maureen Cole and died at the age of thirteen, having fought every dog in Kent! He qualified CDex, UDex and once beat Rudi Eulenspiegel in AOV at Crufts. Adda went to Mrs Gawthrop, a founder member of the English Rottweiler Club, who migrated to South Africa. Finally, Anne went to the dear lady who gave me these details, Mrs Joan Wheatcroft of the Argolis kennel.

The mating was repeated and the 'B' litter was whelped in October 1957. One dog, Bruin of Mallion, went on to have a remarkable career for his owner, Maud Wait. He qualified as a Working Trial Champion (WTCh) – the first Rottweiler to do so – after having already gained distinction with CDex, UDex and TDex qualifications. There were no challenge certificates (CCs) on offer in those days, otherwise he would no doubt have become a show champion. He won Best Exhibit under Bill Siggers at the Camberley Open. He was also able to pass on his abilities to his progeny; the only other two Rottweiler Working Trial

A superb Rottweiler head study – Bruin of Mallion (Photo: courtesy Joan Wheatcroft)

Four Rottweilers of the 1960s – (left to right) Lenlee Fern, Lenlee Leeruan, Bruin of Mallion and Lenlee Delight. (Photo: courtesy Joan Wheatcroft)

Champions were his son and his grandson. His son was Lenlee Gladiator, owned by Mr Osborne; Gladiator qualified CDex, UDex, TDex and PDex. His grandson was Jacinto's Bolero CDex, UDex, TDex and WDex (Working Dog). Bolero was owned by Mr Terry Hadley.

In the context of the working Rottweiler, Mrs Mary Macphail deserves special mention. She has concentrated on this aspect of the breed since she acquired her first Rottweiler, the Bombardier, mentioned earlier. The occasional litters that she breeds have in-depth working pedigrees and the Bombardier's son, Champion Horst from Blackforest CDex, is the only show champion with a working trial qualification. Horst's sons, Meister Maik CDex, UD, owned by Mrs Macphail, and Meister Mattais UDex, owned and trained by Mrs Ockenden, have carried on the Rottweiler working tradition.

The sixth Rottweiler imported to the UK was a bitch called Bim Eulenspiegel, bred by Miss Bruns and purchased by Mrs Chadwick. Bim was whelped on 19 May 1958. Her sire was the 1957 *Bundessieger*, Arros vd Kappenbergerheide ScH2, whilst her dam was the elegant bitch Sonne Eulenspiegel. It is worth noting that Arros's influence was to come again to England in the form of Ch Castor of Intisari who is discussed later. Bim had little impact on the English scene as, sadly, she died of distention in 1961.

The next UK import was the bitch Vera v Filstalstrand, bought by Roy-Smith in partnership with Mary Macphail. Her pedigree is shown in Pedigree 5. Vera had been mated to one of the top German sires, Droll vd Brötzingergasse SchH2. She whelped on 2 December 1960 and one of her sons, Rintelna the Dragoon, went on to become the first Australian champion. The other son was Rintelna the Detective who went to the police and her daughter was Anouk from Blackforest owned by Mary Macphail.

Pedigree 5

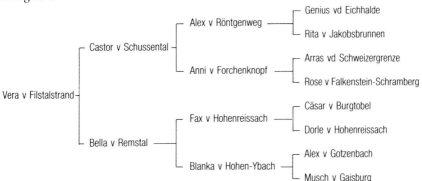

The number of imports, mainly from Germany but also from Scandinavia and Holland, increased in the 1960s and 1970s and one that had a particular influence was Ch Chesara Luther, imported from Holland by Mrs Elsden. Luther's sire was Dutch Ch Baldur v Habenichts. Baldur was sired by Arras v Kanzachtal out of Brava van de Legioenen. Luther was mated to several good bitches, the most significant of whom was Chesara Dark Destiny who became the first English champion, acquiring her title in 1966. Mrs Elsden has enjoyed considerable success with the breed, and up to 1970 had bred and owned more champions than the total of other Rottweiler champions in the UK. Another of Mrs Elsden's imports who had an enormous impact, initially in Britain and later in Australia, was the Swedish dog Ch Chesara Akilles, who was bred by Mr R. Hamburg and whelped on 6 June 1966. He was the most successful of the Elsden imports and appears in many pedigrees, his own appearing in Pedigree 6. Akilles is of particular interest to Australians and is discussed in the chapter on Rottweilers in Australia.

Bärbel v Grevingsberg SchH1 whose name appears in many pedigrees (Photo: courtesy M. Bruns)

Pedigree 6

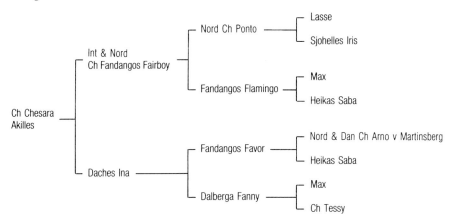

In 1968 Mrs Joan Woodgate, of the Gamegards kennel, imported a dog from Germany called Lars vd Hobertsberg, bred by the Chief Breed Warden Friedrich Berger. Lars had an outstanding pedigree, with Harras v Sofienbusch being a great grandsire on his father's side, whilst Axel vd Kappenbergerheide was on his dam's side. In addition to the bitch Jentris Gloriosa, who was to have influence in Australia, Lars also sired Attila Ajax, out of Gamegards Border Rising, who was exported to Mr Mummery in Australia. Lars's short pedigree is detailed in Pedigree 7.

Pedigree 7

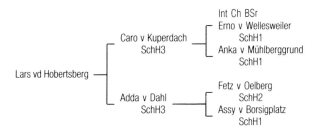

In 1970, Joan Woodgate imported a second dog, the Bulli v Hungerbühl son, Bulli v Waldachquelle. The elder Bulli was perhaps the most famous post-war dog in Germany, with a prodigious show and stud record. The younger Bulli died very young, but not before he had sired some excellent litters. His progeny is well represented in Australia. He was made a champion in 1974 and his short pedigree is shown in Pedigree 8.

Pedigree 8

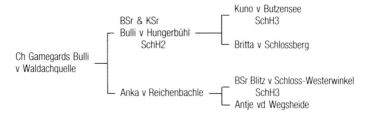

The most important stud to come to Britain in the 1970s was Castor of Intisari who was imported from Denmark by Mr and Mrs Peter Radley in 1973. Castor's pedigree reads like a Who's Who of Rottweilers, as can be seen in Pedigree 9. He soon became an English champion and was the leading stud in the mid 1970s. His dam, Ursula, was mated to Int Ch Farro vh Brabantpark in 1972 and the resulting litter's influence was felt not only in England, but also in America and Australia.

Pedigree 9

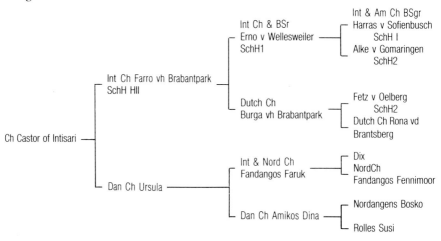

The stud dog of the years 1977–8 was Ch Auscott Hasso v Märchenwald who was purchased by his owner, Gordon McNeil, while he was serving with the British Army in Germany. Hasso's litter sister, Hexe, was, in the author's opinion, one of the outstanding Rottweiler bitches in Europe at that time. The other sister, Hella, became an American champion. Hexe died in 1979 without having produced a litter, a tragedy for her owner, Arthur Gallas, and for Rottweilers generally. Hasso's short pedigree is seen in Pedigree 10.

Ch Castor of Intisari, the most important UK stud of the mid 1970s (Photo: courtesy Peter Radley)

Pedigree 10

Ch Ausscot Hasso v Marchenwald
- Elko v Kastanienbaum SchH1
  - Elko v Kaiserberg SchH1
  - Gitta v Bucheneck SchH1
- Cora v Reichenbachle SchH1
  - IntCh Alex v Dobetal SchH2
  - Antje vd Wegscheide

One may recall that Mrs Gray had sent her Rottweilers to Ireland when war was declared and that they then disappeared without trace. It appears, however, that the Rottweiler saga was in fact perpetuated in Ireland, although no records are available. Mrs Gawthrop mated her bitch, Adda of Mallion, to Ajax v Fuhrenkamp and sold a dog from the litter, Binjum Zabern, to Mr Kelly in Ireland. Mr Kelly mated the dog to a bitch he already owned, Dimitie of Mallion, and from that litter came the most distinguished dog Mr Kelly was to breed – Manzai Kala Koota, CDex, UDex, TDex. His owner, Ivor Fisher, is one of the outstanding trainers in the UK and was introduced to the breed quite fortuitously. While in a dentist's waiting room he saw a picture of Caspar of Mallion in *The Field*. His favourable impression was immediately reinforced when he left the surgery. A small man, leading a very large Rottweiler,

Chesara Dark Intuition, owned by Pat Lanz (Photo: courtesy Pat Lanz)

happened to walk down the street at that precise moment. The man was Joe Joseph and the dog, most appropriately, was called Mighty Man of Stepney. The two men met and the result of the ensuing conversation was that the Rottweiler Club numbers were swelled by two! They proved, however, to be of more than usual significance. Mr Fisher and working Rottweilers are synonymous, whilst the Josephs, breeding under their Bhaluk prefix, have bred, and continue to breed, many beautiful Rottweilers.

The Police and Rottweilers

It is inconceivable to anyone with even a vague idea of a working dog's capacity, that they are not used more often by our law enforcement agencies. The enormous power of a dog's senses, especially those of smell and hearing, can be utilised efficiently for crime prevention, crowd control, tracking and drug detection. The British police are using dogs with increasing success and it is pleasing to see that Rottweilers are much sought-after. Airedale terriers had been used early in this century, but most of the trained dogs were seconded for national service during the First World War. German shepherd dogs were introduced after the Second World War, but the dog squad was not properly organised until the 1950s. The main area of success was in the railway yards where thieves raided goods trains to keep a flourishing black-market operation supplied; this received a mortal blow when dog patrols were introduced on a wide scale. There are few Rottweilers in the police force because the latter generally used to rely on dogs donated by the public and few Rottweilers come into this category. Further, the long association of the police with the German shepherd is not easily breached, especially as the force now breeds its own dogs and has imported stock from Germany for this purpose. Nonetheless, there have been, and will continue to be, a number of good Rottweilers in various police squads.

The first Rottweiler to be so used was Abelard – from the first Mallion litter, whelped in February 1956. He was handled by Sgt Roy Hunter for the Metropolitan police and set a very high standard. The second dog was Rintelna the Detective, born in quarantine on 2 December 1960. Otto, as he was called, worked for the Peterborough police and was handled by PC George. Abelard's brother, born in the fifth Mallion litter, in April 1963, was the next to join up. He was Ernst of Mallion and his tour of duty took him to the Hull dockyards. The home counties, particularly Surrey and Sussex, have used Rottweilers in preference to other breeds; there were two highly skilled Rottweilers with the West Sussex police – Lenlee Maxim UDex, WDex, handled by PC Bostock, and Boyd of Aarons UDex, handled by PC Sturgess.

The Rottweiler Club

The formation of the Rottweiler Club in the UK was due to the efforts and energy of Mrs Wait, ably assisted by Mrs Macphail. All Rottweiler owners were invited to attend a meeting that followed the judging at Crufts on 6 February 1960. Those present were: Captain Roy-Smith, who became the first chairman, Mrs T. Gray, who became the first president, Mrs M. Wait and her husband, Mrs J. Wheatcroft and her daughter, Penny, Mr and Mrs F. Jessop, Mr Wright, Mrs Charles, Mrs Chadwick, Mrs Bensley, Mrs Gawthrop, Mrs Macphail, Mr Kelly and Mr McGloin (who later became the second chairman).

From that initial meeting, the club was founded, with twenty-five members, and these have now swelled to about 700, which figure includes members living in such far-away places as the USA, Australia, South Africa and many other countries. The club issues regular newsletters and a yearbook. Today there are many branches of which the most active are the Northern, formed in 1974, the Midland and the Scottish, formed a year later. The club created a welfare scheme, with its own constitution, and this has also gone from strength to strength and, today, has representatives in some fifty-six areas who take care of, and find good homes for, Rottweilers that, for one reason or another, need to be rehoused.

A second breed club was created some time after the original club called the British Rottweiler Association. Whilst in many breeds the arrival of a second club is not always conducive to over-all harmony, it is to the breed's credit that both clubs in the UK enjoy a friendly relationship with each other. The BRA also has a membership of about 700 and other regional clubs are opening up, so the UK club scene is obviously both healthy and growing. All Rottweiler owners are certainly advised to join one of the clubs where they may participate in the many activities and be kept informed on all aspects of their chosen breed.

Table 4: English Rottweiler Champions 1966–85

Year	Name	Sex	Year	Name	Sex
1966	Chesara Dark Destiny	B	1970	Horst from Blackforest	D
1967	Erich of Mallion	D		Hildegarde from	
	Chesara Luther	D		Blackforest	B
	Chesara Dark Soliloqy	B		Chesara Dark Jasmin	B
1968	Chesara Akilles	D	1971	Chesara Dark Opal	B
	Chesara Dark			Ero von Buchaneck	D
	Inquisitor	D		Retsacnal Gamegard	
	Portia Moriconium	B		Gallant Attempt	D
1969	Chesara Dark Gossip	B	1972	Chesara Dark Kruger	D

Year	Name	Sex
	Borgvaale Bonita	B
1973	Bhaluk Princess Birgitta	B
	Borgvaale Balthazar	D
	Chesara Dark Warlord	D
	Jentris Gerontious	D
1974	Borgvaale Vonda	B
	Chesara Byxfield Akela	D
	Gamegard Bulli von Waldachquelle	D
	Robvale Max-i-Million	D
1975	Prince Gelert of Bhaluk	D
	Cheddi Bonnie of Cenlea	B
	Chesara Dark Pageant	B
	Borgvaale Halla of Helvetia	B
	Attila Briseis	B
1976	Castor of Intisari	D
	Jambicca the Superman	D
	Chesara Dark Leila of Auwil	B
	Dusky Victoria of Vaelune	B
	Schutz from Gamegards	D
1977	Adoram Cordelia	B
	Chesara Dark Julia	B
	Poirot Camilla	B
	Vaelune Alexis	D
1978	Adoram Lennart of Intisari	D
	Linguards Jupiter	D
	Borgvaale Lion City of Ritonshay	D
	Byxfield Demetris of Herberger	D
	Whitebait Touch Wood	D
	Anelie of Basslaw	B
	Cass'es Lass of Potterspride	B
	Gbos Gaytimes	B
	Grafin Tansy Baronin	B
	Panevors Proud Kamile	B

Year	Name	Sex
	Princess Malka of Bhaluk	B
1979	Ablaze of Jambicca	B
	Ausscot Hasso von Märchenwald	D
	Chesara Dark Roisterer	D
	Gbos Goshawk	D
	Graefin Tamsley Witt	B
	Javictreva Team Mascot of Panelma	D
	Panevors Proud Kinsman	D
	Upend Gallant Gairbert	D
1980	Fryerns Advocator	D
	Herberger Count Ferro	D
	Herberger Countess Natasha	B
	Isaela the Saxon	D
	Jagen Dust My Blues	D
	Poirot Edwina	B
	Ronpaula Bold Avenger	D
	Vaelune Denethor	D
	Jagen Mr Blue	D
1981	Ausscot Cover Girl	B
	Chesara Dark Charles	D
	Jagen Asterix	B
	Linguard Norge	D
	Madason Dauntless	D
	Nedraw Black Sunshine	B
	Nobane Bianka	B
	Rudi Anton Bali	D
1982	Ausscot Donnerstag Desera	D
	Chesara Dark Hermina	B
	Chesara Dark Hunters Dawn from Yorlander	B
	Kara of Heramine	B
	Panevors Proud Chickasaw	B
1983	Caprido Minstrel of Potterspride	D

Year	Name	Sex
	Panelma the Highwayman	D
	Panevors Proud Marksman of Jarot	D
1984	Penley Goldfinch	D
	Rottsann Classic Gold	B
	Upend Gay Quilla	B
	Ausscot Franzel of Upend	B
	Varenka Rare Secret	B
	Chesara Dark Rachel	B
	Rottsann Classic Crusader of Vormund	B
	Jagen Blue Aria	B
	Herberger Touch of Brilliance from Vanhirsch	D
1985	Cuidado the Dandy	D
	Poirot Led Zeppelin	D
	Panelma the Adventurer	D
	Varenka Magic Madam	B
	Yorlander's Grecian Girl of Vormund	B
	Rich Bitch of Potterspride	B
	Lara Vorfelder Beauty of Lloydale	B
	Jagen Blue Dale	B
	Jagen Blue Trigo	B
	Caprido Operetta from Thewina	B
	Jambicca Dear Dazzler of Torrentia	B

Table 5: Post Second World War Rottweiler UK Imports

Year	Name	Origin	Sex	Importer	Kennel
1953	Ajax v Fuhrenkamp	Germany	Dog	Capt Roy-Smith	Rintelna
1953	Berny v Weyher	Germany	Bitch	Capt Roy-Smith	Rintelna
1954	Quinta Eulenspiegel	Germany	Bitch	Joanna Chadwick	Mallion
1954	Rudi Eulenspiegel	Germany	Dog	Joanna Chadwick	Mallion
	Lotte v Osterburg	Germany	Bitch	Capt Roy-Smith	Rintelna
1958	Bim Eulenspiegel	Germany	Bitch	Joanna Chadwick/ Mr Newton	Mallion
1960	Vera v Filstralstrand	Germany	Bitch	Capt Roy-Smith/ Mary Macphail	Rintelna Blackforest
	Ajax vd Lonneker Bult	Holland	Dog	Mr Britton	
	Chesara Luther	Holland	Dog	Judith Elsden	Chesara
	Cabiria vh Brabantpark	Holland	Bitch	Maud Wait	Lenlee
1964	Akilles	Sweden	Dog	Judith Elsden	Chesara
1965	Rodsdens Jett v Sofienbusch	USA	Dog	Mary Macphail	Blackforest
	Blanka Ostertal	Germany	Bitch	Mr and Mrs McLean	
1967	Basula v Sachenhertz	Germany	Bitch	Joan Woodgate	Gamegards
1967	Ero v Buchaneck	Germany	Dog	Mr Baldwin	Taucas
1968	Lars vd Hobertsburg	Germany	Dog	Joan Woodgate	Gamegards
1970	Bulli vd Waldachquelle	Germany	Dog	Joan Woodgate	Gamegards
1973	Castor of Intisari	Denmark	Dog	Mr and Mrs Radley	Intisari
	Hasso v Marchenwald	Germany	Dog	Gordon McNeil	Ausscot
1974	Lord vd Grurmannsheide	Germany	Dog	Mrs Bowring	Herburger
	Arno v Ross	USA	Dog	Mrs Bowring	Herburger
	Torro Triomfator	Holland	Dog	Judith Elsden	Chesara
	Tara Triomfator	Holland	Dog	Judith Elsden	Chesara
1975	Villa Zayanara	Sweden	Dog	Ann Glossop	Sangett
1982	Samson of Gregarth	Sweden	Dog	Karen Kruger	Bergsgarden
1984	Fella v Siedlerpfad	Germany	Bitch	Mr Hosband	Poldark
	Dolf v Rebenhang	Germany	Dog	Joan Woodgate	Gamegards
	Ida vd Mauth	Germany	Bitch	K and B Hindley	Yorlander

4 The Rottweiler in America

The first Rottweiler to be registered with the American Kennel Club (AKC), in 1931, was the bitch Stina v Felsenmeer (Blucher v Felsenmeer x Alma), imported by August Knecht of New York. Stina had been bred in Germany by Adolf Wagner of Ziegelhaussen. However, it is known from German stud book records that one Otto Denny bred a litter in the USA, which whelped in September 1930, thus being the first litter to be bred in the United States. This, of course, means that one bitch, at least, existed in America before Stina, and before the AKC gave recognition to the breed in 1931.

In 1932, Knecht registered the earlier imported dog Arras v Gerbermuhle (Gallus v Bockenheim x Asta v Bethmannspark) which he mated to Stina to produce the first recorded litter registered with the AKC. The pups, under the Wellwood prefix of Knecht, were Alma 812850, Ada 812851, Alda 812852 and Asta 812853. The German stud books indicate that two further pups were in this 'A' litter, these being Arno and Alpha, and why these were not registered with the AKC is not known. It should be pointed out that a number of the early German migrants to the USA continued to register litters with the ADRK as well as with the AKC. One must assume they were breeders of high repute in Germany as the ADRK accepted these registrations without being able to check out the litters, which is their normal procedure. Further, the AKC accepted the breed onto their register in 1931, even though it had no standard for the Rottweiler.

The breed made little impact in the USA until the 1960s, and between 1931 and 1944 only ninety-three dogs were registered with the AKC. Even after the Second World War, Rottweilers figured far more in obedience classes than in those for conformation. The first show champion, made up in 1948, was Zero, owned and bred by Noel P. Jones of Idaho; from the same litter came Zola, owned by Mrs Erna Pinkerton, who was to be the second champion. Mr Jones not only held the first breed matches in his backyard, but was also instrumental in forming the first breed club in the USA. He was also the handler of the first Rottweiler to win the Working Group, this being Ch Kurt (Kris x Delga). The first champion to qualify for an obedience title in 1949, was Ch Zada's Zenda CD, owned and handled by that redoubtable Rottweiler character Barbara Roloff (Hoard-Dillon), who has bred over forty champions and easily leads the list of American champion breeders.

Two other early pioneers of the breed in America during the 1940s were Martin Hermann and Arthur Eichler. Hermann, from Dusseldorf, emigrated in 1929 and, after working with several breeds, including the Dobermann, set up his own Von der Heid kennels in Ohio during 1945. He imported a male weighing over 73kg (160lb), called Tropf v Hohenreissach, and it was this dog that was used to illustrate the first American standard of the breed. Hermann adopted the kennel name of Crestwood and this was to be a most influential name in many early American pedigrees, as will be seen.

Eichler imported a most important dog in Gero v Rabenhorst, as he was to become the first Rottweiler to qualify CD in the USA. This title was gained in 1939, with CDX following in 1940. In spite of his bulk, Gero was still able to perform his UD exercises and won another first for the breed when he qualified in 1941. He continued in obedience classes until 1948, by which time he was eleven years old. The Eichlers were dominant in the obedience ring during the early years and the first six Rottweilers to gain obedience titles were either bred or owned by them.

Another prominent kennel begun in 1945 was that of Palos Park, which was owned by Eugene Schoelköpf. Eugene had emigrated from Frankfurt in 1923 and had an impressive grounding in the breed as his father, an early German Rottweiler Club member, owned the Zuffenhaussen kennel and is mentioned in Volume 1 of the German stud book in respect of the twelfth entry, Leo v Nachen.

Schoelköpf started his kennel with a bitch, Ami of Crestwood (Queenie), who was whelped in December 1944 and bred by Martin and Henrietta Hermann. Next a dog was imported, Dasso v Echterdingen, and then a bitch, bred by Jakop Köpf, called Seffe v Gaisburg. Dasso became a champion in April 1951, with Seffe gaining a similar honour in September of the same year. He mated Dasso to Queenie and this was to prove a litter of considerable impact. From it, Alma was to become a champion and was retained; Asto was also to be a champion; whilst Asta became the foundation bitch of the Roberts Park kennels which was to produce many superb Rottweilers. The Schoelköpfs helped to found the Medallion Club and are charter members of it – there are twenty-five in all.

By a strange coincidence, on the very day Eugene Schoelköpf visited the Crestwood kennels to purchase his first bitch, so did another person destined to become a household word among the Rottweiler fraternity. This was Mr Pat Rademacher who purchased a dog, August der Grosse, who was a son of Tropf out of Asta of Crestwood. Pat Rademacher and his sister, Joan Klem, were to build up what is now one of the world's most famous Rottweiler kennels – that known as Rodsden's. This kennel has imported more German Rottweilers than any other kennel in the world and their most famous import was the legendary Harras v Sofienbusch. However, after acquiring August, Rademacher then purchased another dog, called Erwin, whose pedigree is shown in Pedigree 11. He also acquired an Erwin daughter, Alva of Crestwood. He mated Alva to August to produce his first litter in March 1947. One of the litter, Astrid of Crestwood, was sold to Rademacher's sister, Joan, who worked her in obedience before mating her to Ch Dasso to produce her first litter.

Rodsden's first import was a bitch, Quelle vd Solitude, bred by Herr Vogel from good working stock – her sire was Droll vd Brötzingergasse and her brother, Quick, was the 1966 *Leistungssieger* (working champion). Quelle became an American champion and also qualified CD. She was mated to Harras and produced the famous 'K' litter which probably influenced the American scene more than any other mating.

Pedigree 11

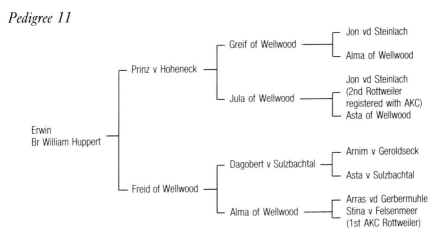

```
                                              ┌─ Jon vd Steinlach
                           ┌─ Greif of Wellwood ─┤
                           │                  └─ Alma of Wellwood
        ┌─ Prinz v Hoheneck ─┤
        │                  │                  ┌─ Jon vd Steinlach
        │                  └─ Jula of Wellwood ─┤  (2nd Rottweiler
        │                                     │  registered with AKC)
Erwin ─┤                                      └─ Asta of Wellwood
Br William Huppert
        │                                     ┌─ Arnim v Geroldseck
        │                  ┌─ Dagobert v Sulzbachtal ─┤
        │                  │                  └─ Asta v Sulzbachtal
        └─ Freid of Wellwood ─┤
                           │                  ┌─ Arras vd Gerbermuhle
                           └─ Alma of Wellwood ─┤  Stina v Felsenmeer
                                                  (1st AKC Rottweiler)
```

The foregoing can be no more than a glimpse of the people and dogs whose influence has been of lasting importance. Many early breeders and their stock have been omitted, not because their part in the development of the breed in America was not of importance, but simply because to cover them all would fill a volume in itself.

Best in Show Winners

Due to the pyramid structure of judging – which applies to most countries including the UK and Australia – Rottweilers in America have

Ch Dux v Hungerbühl SchH1 has proved to be one of the really outstanding American sires of all time. He was a brother of the famous Bulli v Hungerbühl (Photo: courtesy Mrs Rademacher)

achieved greater individual fame than their forbears in Germany where judging is restricted to breed level.

The first Rottweiler to win Best Exhibit in an all-breeds championship show was Ch Kato v Donnaj CDX, TD who was bred by Laura Coonley and owned by Jan Marshall who also handled him throughout a career in which he was eighty times Best of Breed and five times Best of Group. He was sired by Rodsden's Kluge vd Harque CD out of Ch Franzi v Kursaal (German import). The occasion of his epic victory was the Merrimack KC show in May 1971. The very next day his brother, Ch Rodsden's Duke Du Trier, also won the supreme award at the Illinois Valley KC show! Duke was owned by Dr and Mrs Olson and handled by Richard Orseno. Duke went on to gain a similar win in Ontario, to become the first all-breeds winner in Canada for the breed.

The third Best in Show winner was the German import Ch Erno v Ingenoff (Dux v Stüffelkopf SchH1 x Dedda v Kursaal SchH1) whose win was gained in August 1975. Erno was imported by Harry Isaacs but owned later by Charles Hill and had been a junior winner in Germany.

He was a fine specimen, as his breeding would suggest, and both Friedrich Berger and Mary Macphail spoke highly of him.

The next dog to be mentioned was never a BIS winner, although he did have an excellent ring record, but his value as a stud cannot be other than immeasurable on the American show circuit. He was Ch Dux v Hungerbühl, a full brother to the immortal Bulli v Hungerbühl. Dux was imported by Elizabeth Eken and Rodsdens, and was the top producing male for three consecutive years. He qualified SchH1 and was awarded CACIB whilst still in Germany. When awarding him BOB in the USA, Heinz Eberz, in his critique, stated 'faultless in all parts' – praise indeed. Dux was a superb mover, excellent in colour and very masculine. He sired thirty-six champions – the greatest number for an American sire. One of his sons, Ch Rodsden's Bruin v Hungerbühl CD, out of Ch Rodsden's Frolich Burga CD, TD, won BIS honours on no less than five occasions. Bruin was breeder-owned by J. and G. Kittner, and gained his first BIS in July 1979, making him the seventh Rottweiler to do so.

Ch Freeger's Ondra CD, bred by Mrs Freeman and Mrs Nightingale (Photo: John Ashby)

Just two weeks after Erno won BIS, this award was gained by Ch Duke's Derek v Altmeister, making him the fourth such winner and the first son of a BIS winner to achieve such a win. Derek was out of Dees v Odenwald, owned by Annie Anderson. The fifth BIS winner was Ch Shearwater Cochise who was sired by Arras v Kinta, a dog with a most impressive champion-producing record.

The next BIS winner was to be Am & Can Ch Donnaj VT Yankee of Paulus – the second such winner to be owned by Jan Marshall. He was bred by Pauline Rakowski and is truly an American, having been born on 4 July 1975! His dam was Ch Amsel v Andan CD and it is interesting to note that her sire was Ch Kato v Donnaj, thus emphasising the enormous influence of Harras v Sofienbusch who was Kato's great grandsire. As mentioned, Ch Bruin was the seventh BIS winner, whilst the eighth was Ch Oscar vh Brabantpark who also boasts Harras in his pedigree. Oscar was imported from Holland as a five year old by Clara Hurley and Michael Grossman. He was both a Dutch and Belgian champion and he burst like a meteor across the American show scene, going BOB under Herr Berger and likewise under Mary Macphail. Tragically, he died a few days after Christmas 1979, a great loss to those who admired him – and even more so for his owners. His BIS win was at Orange Empire Dog Club, under Australian Peter Thomson, in July 1979. During his brief career he collected fifty-four BOB awards and four Best of Groups.

The ninth winner was Ch Van Tieleman's Cisco CD who gained his win in 1980 and is the youngest of the breed to go BIS. He was only seventeen months old when he won at Ephrata-Moses Lake Kennel Club show under Sue Kauffman, thus bettering the achievement of Duke's Derek who was thirty-two months old when he won his BIS. Cisco was by Ch Trollegens Frodo CD out of Jaheriss Gunda.

The tenth winner was the impressive dog Ch Rhomarks Axel v Lerchenfeld, bred by Walter and Ingrid Rhodes. Axel can boast over thirty BOB and nine Group wins and was sired by Ch Elexi vd Gaarn out of Ch Chelsea De Michaela CD.

The BIS at Durham KC, in 1982, was to be Ch Azuro v Rowehaus who was also to win BOB at Westminster the following year. He was by Ch Georgian Court Bruin out of Ch Fuller's Roxy v Hause Hagele, and bred by Milan Rowe Jr.

The twelfth and last Rottweiler to gain a BIS win was Ch Donnaj Green Mountain Boy who has achieved this award on three occasions, the first being in 1982. His ring record is unsurpassed in the USA and

The author with an eight-week-old puppy

Am and Can Ch Groll v Haus Schöttroy CD, bred by Theodor Oymann and owned by Mrs Freeman (Photo: W. Gilbert)

he has sired many champions which is not surprising when one considers he is the third of four generations to have won BIS awards. Only one other BIS winner was older than Mountain Boy when gaining BIS and that was Ch Oscar who was five years and nine months – Mountain Boy was just one month short of his fifth year. Out of interest, it can be stated that the average age of BIS Rottweilers, over the twelve dogs covered, and at the point at which they won this award is three and three-quarter years old.

Int Ch Harras von Sofienbusch SchH 1

No account of Rottweilers in America (or indeed anywhere) would be complete without special reference to this magnificent triple *Sieger* whose influence has been so far-reaching. He is discussed in the German chapter on great producers (see p 32), but here we will look at his record in the USA. He was mated just ten times in America, producing forty-six offspring, of which seventeen became champions;

Int Ch Bulli vom Hungerbühl (whelped 1966), bred by Lothar Born, owned by Christian Kohler (courtesy Christian Kohler)

Osco v Schwaiger Wappen (whelped 1982), bred by Xavier Meixner, owned by I. Kugel-Staiger

Int Ch and Triple Bundessieger *Harras v Sofienbusch SchH1, probably the greatest influence of all on the breed in the USA* (Photo: courtesy Mrs Rademacher)

Ch Kluge vd Harque CD, a Harras son, was himself a great sire. (Photo: courtesy Mrs Rademacher)

his name appears in the pedigree of some 100 American champions. However, pure statistics are not entirely reliable in making assessments with regard to a dog's influence on a breed. Other factors, such as the number of bitches available, their quality and compatability, all play vital roles. One must not forget either, the large number of puppies that are not shown or even registered. Of the ten matings, only one was outside Rodsden's kennel, when he was mated to Dorothea Gruenerwald's Abington's Aphrodite who produced just one bitch, Ch Lorelei – herself the dam of six champions. Had Harras been used less sparingly, one can only wonder at the potential magnitude of his influence.

His mating to Ch Quelle vd Solitude produced the Rodsden's 'K' litter of which two were outstanding. Ch Rodsden's Kurt vd Harque was the first Rottweiller to win consistently in group, whilst Ch Rodsden's Kluge vd Harque CD sired thirty-four champions and twenty-three offspring who qualified for obedience degrees, including the first Rottweiler to gain SchH2 in the United States. Kluge sired the first two BIS winners already discussed, whilst one of their sons also went BIS, thus reflecting Harras's ability to pass on his quality.

Int Ch Erno v Wellessweiler was the 1966 Bundessieger *imported by Muriel Freeman, and was a Harras son* (Photo: courtesy Mrs Freeman)

The sons of Harras who were imported to the USA also proved of great influence. Int Ch BSr WS & Am Ch Erno Wellesweiler SchH1 was possibly the most notable of these. He was imported by Muriel Freeman. A Dutch son of Erno, Ch Falco vh Brabantpark, was imported by Joan Klem and Mr Chambers. Falco sired twenty-three champions and twenty offspring with obedience titles. On the working side, America's first UDT bitch, Ch Rodsden's Wilma vd Harque, was a Harras grand-daughter as was Ch Quelle vd Harque SchH2 – a Kluge daughter.

Rodsden's imported another son, Ch Bengo v Westfalenpark CD, whilst Barbara Hoard-Dillon of Panamint kennels imported Ch Bullino vd Neckarstroom from Holland.

In summarising Harras, it can be said that whilst other Rottweilers have performed with greater distinction in the ring, and many of the later studs have produced more champions, when one considers the era in which he lived and the quality of bitches available at the time, one must conclude that America owes a great deal to this remarkable dog. Both Ch Dux and Ch Bulli were mated a great many more times than Harras, but only time will tell whether their influence, in depth, will equal his. Chart 7 illustrates only part of Harras's influence in the USA.

Chart 7: This male descent line illustrates just one area of the influence of Harras v Sofienbusch

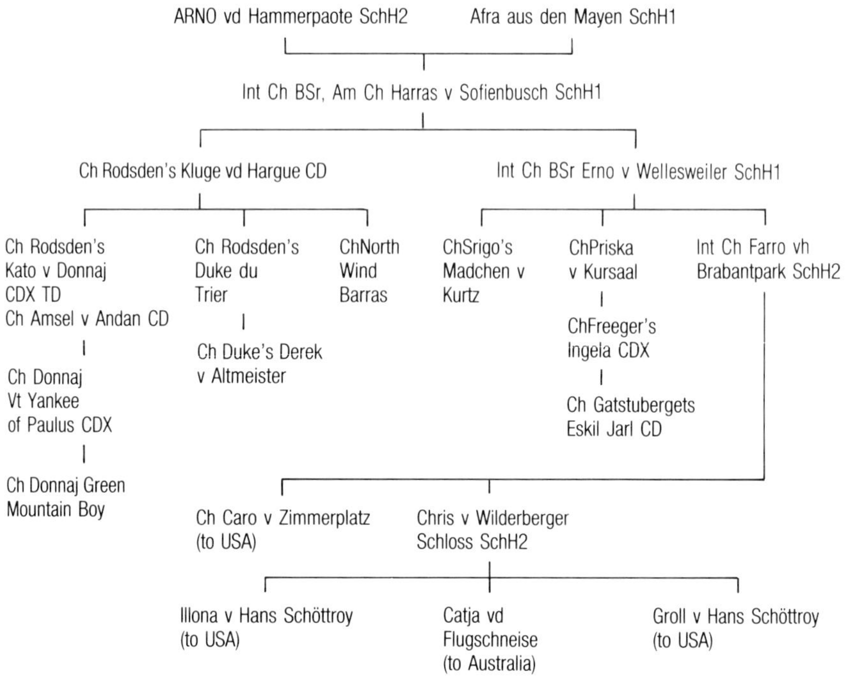

ARNO vd Hammerpaote SchH2   Afra aus den Mayen SchH1

Int Ch BSr, Am Ch Harras v Sofienbusch SchH1

Ch Rodsden's Kluge vd Hargue CD   Int Ch BSr Erno v Wellesweiler SchH1

Ch Rodsden's Kato v Donnaj CDX TD
Ch Amsel v Andan CD

Ch Donnaj Vt Yankee of Paulus CDX

Ch Donnaj Green Mountain Boy

Ch Rodsden's Duke du Trier

Ch Duke's Derek v Altmeister

ChNorth Wind Barras

ChSrigo's Madchen v Kurtz

ChPriska v Kursaal

ChFreeger's Ingela CDX

Ch Gatstubergets Eskil Jarl CD

Int Ch Farro vh Brabantpark SchH2

Ch Caro v Zimmerplatz (to USA)   Chris v Wilderberger Schloss SchH2

Illona v Hans Schöttroy (to USA)

Catja vd Flugschneise (to Australia)

Groll v Hans Schöttroy (to USA)

Rottweiler Clubs in America

The USA is served by a network of clubs, coast to coast. Of these, four have gained official recognition from the AKC – the fifth, and oldest, recognised club having been defunct since 1966. This latter club, the Rottweiler Club of America, was formed in 1948, under the presidency of Ian Mill. A mixture of lack of support and internal politics brought about its demise.

The present parent body is the American Rottweiler Club which was organised in 1971 and had, as its first delegated president, in 1972, Mrs Bernard Freeman. The club produces a newsletter, called *Ark*, and has produced editions of a work called *Rottweiler Pictorials*. These contain hundreds of photographs depicting leading dogs and their pedigrees and are certainly now very much collectors' items. The parent club is responsible for drawing up any revisions to the standard, which it then places before the AKC for their adoption.

Of the other three recognised clubs, the oldest is the Colonial Rottweiler Club which was the brainchild of Arthur M. Rich. The club was formed in 1956 and its first president and co-founder was William C. Stahl. Many devotees of the breed who joined the club at its inception have since become famous Rottweiler personalities. These include Muriel Freeman, one of the very few Americans to have been invited to judge in Germany (she is the owner of the Freeger prefix); Felice Luburich of Srigo kennels, second only to Barbara Dillon as a champion breeder; Mr and Mrs Rau and their daughter, Karen; Mrs Grantham and her son, Earl; Mr Zinnanti and others.

The Medallion Rottweiler Club was formed in 1959, with Mrs Seymour Levine as its first president. Among its charter members were Joan and Richard Klem, Mr and Mrs Rademacher, Mr and Mrs Schoelkopf, Werner Gessner and other now highly respected breeders. The club issues a newsletter and also a most interesting new-member information kit which includes the AKC and ADRK standards, as well as a code of ethics and other useful aids. Its speciality shows have been judged by many international judges, including Herr Berger, Mary Macphail, Heinz Eberz and Gerd Hyden.

The youngest of the original speciality clubs is the Golden State Rottweiler Club, based in Los Angeles. The club was formed in 1962 with Mrs von Rettburg as its first president. It was originally founded as the Southern California Rottweiler Fanciers Club, but quickly outgrew its local status. It received recognition from the AKC in 1969, and amongst its active early members were Mrs Fitterer (a former president of the Medallion Club), Margareta McIntyre and Mrs Camarillo. The club is probably the largest of the breed clubs in the USA and issues an excellent monthly newsletter. This contains information about the breed, not only in America, but also elsewhere, and all additions to Biodex. This latter item was the brain child of Clara Hurley and is a record of the hip status, not only of dogs and their litters, but also of their forebears where this is known.

Each of the clubs discussed is an autonomous body, although there is much co-operation between them. The AKC exercises some control over these clubs but, in theory at least, the ARC has no control over the speciality clubs or their members. The clubs can influence ARC policy by representation.

The enormous increase in the number of Rottweilers in the 1970s promoted the growth of a number of localised breed clubs. Currently, in addition to those already mentioned, there are ten which includes the Canadian Rottweiler Club in Ontario. The others are based in Dallas (Texas), Georgia (Dogwood Club), Houston Bay Area Club (Texas), Mid-South Club (Tennessee), Greater Detroit (Michigan), Orange Coast (California), Tejas (Texas), Tidewater (Virginia) and the Western Rottweiler Owners, in California. The latter club is unusual in that it has no constitution and its members do not meet on a regular basis. Its objective is the education of Rottweiler owners in the enjoyment and improvement of the breed. It issues a newsletter which is sent, free, to its members and serves all interested owners, regardless of any other club to which they may belong.

America has secured the future of the Rottweiler and, by supporting local and national clubs, those who own the breed will help to perpetuate the good image so important to such a powerful dog. Friedrich Berger is reputed to have said that soon the Germans will have to look to America for imports, and there may be an element of truth in such a remark. America has imported many of the finest dogs in Europe over the years and has a wealth of quality in its gene pool. The breed in America is young by German standards and without a breed warden system. For a people who would never accept the sort of discipline imposed by the ADRK, it is the breed clubs who must guide and protect, at all costs, the character of the Rottweiler. The present-day number of advertisements for 31in/160lb attack dogs is most disturbing and only the growth of responsible breed clubs can counter this sort of unwanted promotion.

Table 6: American Imports Prior to the Second World War

Name	Whelped	Registered	Sire and Dam	
Stina v Felsenmeer	03.08.29	12/31	Blucher v Felsenmeer/Alma (Gruner)	
805867			6116	13702
Irma vd Steinlack	09.04.29	12/31	Franzi vd Kinzig/Zilly vd Steinlack	
805869			11302	
Jon vd Steinlack	09.04.29	12/31	Franzi vd Kinzig/Zilly vd Steinlack	
			11302	
Arras vd Gerbermuhle	22.08.26	2/32	Gallas v Bockenheim/Asta v Bethmannspark	
812849			9239	9140
Cora v Palais	29.11.26	6/32	Jack v Rennplatz/Afra v Schlosshirsehorn	
830052			11405	7676
Arras v Schmiden	26.05.27	6/32	Lord v Stuttgart/Arni v Memmberg	
830053			11437	10849
Dagobert v Sulzbachtal	02.08.26	12/32	Arnim v Geroldsec/Asta v Sulzbachtal	
850526			9005	9774
Zilly v Steinlack	13.09.26	12/32	Crallo v Wittlingen/Trudi v Steinlack	
850528			8902	12224
Janko v Steinlack	04.09.29	10/33	Franzi v Kinzig/Zilly v Steinlack	
891287			11302	
Jorg v Steinlack	04.09.29	12/34	Franzi v Kinzig/Zilly v Steinlack	
963137			11302	
Baya v Jackobsbrunnen	29.04.33	8/35	Hackel v Köhlerwald/Cilla v Rotenwald	
A8018			15691	17053
Holmes v Zuffenhausen	23.09.33	8/35	Egon v Hannover/Balka v Vergissmeinnicht	
A9247			16606	17630
Edo vd Liebenburg	08.04.35	4/37	Karmin v Hohenzollern/Aga vd Liebenburg	
A143973			18642	18393
Casey v Filderblume	10.06.36	3/38	Lord v Gaisburg/Blanka v Filderblume	
A217961			20175	20594
Cora v Schloss Kilchberg	21.07.36	3/38	Barry vd Leinburg/Bella v Adlerhorst	
A217962			17582	18593
Flora v Jackobsbrunnen	28.04.37	9/38	Oleo v Gaisburg/Anni v Jackobsbrunnen	
A256981			20853	19134
Bachus v Universum	21.11.36	9/38	Ido v Zuffenhausen/Afra v Reutlingen	
A256780			20497	19956
Arras v Birkenwaldchen	04.04.35	11/38	Arras v Steinbuhl/Cora v Greifenbachtal	
A268109			17588	17945
Barbel v Rommerberg	04.11.32	11/38	Bruno v Pfalzgau/Elli v Hauptwache	
A268980			16958	14335
Gero v Rabenhorst UD	21.09.37	1/39	Carlo v Leinburg/Barbel v Rommerberg	
A268387			18952	
Tropf v Hohenreissach	29.03.37	4/39	Ido v Zuffenhausen/Lore v Hohenreissach	
A306385			20497	21108

Post-war to 1950

Name	Whelped	Registered	Sire and Dam	
Astra v Weinberger	28.02.46	2/49	Arno v Hohenheim/Billa v Biberach	
W112477			24949	25017
Basta of Conny (Denmark)	05.07.48	5/50	Basta/Jegindo Conny	
			DKK101099	DKK107947
Danmark (Denmark)	11.09.47	5/50	Morso Joker/Tonny	
W178351			DKK101099	DKK859979
Dasso v Echterdingen	09.01.48	7/50	Alex v Zabergau/Burga vd Ammerquell	
W189828			25770	24981
Seffe v Gaisburg	24.04.48	7/50	Glanz v Walzbachtal/Luci v Gaisburg	
W189827			26088	26279

5 The Rottweiler in Australia

Compared to the UK and the USA, Australia was much slower in recognising the great potential of the Rottweiler, and it was not until 1962 that the first pair was imported. In part, this may reflect the extremely stringent quarantine laws of the past, which are only slightly less demanding today. These will be discussed later in this chapter.

When Captain Roy-Smith emigrated to Perth in 1962, he took with him a dog, Rintelna the Dragoon (Droll v Brötzingergasse x Vera v Filstilstrand) and a bitch, Rintelna the Chatelaine (Ajax v Fuhrenkamp x Rintelna Lotte v Osterberg). (Roy-Smith is discussed on pp 42–3.) The Dragoon had been mated with the Chatelaine prior to emigration and the litter was born in quarantine on 2 September 1962. Unfortunately, suitable buyers could not be found, so all the pups, save one, were put down. The surviving bitch, Rintelna the Empress, was sold to Mr de Jonge of Adelaide who had been in the Dutch police force before emigrating, and was therefore acquainted with the Rottweiler.

Ch Rintelna the Dragoon, the first Rottweiler in Australia to become a champion, imported by Captain Roy-Smith, is seen here as a seven-month old puppy (courtesy Captain Roy-Smith)

Rintelna the Chatelaine, the first Rottweiler bitch in Australia, imported by Captain Roy-Smith, is seen here at nine months of age (courtesy Captain Roy-Smith)

That the first of a new breed in a country should find difficulty in being placed seems incredible today – the more so when it is realised that the *Blackwood Times* had published an article, with pictures, on the Rottweiler in their edition of 26 October. Although there was interest in this new variety, there were no takers!

On 13 July 1963, a repeat mating of the Dragoon to the Chatelaine resulted in three puppies – the 'F' litter. One bitch was given to the Guide Dog Association, whilst a dog, Rintelna the Field Marshal, and the second bitch, Rintelna the Fatale, went to Douglas Mummery of Victoria, who registered them with the state kennel club in June 1964. Mr Mummery's kennel name of Heatherglen thus followed that of Rintelna into the annals of Australian Rottweiler history. Roy-Smith moved to Ipswich in Queensland, where the 'G' litter was born on 8 May 1966. Rintelna the Grenadier was retained by Roy-Smith and Rintelna the General came to the author who adopted the kennel name of Auslese (the German term for specially selected grapes seemed particularly apt as the author is a keen wine lover and the breed his special selection from all other breeds). Both the Dragoon (Roly) and the Chatelaine (Lola) were shown by Roy-Smith, and Roly became a

Pilgrimsway Loki, bred by Mrs Garland, imported by Mr Mummery, is seen here with a young admirer (Photo: courtesy Mr Mummery)

champion at his last show, on 19 January 1967, under Mrs Frazer. Rintelna Rottweilers were unopposed at this time and Rintelna the Grenadier became a champion on 1 June 1968, whilst his brother, the General, gained his title in March 1969, to become the author's first male champion.

The Chatelaine produced eight puppies in January 1967, but all died of an infection. The Dragoon developed a tumour and was destroyed on 24 March 1967, whilst the Chatelaine, who had produced another litter in 1967, developed cancer and was destroyed on the 3 July 1967, barely three months after her mate. Thus ended the history of Roly and Lola, the first Rottweilers to go to Australia.

The next Rottweiler import was Pilgrimsway Loki (Rintelna the Bombardier x Brunnhilde of Mallion) who was registered in July 1963 by his importer Mr Mummery. Loki was a dog of immense character who made an instant impression on Australians and was held in awe by all who came into contact with him. Loki was mated to Rintelna the Fatale on many occasions, the first of which resulted in a litter whelped in June 1964. From this same pairing, a litter was whelped in December 1965 and in that litter was Heatherglen Chablis Khan – a most important Rottweiler to the author, as it was his first!

Chab was to be my constant companion for many years and it was a very sad day when he died in 1973. He was quite a remarkable character; he worked cattle and sheep, retrieved from land or water, and filled all villains with unholy terror! He featured in a film of the Rottweiler working sheep, made in 1968 for the Colonial Rottweiler Club in the USA. Some years later an American lady made my day by saying, 'You are well known in Hollywood because of your films' – a great compliment to someone who could not even load a movie camera!

Rintelna the Empress (the bitch purchased by Mr de Jonge) was mated to Loki, producing, among others, the dog Marthleen Balthazar who was whelped on 2 May 1966. He became a champion in 1968, gained his CD in 1969 and his CDex in 1970, and was the best specimen from the Loki/Empress matings. In March 1965, Mr Mummery imported Lenlee Gail who had an excellent working background. Her sire was Bruin of Mallion CDex, UDex, WT Ch, TDex, out of Lenlee Neeruam Brigitte CDex, UDex; she was bred by Maud Wait. Gail was mated several times to Loki and produced a number of puppies that were to be significant in the development of the breed in Australia. Heatherglen Rudi, whelped in February 1966, was the first of these; he was never shown but sired excellent stock. Heatherglen Cliquot, whelped in November 1966, came to the author and became the first Victorian champion and the first bitch champion in Australia. Pilgrimsway Loki died of a heart attack on Christmas day 1971, whilst Lenlee Gail died in 1972, so ending the second chapter of the breed's history 'down under'.

All of the early Australian Rottweilers, as detailed, came from Rintelna/Loki/Gail matings and the degree of inbreeding was, therefore, higher than is found once a breed is well established. In the desire to improve the gene pool of my own kennel, I contacted The Kennel Club in London who introduced me to Mary Macphail, the renowned trainer and judge of Rottweilers. Through Mary's good office, we were fortunate enough to import a bitch puppy, Chesara Dark Impression, from Judith Elsden. Impression's sire was Chesara Luther, a superb Dutch import and the second champion of the breed in the UK. Her dam was Chesara Dark Destiny, the first British champion. Rudi, as we called her, left an indelible imprint on the breed and for many years most of the leading Rottweilers in Australia had her name in their pedigrees. Her offspring were to become the foundation bitches for many now-famous kennels.

The rabies scare of 1971 resulted in a clamp-down on any imports

An informal photograph of the author with his dogs (left to right) Ch Auslese Beaujolais, Ch Auslese Niersteiner and Auslese Lirac (Photo: Max Neilson)

into Australia, but, when this was lifted in the following year, a flood of dogs arrived. Mr Mummery imported four: Attila Ajax (Lars vd Hobertsberg x Gamegards Border Rising); Chesara Dark Nobleman (Chesara Akilles x Chesara Dark Memory); Chesara Dark Wishful (Ero v Buchaneck x Chesara Dark Katrin), and Baroness Delviento (Chesara Dark Inquisitor x Chesara Dark Gamble). Except for Lars, all the others had sires who were British champions.

Akilles, from the famous Fandangos line in Sweden, was the top British sire at the time and I was anxious to acquire a quality bitch to put to him. Again through Mary Macphail, we acquired Jentris Gloriosa (Lars vd Hobertsberg x Chesara Dark Revelry). Gloriosa was mated to Akilles before being exported in 1971 and whelped ten pups, but only four survived. Two were dogs and both became champions – Auslese Bacchus and Auslese Beaujolais. Both left their influence on the breed and Beau was the first Rottweiler to go Best in Show at an all-breed championship show.

Mrs Terry imported a bitch, Black Shiva (Ch Chesara Dark Kruger x

Bathsheba Black Velvet), which was bred by Mr R. Johnson. From the mid 1970s onwards, the number of imports rose steadily, and these included a number of progeny sired by the British champion Gamegards Bulli vd Waldachquelle, of whom much was expected. The bitch Attila Bathsheba, out of Attila Astrid, was one of these and was purchased by Mrs Biltris. Bathsheba was mated to Upend Gallant Elf prior to export, and served her quarantine in New Zealand where her litter was born. Sheba won her New Zealand champion title before going on to Australia – together with a son, Korobeit Hud, and a daughter, Korobeit Helga.

A Bulli son, Jentris Kyrie, out of Jentris Gypsophilia, was imported by Mrs Seymour-Johns of New South Wales. Kyrie sired Finforest Emmanuelle who became a champion and also the first Australian Rottweiler to qualify UD. She was owned by Sally Larha and trained by Joan Bull who also took her to her TD title. Another Bulli son, imported by Jenny Anvers, was Gamegards Mayhap out of Brooklow Cool Angel of Manisus. Mayhap was the most influential of the Bulli sons. Gamegards Zodiac, out of Gamegards Double Dare, was a further Bulli son imported, but later transferred to Tasmania. One has to say that Bulli's influence in Australia was disappointing when compared with that of his father in Germany.

In 1978 Mr Mummery imported Chesara Dark Boris (Toro Triomfator x Chesara Dark Olga); Herberger Count D'Arcy (Lord vd Grurmannsheide x Rawtor Succo Emma of Herburger) and Adoram Matheson (Ch Castor of Intisari x Adoram Horsa). The first South Australian import was made by Mrs Naughton who brought in Vadenza Valhalla (Ch Auscott Hasso v Marchenwald x Auscott Capucine), whilst Borgvaale Sunday Morning (Arkle of Cenlea x Chesara Dark Jasmine) was imported to New South Wales, but later transferred to the west. Mr Goedemonte, of the Brabantsia kennels in Western Australia, imported Chesara Dark Rustler (Torro Triomfator x Borgvaale Venus) and Guiding Flame (Ch Auscott Hasso v Marchenwald x Owlcroft Anita). In Victoria Mr and Mrs Inkster imported Janbicca Supersonic (Ch Janbicca the Superman x Herburger Countess Katya) and Attila Honour (Attila Watchful x Attila Chione).

The first import from Germany was undertaken by the author when he acquired Catja vd Flugschneise who was purchased by the Chief Breed Warden Friedrich Berger; she was mated to Ch Castor of Intisari before being exported with four of her progeny. On a trip to Europe in 1981 we reviewed some 1,200 Rottweilers and purchased two who, it is hoped, will continue to improve the Australian gene pool. These were Felix v Mägdeberg (Brando v Haus Neubrand x Biene v Hohenhameln) an excellent dog, and the bitch Echo v Mägdeberg (Cliff v Luckshof x Babette v Magdeburg).

The first import from the USA was made in 1982 by Mrs Pat Hall of Stromhall kennels, who acquired Powderhorn Fetz of Wencrest sired by the superb triple champion Oscar vh Brabantpark out of Illona v Haus Schottroy. The addition of Fetz's line can, in theory, only improve the present range of Australian bloodlines, although only time will tell, and it is to be hoped that the future of the breed will be the better for these importations.

As this book goes to press the author has four exciting imports in progress. One is a young Eulenspiegel bitch from Marieanne Bruns, a bitch puppy from a German import mated to an English champion, an excellent dog from Dr Carla Lensi in Italy and the 1986 Youth *Sieger* Graf v Grüntenblick.

In most cases the pedigrees of the imported dogs can be traced by reference to the chapter on the breed in Britain, from where nearly all Australian Rottweilers have originated.

The Show Scene

In the 1960s and early 1970s, Victoria was the only state to show the Rottweiler. Half a dozen entries were normal, and it was not until the 1972 Melbourne Royal that good numbers were exhibited. At that show there were forty-nine entrants to be judged, under Mrs Lindhe of Sweden. BOB went to Ch Auslese Pommery, and BOS to Auslese Contessa, owned by Mr Henderson. The first large entry for a speciality was 153 at the seventh Victorian Championship Show which was judged by Muriel Freeman from the USA. Her BOB was Ch Heatherglen Franz CD, whilst BOS was Auslese Bold Kristy. The respective owners of these dogs were Miss Brenda Rawson and Mr and Mrs Young. A dog that was a prolific winner during the period 1973–7, as well as an advertisement for the breed, was Mrs Terry's Ch Uplands Lados who was seldom beaten and won challenges at the royal shows in Melbourne and Sydney. Ch Auslese Pinot was another good winner and, indeed, beat Lados for BOB on all the occasions they met.

Many present-day Rottweiler owners and breeders may be unaware of a point of interest, not documented in contemporary works, concerning Captain Roy-Smith who returned to England in 1977 and took with him Ch Auslese Bold Baggage, with the intention to commence breeding operations with her. She gained a Res CC under Muriel Freeman at the club championship of that year and remains the only Australian Rottweiler to have been exhibited at Crufts. Roy-Smith's plans did not work out, and he later returned to Australia where he died in 1981. Bold Baggage was given to Mrs Joan Wheatcroft and, at the time of writing, is eleven years old and a much loved member of the family.

Pedigree 12

FELIX V MÄGDEBERG (Imp Germany) G0095710G10

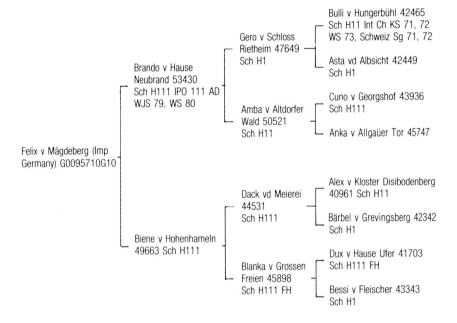

Felix v Mägdeberg (Imp Germany) G0095710G10

- Brando v Hause Neubrand 53430 Sch H111 IPO 111 AD WJS 79, WS 80
  - Gero v Schloss Rietheim 47649 Sch H1
    - Bulli v Hungerbühl 42465 Sch H11 Int Ch KS 71, 72 WS 73, Schweiz Sg 71, 72
    - Asta vd Albsicht 42449 Sch H1
  - Amba v Altdorfer Wald 50521 Sch H11
    - Cuno v Georgshof 43936 Sch H111
    - Anka v Allgaüer Tor 45747
- Biene v Hohenhameln 49663 Sch H111
  - Dack vd Meierei 44531 Sch H111
    - Alex v Kloster Disibodenberg 40961 Sch H11
    - Bärbel v Grevingsberg 42342 Sch H1
  - Blanka v Grossen Freien 45898 Sch H111 FH
    - Dux v Hause Ufer 41703 Sch H111 FH
    - Bessi v Fleischer 43343 Sch H1

Pedigree 13

ECHO V MÄGDEBERG (Imp Germany) G0095709G10

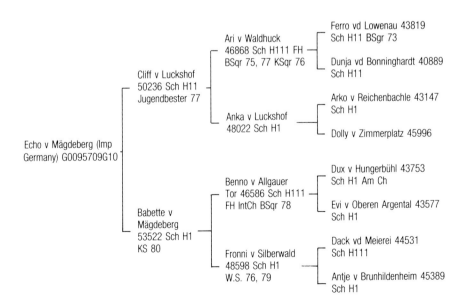

Echo v Mägdeberg (Imp Germany) G0095709G10

- Cliff v Luckshof 50236 Sch H11 Jugendbester 77
  - Ari v Waldhuck 46868 Sch H111 FH BSqr 75, 77 KSqr 76
    - Ferro vd Lowenau 43819 Sch H11 BSgr 73
    - Dunja vd Bonninghardt 40889 Sch H11
  - Anka v Luckshof 48022 Sch H1
    - Arko v Reichenbachle 43147 Sch H1
    - Dolly v Zimmerplatz 45996
- Babette v Mägdeberg 53522 Sch H1 KS 80
  - Benno v Allgauer Tor 46586 Sch H111 FH IntCh BSqr 78
    - Dux v Hungerbühl 43753 Sch H1 Am Ch
    - Evi v Oberen Argental 43577 Sch H1
  - Fronni v Silberwald 48598 Sch H1 W.S. 76, 79
    - Dack vd Meierei 44531 Sch H111
    - Antje v Brunhildenheim 45389 Sch H1

Pedigree 14

YUCCA EULENSPIEGEL (Imp Germany) ADRK 68383

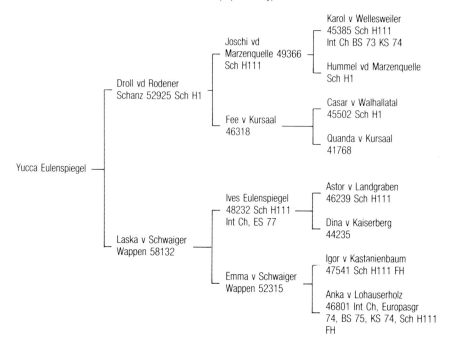

```
                                                        ┌─ Karol v Wellesweiler
                                          ┌─ Joschi vd  │  45385 Sch H111
                                          │  Marzenquelle 49366  Int Ch BS 73 KS 74
                                          │  Sch H111   │
                       ┌─ Droll vd Rodener │            └─ Hummel vd Marzenquelle
                       │  Schanz 52925 Sch H1           │  Sch H1
                       │                  │             ┌─ Casar v Walhallatal
                       │                  └─ Fee v Kursaal  45502 Sch H1
                       │                     46318      │
                       │                                └─ Quanda v Kursaal
Yucca Eulenspiegel ────┤                                   41768
                       │                                ┌─ Astor v Landgraben
                       │                  ┌─ Ives Eulenspiegel  46239 Sch H111
                       │                  │  48232 Sch H111  │
                       │                  │  Int Ch, ES 77  └─ Dina v Kaiserberg
                       └─ Laska v Schwaiger │                 44235
                          Wappen 58132    │                ┌─ Igor v Kastanienbaum
                                          │                │  47541 Sch H111 FH
                                          └─ Emma v Schwaiger │
                                             Wappen 52315  └─ Anka v Lohauserholz
                                                              46801 Int Ch, Europasgr
                                                              74, BS 75, KS 74, Sch H111
                                                              FH
```

Pedigree 15

Poldark Mary Rose (Imp UK) L5937403L

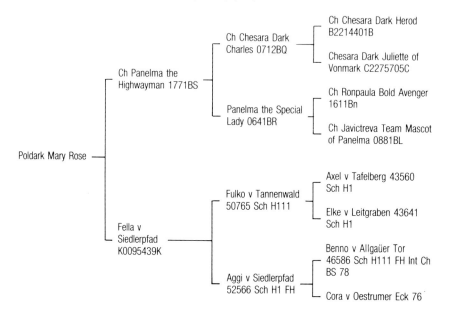

```
                                                        ┌─ Ch Chesara Dark Herod
                                          ┌─ Ch Chesara Dark  B2214401B
                                          │  Charles 0712BQ │
                       ┌─ Ch Panelma the  │             └─ Chesara Dark Juliette of
                       │  Highwayman 1771BS│                Vonmark C2275705C
                       │                  │             ┌─ Ch Ronpaula Bold Avenger
                       │                  └─ Panelma the Special  1611Bn
                       │                     Lady 0641BR │
                       │                                └─ Ch Javictreva Team Mascot
Poldark Mary Rose ─────┤                                   of Panelma 0881BL
                       │                                ┌─ Axel v Tafelberg 43560
                       │                  ┌─ Fulko v Tannenwald  Sch H1
                       │                  │  50765 Sch H111  │
                       │                  │             └─ Elke v Leitgraben 43641
                       └─ Fella v         │                Sch H1
                          Siedlerpfad     │                ┌─ Benno v Allgaüer Tor
                          K0095439K       │                │  46586 Sch H111 FH Int Ch
                                          └─ Aggi v Siedlerpfad │  BS 78
                                             52566 Sch H1 FH └─ Cora v Oestrumer Eck 76
```

Pedigree 16

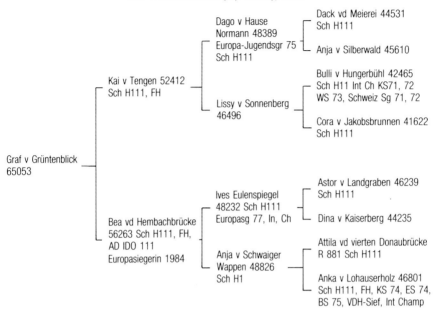

GRAF V GRÜNTENBLICK (Imp Germany) 65053

Graf v Grüntenblick
65053

- Kai v Tengen 52412
  Sch H111, FH
  - Dago v Hause
    Normann 48389
    Europa-Jugendsgr 75
    Sch H111
    - Dack vd Meierei 44531
      Sch H111
    - Anja v Silberwald 45610
  - Lissy v Sonnenberg
    46496
    - Bulli v Hungerbühl 42465
      Sch H11 Int Ch KS71, 72
      WS 73, Schweiz Sg 71, 72
    - Cora v Jakobsbrunnen 41622
      Sch H111
- Bea vd Hembachbrücke
  56263 Sch H111, FH,
  AD IDO 111
  Europasiegerin 1984
  - Ives Eulenspiegel
    48232 Sch H111
    Europasg 77, In, Ch
    - Astor v Landgraben 46239
      Sch H111
    - Dina v Kaiserberg 44235
  - Anja v Schwaiger
    Wappen 48826
    Sch H1
    - Attila vd vierten Donaubrücke
      R 881 Sch H111
    - Anka v Lohauserholz 46801
      Sch H111, FH, KS 74, ES 74,
      BS 75, VDH-Sief, Int Champ

Pedigree 17

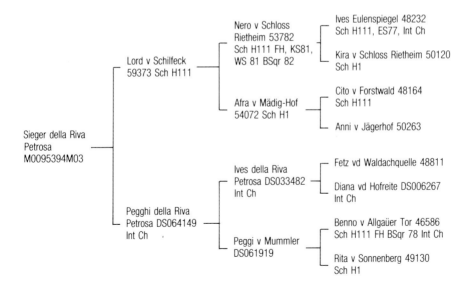

SIEGER DELLA RIVA PETROSA (Imp Italy) M0095394M03

Sieger della Riva
Petrosa
M0095394M03

- Lord v Schilfeck
  59373 Sch H111
  - Nero v Schloss
    Rietheim 53782
    Sch H111 FH, KS81,
    WS 81 BSqr 82
    - Ives Eulenspiegel 48232
      Sch H111, ES77, Int Ch
    - Kira v Schloss Rietheim 50120
      Sch H1
  - Afra v Mädig-Hof
    54072 Sch H1
    - Cito v Forstwald 48164
      Sch H111
    - Anni v Jägerhof 50263
- Pegghi della Riva
  Petrosa DS064149
  Int Ch
  - Ives della Riva
    Petrosa DS033482
    Int Ch
    - Fetz vd Waldachquelle 48811
    - Diana vd Hofreite DS006267
      Int Ch
  - Peggi v Mummler
    DS061919
    - Benno v Allgäüer Tor 46586
      Sch H111 FH BSqr 78 Int Ch
    - Rita v Sonnenberg 49130
      Sch H1

Pedigree 18

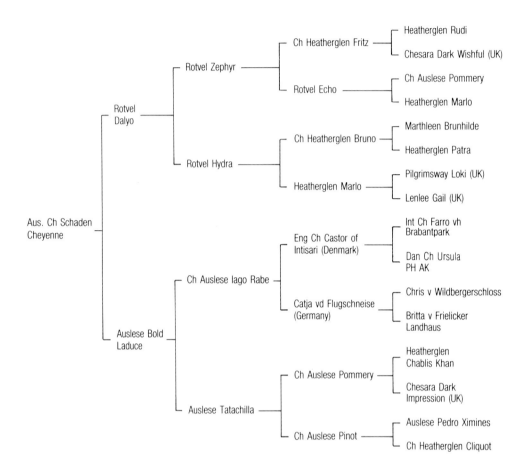

Ch Tayvelka Noble Event (sire Vadenza Valhalla, UK import), bred and owned by Mr and Mrs Taylor, was BIS Rottweiler Ch Show in 1984, under Herr Fausner (Photo: Alan Hutchison)

An excellent study of Mrs Goble's Ch Schaden Cheyenne – a leading winner of the mid 1980s in Australia

Returning to Australia, the first champions in the west of the country were those owned by Mr Goedemonte. He purchased the Auslese dogs Givry, Lambray and Mercury. The first two gained their titles in 1975, with Mercury gaining his in 1976. Other Western champions were Auslese Bold Guido, Auslese Bold Ballad, Brabantsia Tanja, Brabantsia Faru and Kemmelberg Lady Leah.

In the early 1980s, three dogs are already proving themselves prolific show winners and reflect great credit on their breeders, Mr and Mrs T. Lowther, as well as on their owners Mr and Mrs John Weir. Ch Tarquinian Ambassador (Kerusgal Houdini x Kerusgal Black Iolanthe) and his sister, Ch Tarquinian Adante, had collected no less than ninety-six CCs between them inside their first five years. Ch Tarquinian Dejanira (Kemmelberg Black Watch x Zambax Lars Amanda), not wishing to be outdone, acquired thirty-one CCs by the tender age of twenty-one months. Another dog with many wins is Tayvelka Noble Marcus (Chesara Dark Nobleman x Asgardweiler Renata), owned by Mr and Mrs Borg. A promising young dog is Mrs Goble's Ch Schaden Cheyenne whose pedigree is shown in Pedigree 18, and who continues to be a consistent show-winner.

Pedigree 19

DUAL CHAMP AUSLESE BOLD GAMMON AOC

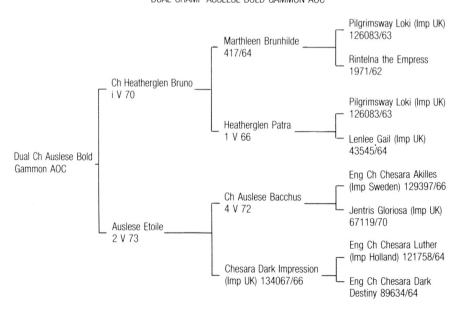

A bitch that has proved an outstanding winner of the 1980s is T. J. and J. E. O'Brien's Ch Saarlund Quanabie Mist whose pedigree appears below.

Pedigree 20

CH SAARLUND QUANABIE MIST

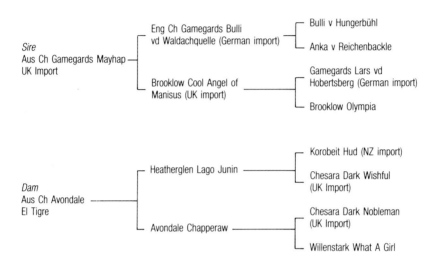

Obedience

Unlike the early days in the USA, the Rottweiler was at first neglected in Australia as far as obedience tests were concerned, but, happily, has enjoyed considerable success in this area in recent years. At Auslese, we have always been conscious that Rottweilers are all about working and have concentrated our efforts on the farm where our dogs are essential in working sheep and cattle, as well as being excellent all-round gundogs.

Obedience classes were held on the farm under the State's finest instructor, Michael Tucker, and in all other parts of the country owners have found how well the breed is suited to working tasks. In Victoria, John Stewart concentrated on training and his skill was rewarded when Tarquinian Apache CDex, UDex, TD was awarded the title Australian Obedience Champion. In New South Wales, Finforest Emmanuelle has already been discussed (see p 81). Another excellent worker was Mr Maruff's Leoleon Pinto CDex, TD (Heatherglen Ginaldus x Heatherglen Emmy). An outstanding obedience dog was Ch Stomhall Torrey CD, CDex, UD, TD (Chesara Dark Nobleman x Anverdons Olympia) owned and trained by Pat Hall. He was group winner on three occasions

Ch Robstans Our Dulcinea, bred and owned by Mr Gration, was the 1984 Rottweiler Ch Show bitch challenge winner (Photo: Alan Hutchison)

Ch Stromhall Torrey CDex, UD, TD – BIS Rottweiler Ch Show 1983 – was an outstanding obedience winner for his owner, Pat Hall. (Photo: Alan Hutchison)

one being at the Sydney Royal. Torrey was, unfortunately, killed when only six years old. The supreme honour of Australian dual champion, the only one at present, goes to Auslese Bold Gammon (Heatherglen Bruno x Auslese Etoile). 'Gabby' was an ornament to the breed and a great credit to her owner, Helen Read. Apart from winning every obedience title she had an outstanding show record and was recognised by all visiting specialists, such as Thelma Gray, Muriel Freeman and Marguereta McIntyre, winning a reserve CC, a CC and a BIS.

The obedience scene in Australia is now very healthy and in Victoria and New South Wales over forty Rottweilers have qualified in both show and working tests. Clearly, such testing is a better yardstick of judging a breed than merely parading it around a show ring, which tells one very little about its ability to perform the role for which it was intended. It is hoped that the present trend, to both work and show dogs, continues to gather momentum which must be in the breed's greatest interests.

Rottweiler Clubs in Australia

The first Rottweiler club in Australia was that of Victoria, formed in 1971 by a group of enthusiasts. They approached the Mayor of Rottweil for permission to use the crest of the town as the club emblem. This was granted. The club conducted its first parade in 1972, and its first championship show in March 1973. It has grown enormously, reflecting the popularity of the breed, and now has over 350 members. Wisely, it has adopted a policy of inviting breed experts from overseas, and entries at shows are large, that of the 1984 speciality being 206. The judges were Mr Fausner (Germany) and Mrs Hyden (Sweden). There were 232 entries in 1986 judged by Mrs Macphail (UK).

The New South Wales Club was formed in 1974, followed soon after by the South Australian. Each runs its own speciality and both are keen on the obedience side, especially the former. The Rottweiler explosion will test the capacities of all clubs but, with the experience and assistance of those already well established in the breed, future clubs should meet the challenge and help in the proper development of the breed.

Quarantine Regulations

The rules that govern the importation of dogs into Australia are probably the strictest of any country in the world, and this must directly affect both the spread and quality of stock. We have been most fortunate in Rottweilers in that the imported dogs, in the main, have all been of high standard, and most visiting breed experts are impressed with the quality of the stock they see.

Willenstadt Alana, bred by Ms Margaret Hayward and owned by Miss McClenaghan, was the 1984 Rottweiler Ch Show Best Puppy – she was sired by the American import Powderhorn Fetz of Wencrest (Photo: Alan Hutchison)

In past years, the regulations demanded that any dog imported from any country other than the UK, Eire or New Zealand, must first spend six months in quarantine in the UK to be followed by a further six months of residence. The dog was then eligible for entry to Australia where it underwent a further three months' quarantine. This made importing both a lengthy and expensive undertaking, and clearly restricted the number of dogs that were available as potential breeding partners. Happily, the regulations have now become more favourable, and dogs need spend only one month as a resident in the UK after their quarantine period, and only two months in Australia – even so, it is still a long and costly procedure to import. Thus apart from time and financial considerations, there is also the question of the effect on the dog itself – most imports being young suffer from the lack of a stable homelife at a crucial period of their development. Any person contemplating an import should, therefore, give every aspect careful consideration and be sure that the import has real relevance, both to their own plans and to the breed in the wider sense.

6 The Rottweiler in Scandinavia

Although Finland is not part of Scandinavia, it is convenient to include it in this chapter as being one of the four most northerly strongholds of the Rottweiler. The other three countries are Norway and Sweden, the two true Scandinavians of that peninsula, and Denmark, historically regarded as being part of Scandinavia, although lying to the south of it and joining West Germany as part of the western European mainland. All four countries are members of the FCI and, in addition, have a common kennel union – The Scandinavian – formed in 1889. Danish dogs are exhibited in western European shows, there being no quarantine restrictions on movement, but those of the other three countries exhibit only amongst themselves, as they are subject to quarantine regulations.

Norway

The Rottweiler has been established in Norway for many years and was certainly in evidence prior to 1919 when the first of the breed was registered there. The Norwegian Rottweiler Club was formed in 1933. The club was conscious of the need to preserve the breed's working qualities and has retained this objective to the present day. In Norway the Rottweiler is very much a utility companion dog and this is reflected in the interest shown in working tests. The premier event of the year is held in the autumn, over two days, and the dogs are tested for obedience, tracking, searching and agility, along *Schutzhund* lines. Man-work, however, is prohibited under Norwegian law and is not included in the tests.

Snow rescue work is one very important role for the breed in a country with both heavy snow falls and much forestry in which it is easy to get lost. Norwegian rescue dogs do not carry a cask of brandy attached to their collars, but, instead, have a loose flap of leather. When a lost person is traced, the dog will return to the handler holding the leather which indicates that a find has been made. He does not bark or attempt to help; this may cause shock or alarm. The handler is then led to the person. There is a special club, called the Drunkshund Club, which concentrates on training dogs for this type of work.

Rottweilers are also used for draught work, pulling sledges in the

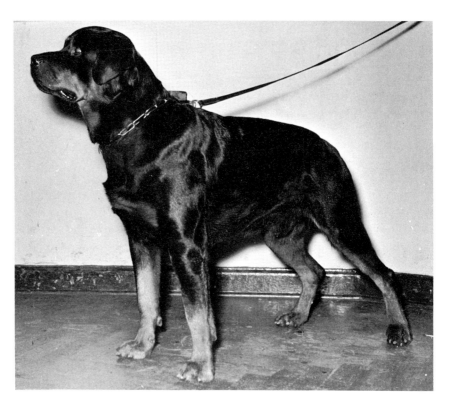

Dan and Nor Ch Arno v Martinsberg was imported from Germany by Mrs Hyden and sired the first Fandangos litter, all of which became champions (Photo: Tjänst)

winter and acting as pack animals during the summer. In this latter pursuit they wear a specially designed harness which holds two rucksacks, and are thus able to be very much a part of the family when hiking trips are undertaken. We saw one of these dogs in Trondheim and his master, a priest, claimed he was 'the best Rottweiler in the world' – but isn't every Rottweiler we own always the best?

Dog shows are run on similar lines to those in the UK and elsewhere, but the classes are different and a critique is written when the dog first enters the ring. These can be queried by handlers, and the judges are happy to discuss the exhibit's merits and failings. Dogs are graded according to the German system, but numbers 1, 2, 3, and so on, replace V, Sg and G. All dogs graded 1 return, with the best dog winning and going on for Best of Sex. The two winners are then judged to find Best and Reserve Best Exhibit.

On the show scene, Norwegian bloodlines have been influenced by good imports from Sweden. One such dog was Ch Ponto, bred in the Fandangos kennel. Before leaving Sweden Ponto was mated to Fandango Flamingo producing Int Ch Fandangos Fairboy who was not only to sire many quality Norwegian Rottweilers, but also Ch Chesara Akilles whose influence in the UK and in Australia has been cited in the appropriate chapters. Imports from Germany, surprisingly, have made no great impact in Norway, and Sweden remains the country whose bloodlines seem to blend best with the sound lines now well established in Norway. The main German influence was through Swedish champion Tell vd Hackerbrücke imported into Sweden by Mrs Hyden.

Sweden

The first Rottweiler registered in Sweden was the bitch Syda v Karlstor, in 1914, whilst the first dog of major influence was to be Arbo v Torfwerk 954 who was imported in 1921. Arbo and his litter brother, Arco 955, exercised an enormous influence on the breed, and, whilst Arbo was overshadowed by Arco in Germany, he did prove to be of great importance in Sweden. His son, Aspinas Bjorn, was the first Swedish working and show champion and the two were to be the foundation dogs of most Swedish bloodlines.

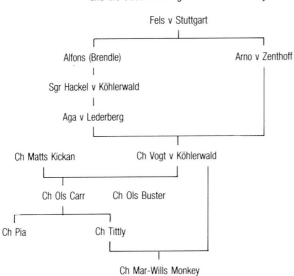

Chart 8: The influence of Fels v Stuttgart on Scandinavia and the close breeding of Mar-Wills Monkey

Bjorn was famous in police circles for stolen goods' recovery and when, in 1928, an insurance company donated a special trophy for the best practical performance at the Swedish Kennel Show; with Bjorn in the field, there could be only one winner!

Swed Ch Faunus Xante was both beauty and working show winner for the Faunus kennel
(Photo: Andreas. Courtesy: Mrs Hyden)

In 1934 Mr N. Carlsson imported two dogs, one of which was to have lasting influence in Sweden. This was Dutt vd Hackerbrücke, who traced his ancestry back to Alfons (Brendle) through his sire, Ido v Köhlerwald; the Dutt son, double champion Asteruds Treu, proved an excellent sire. Mr Carlsson's other 1934 import was the Hackel daughter, Blanka v Vogelsklause, but she did not have the hoped-for influence.

Another dog of singular importance was Vogt v Köhlerwald who was imported in 1939 by the Mar-Wills kennel owned by Mr Ronnstrom. Vogt was a fine show dog and became a champion after three shows. He had graduated SchH3 and had been used at stud in Germany prior to export, his progeny having influence both in the UK and Australia through Ch Chesara Akilles. Vogt's mating to Ch Matts Kickan produced Ch Ols Carr, one of the greatest of Swedish producers. A repeat mating produced double champion Ols Buster. Ols Carr produced some particularly fine bitches and two outstanding examples of these were Ch Pia and Ch Tittly. Tittly was mated back to Vogt to produce Ch Mar-Wills Monkey, one of the best examples of close line-breeding in Sweden.

The Teck blood, through the influence of Fels v Stuttgart, may be seen in chart 8, which also illustrates the close breeding of Mar-Wills Monkey and the influence of Vogt.

The last import from Germany, prior to 1939, was Ch Tell vd Hackerbrücke, imported by Mrs Hyden. His impeccable breeding may be seen in Pedigree 21. One of his daughters, bred to an Ols Carr grandson, had a considerable influence on the breed in Finland, whilst a son, Ajax, was a foundation dog in Norway.

In 1953 Mrs Hyden imported three dogs from Germany, these being Bosko v Kissel and Benno v Haus Adams – both line-bred to Hackel – and Arno v Martinsberg, who overshadowed the first two named. Arno became a Danish and Norwegian champion and the influence of the Gaisburg blood was felt almost immediately. Arno was sired by Arno v Schafenberg out of the *Reichssiegerin* Vroni v Gaisburg. The Fandangos kennel used him over their bitch Heikas Saba, a grand-daughter of Tell vd Hackerbrücke, to produce their famous 'F' litter (letters are misleading in Scandinavia as the same letter is used for different litters). Int Ch Fandangos Fantom was an Arno grandson, whilst Int Ch Cora Korad was a grand-daughter. One of his great grandsons was Ch Chesara Akilles.

Swed Ch Faunus Jasmine, bred and owned by Gun Bergguist and Nils Stenbacka (Photo: courtesy Mrs Hyden)

Pedigree 21

CH TELL vd HACKERBRÜCKE

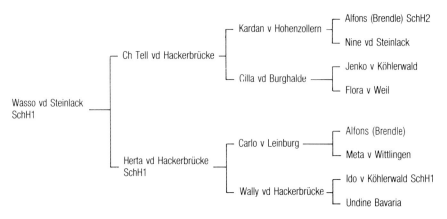

The Nordangens kennel imported two bitches whose Scandinavian influence was considerable. The first was Britta vd Kisalinde who was imported in 1958, and the second was Britta vd Lohnerhoe, imported in 1961. The latter's sire was Arros vd Kappenbergerheide who was sired by the famous Igor v Kohlwald. Britta's influence extended to Britain, the Americas and Australia and is seen in Pedigree 22.

Pedigree 22

Eng Ch CASTOR OF INTISARI

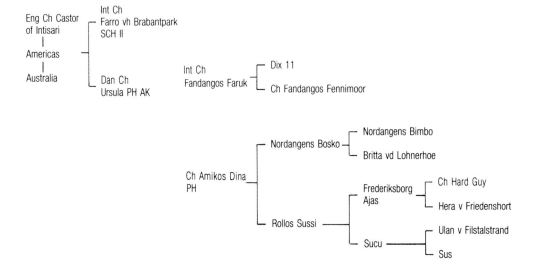

In 1962 the Hydens imported Afra vd Brantsberg from Holland, whilst, in 1971, they also imported Gamegards Far N Away from Joan Woodgate in England. Mrs Hyden, a Rottweiler judge of international standing, has been the unofficial breed warden in Sweden for nearly forty years, whilst her husband, Sven, was active in the working field as far back as 1928 and has judged Rottweilers since 1940.

Denmark

The Danes, as in other Scandinavian countries, are very keen to develop Rottweilers as much as utilitarian companions as guard companions which is very much a German trait. They concentrate on procedures to discover hereditary ability as they feel, with justification, that German methods do not discriminate between this capacity and what the dog has learnt. The aim of most tests is to discover the dog's ability in more than a mere demonstration of aggression. Characteristics such as willingness to play, curiosity, concentration, tendency to hunt, or ability to relax are all tested. Dogs in Denmark are extremely fit and they seem to age better than most Rottweilers. A veteran we saw during his demonstration looked to be no more than three years of age. The handlers are also very fit.

The first import from Germany was the bitch Ruth v Freiheit who was acquired in 1911 by a policeman, Hakon Jorgensen, later to become Director of Police in Denmark. He was very impressed with what he saw of the breed in Germany, and after Ruth had joined the department, a second import, Bello v Neuffen, was purchased. Bello was used sparingly at stud in Scandinavia.

A good dog from Norway, Sjohelles Nero, was imported, but there were no good bitches available in Denmark, so a line was not established; the same is true of Ch Morso King whose influence would, no doubt, have been more meaningful had better bitches been available. In 1947, Nordjyden kennels imported Cita v Rutliweg who was mated to the Norwegian dog Burmand to produce an excellent bitch, Ch Nordjydens Schwiss. Schwiss was mated to the Swedish dog Bosko v Kissel and produced a top Danish dog, Ch Nordjydens Ulla FH.

Two litter sisters – Britta and Black Friedenshort – were imported from Germany in 1956 and, together with Arno v Martinsberg, a grandson of Vroni v Gaisburg, who was used at stud in Denmark, introduced the Gaisburg bloodline into the country. In 1958, the Sussi kennels imported Ulan v Filstilstrand, and in 1960 the Ostjyden kennels imported Clou Eulenspiegel. After whelping her second litter, it was discovered that Clou had entropion and she was put down. The gene was carried by her grandfather, Asso v Wakenitzberg, and was brought

PH Aias, the outstanding Danish Rottweiler who was Klubsieger *in 1978 and* Bundessieger *in 1979, the only non-German dog ever to win these prestigious titles.* (Photo: courtesy Tonni Pederson)

into the UK by Quinta and Bim Eulenspiegel who were also descendants of Asso.

The Frederiksborg kennels imported Hera v Friedenshort PH, AK and she proved to be significant in countries other than Denmark. Her mating to Ch Hard Guy produced Frederiksborg Ajas who, in turn, sired Rollos Sussi, the dam of the most beautiful bitch born in Scandinavia, Ch Amikos Dina PH AK. Dina's grandson, through her daughter Ch Ursula PH, AK, was none other than Ch Castor of Intisari, the top UK stud of the day. Ursula's sire was the most famous of Danish dogs, Int Ch Fandangos Faruk AK, owned by Gunvor of Klinteberg. Faruk produced more than 100 pups, of which a quarter earned working degrees; he was awarded the Swedish Working Dog Trophy, a truly unique distinction.

This review on Danish Rottweilers would not be complete without reference to Aias who was whelped in September 1974, out of Gottschalks Juno by Mentor. He was bred by D. and B. Kandrup of Valby DK and owned by Tonni Pedersen of Bronshoj. Aias was awarded the coveted title of 1978 *Klubsieger* in Germany by Paul Schafer when he beat a record entry of twenty-seven dogs, of whom twelve were rated V; the field included the dog that became *Bundessieger* a few days later – Benno v Allgaüer-Tor. Aias went on to become *Bundessieger* himself a year later.

Ch Rintelna the General with his son. This picture appeared in 1969 with an article in Womans Weekly *(Australia) and put the breed on the map in that country* (courtesy Australian Consolidated Press)

Auslese Ennius (whelped 1984) at the Asia Kennel Union Dog Show

Ch Auslese Ferrara CD (whelped 1985), owned by Mr Zurek (courtesy Mr Zurek)

Finland

In spite of its very small population, Finland has a long and growing association with the Rottweiler. Its club was formed in 1946, with Olavi Pasanen as president, and boasts a membership bettered only by the ADRK, and possibly that of Denmark's club. Mr Pasanen must be singled out in any discussion of Rottweilers and stands without equal in his homeland. He is an international judge, an ambassador for the breed and a major influence in the International Friends of the Rottweiler (IFR). His von Heidenmoor kennels, begun in 1946, are world-famous and his interest in working trials has earned him the rare distinction of the Plaque of Finnish Union of Working Breeds which was awarded to his kennel. The Chief Breed Warden is Mr J. A. U. Yrjölä who has held the appointment for over twenty years.

The first Rottweilers in Finland were registered in 1927 and were Swedish imports, Hammarsbys Buck and Lutz av Meldstein. Imported dogs, other than those from the UK, Sweden or Norway, must undergo four months' quarantine, and this restricted German imports in the early years – mainly due to the expense. Indeed, one novel method of acquiring a Rottweiler just after the Second World War, was to exchange a trained German shepherd dog for a Rottweiler bitch in whelp from Sweden.

Later, however, German imports started to arrive and amongst the more influential were Karo v Jakobsbrunnen, Droll v Wolfsgarten, Benno v Bacherbach, Jim v Fleischer, Gerry Eulenspiegel, Jacky v Haus Schöttroy and Larry v Stuffelkopf. The bitches included Meta vd Solitude, Dora v Goldsteinpark, and Jessy v Haus Schöttroy. Imports came from Sweden and Denmark, with the Swedish dog, Aviemores Fakir, and the Danish dogs, Holmes Blackie and Holmes Buster, being the more influential. In order to strengthen Finnish bloodlines further, their bitches have been mated to German imports into Sweden, such as Droll v St Andreasberg, Castor v Emstal and Ilo v Klösterchen, as well as to top Swedish studs like Fandangos Fair Boy, Fandangos Faruk and the Bergsgardens dogs, King, Dallas and Aiko.

Like the Scandinavians, Finnish breeders and owners are concerned to develop the working side of the breed and much emphasis is placed upon this. Rottweilers are used as guards, police dogs, trackers, drug searchers and even guide dogs for the blind. Mental agility tests are those adopted from the Swedish system which is also used in Denmark, whilst the Finnish breed test for conformation and character is much the same as the German ZTP.

7 The Rottweiler in Other Countries

Having dealt with the breed in those countries where it is already well established, I will now review it briefly in those places where its numbers will most certainly grow in the coming years. Italy has been left to the last, as it seems an appropriate country with which to conclude the historical review of the Rottweiler's development and spread around the globe from its Italian origin.

Brazil

Although the Rottweiler is found in numerous Latin-American countries, it is best established in Brazil. I am told that the breed was exhibited in shows during 1958, but have no records to support this. In 1965, Dimiter Petroff, a director of Lufthansa Airlines, emigrated to Rio de Janeiro with his family, taking with them their Rottweiler who, no doubt, created much interest, although he was never shown or bred from. In 1968, Dr Karl Leisinger, his wife Ursula and their daughters, emigrated to Petropolis and took with them Etzel v Gertrudenhof (Grimm vd Hobertsberg SchH1 x Lita v Schloss Westerwinkel), bred by Gunter Schlotjunker. Etzel was shown at five international shows, being awarded a CACIB at each one. He became the foundation dog of the breed in the country. His lines go back to the great German dog Igor v Kohlwald.

The Leisingers imported a bitch from Germany, Camba v Beselicker-Koph (Gring vd Wigg SchH1 x Zola v Jakobsbrunnen), into their Alcobaca kennels and this, when mated to Etzel, produced the first two litters to be registered in South America. The 'A' litter was not shown, but some of the 'B' litter were, and figured in the breeding programmes of numerous kennels, particularly that of the Frisans. A bitch, Barbarella do Alcobaca, owned by Haroldo Tupinamba, was the top Rottweiler bitch in 1974 and the first Brazilian champion of the breed. Her sire and dam were the leading show winners in 1972 and 1973, with Barbarella displacing her mother in 1974. A litter brother, Int Ch Blaubart Do Alcobaca, owned by Joao Gasper Melo, was the best male in 1975. A litter sister, Int & Grand Ch Britannia Do Alcobaco was the best bitch. Britannia is owned by the author's friend, Luciano Cruz de Oliveira, Rottweiler breeder and judge, and the information on the scene in Brazil is due largely to this gentleman's helpful correspondence.

In 1975 Dr Bernard Vaena imported a well-bred dog, Sangetts Svarte-Tarras (Fin Ch Reza x Fandangos Skade), whilst Tuula Salovaara, in San Paulo, imported further Scandinavian lines in the form of a dog, Beara v Heidenmoor, and a bitch, Ursus v Heidenmoor. The breeder of the dog was the famous judge and Rottweiler authority, Olavi Pasanen, whilst that of the bitch was Aune Jayhiaimen. Another bitch, imported from Finland by Gerald Nobrega, was Attalos Charlotta, bred by Rita Alanen Inkeri.

The same year saw the first import from Britain, which was Herburger Countess Aisha (Ch Castor of Intisari x Trojanus Flavia of Herburger). She was owned by Jose Lima and proved to be the top bitch of 1976 and 1977. North American imports included Int Ch Kuhns Andvari, bred by Prudence Kuhn and owned by Victor Ekner; Kuhlwald's Axel, bred by Norma Harris and owned by Haroldo Tupinamba, and Bergluft Elke, bred by Dorit Rogers and owned by Fernando Frota. One bitch that proved highly successful was the Finnish Ella (Joukanheimo Constantinus x Neiju), bred by Marja Ekman and chosen for the owner, Luciano Cruz, by the Chief Breed Warden, Jokya Yrjölä. Ella became a Brazilian and International champion and was the leading bitch in South America in the late 1970s.

The Rottweiler has made a great impression on South American dog fanciers, especially those of Brazil, and has also been accepted by the army and police forces. The breed is recognised as an obedience dog and is appearing in trials, both working and *Schutzhund*. The greatest impact, however, has been in the family circle where they are rapidly replacing boxers and German shepherds as the number-one choice for companion-guard. There is no breed club, but owners receive information from British and American clubs, as well as from the Finnish Rottweiler Club.

South Africa

As in many countries, the Rottweiler was for years overlooked by South Africans whose companion-guard-dog choice was a German shepherd, a Dobermann or, somewhat surprisingly, a Bull Terrier. Rottweilers had been imported from just prior to the Second World War, but made no impact at all; indeed, from 1945–56, none were registered. After 1956, interest in the breed gathered momentum and, by the mid 1970s, registrations were passing the 600 mark. By 1979 they had reached 2,429 – an immense leap. The trend continued into the 1980s, and by 1983 the figure was 4,740, well ahead of the UK total. Not until 1984

The top winning Rottweiler in South Africa, Ch Tankerville Digby, bred and owned by Mr and Mrs Dudley Bennett (Photo: courtesy Mr Bennett)

was there a halt in the onward march, when the figure dropped to 3,933 – the first country of significance to show such a halt in the rise in popularity.

There is little doubt at all that the popularity explosion of the Rottweiler reflects the society in which we now live, and which seems to have become more violent. Certainly, in South Africa, this has had considerable influence on the fortunes of the breed which is almost exclusively owned by the white population. It is not coincidental that about half of all dogs registered in that country come from the working group, the Rottweiler now being second only to the German shepherd, and continuing to gain support, largely at the expense of the Dobermann which is in decline.

The South African show scene is made difficult because of the great distances between venues, but, nonetheless, it has become a popular pastime with a growing number of people. A most successful breeder-exhibitor over the years has been Mr Dudley Bennett, the president of the South African Rottweiler Club. His foundation dog, Ch St Tuttson Bastian of Tankerville, did much to promote the breed, apart from siring superb stock. Tankerville stock have been regular dog and bitch of the year winners, and the kennel has produced eleven champions. Ch

Tankerville Digby was the first Rottweiler to win Best In Show at an all-breeds show. Digby was out of Tankerville Heidi (a Ch Tuttson daughter) and sired by Mr Bennett's British import, Ch Upend Gallant Luke bred by Barbara Butler who has judged in South Africa.

A number of leading Rottweiler authorities have judged in South Africa and these include Aage Christensen of Denmark, Rainer Vourinen of Finland and Muriel Freeman of the USA. The breed's first championship show was held in 1985 and judged by Adolf Ringer, Commandant of the Austrian Military Dog School. An entry of 109 was attracted, and the honours were shared by Ch Tankerville Digby and his sister, Ch Tankerville Debbie.

South African breeders import from Germany, Scandinavia and the UK, giving them a sound cross-section of leading bloodlines, and it can only be hoped that the nation's renewed internal problems do not adversely affect the onward progress of the Rottweiler in that country. There is a need for the breed's history in South Africa to be carefully researched and I understand that Dr E. Retief is undertaking this task which will be welcomed by enthusiasts in other countries, who find it difficult to obtain detailed information of Rottweiler activities.

Clearly, the Rottweiler is used both by police and armed forces, both having their own breeding programmes, that of the police being near Pretoria and that of the army being at Voortrekkerhougte. Cross-breeding is undertaken – usually to Dobermanns or bloodhounds, although I am informed that such crossing is not restricted to dogs! The army was presented with a male Siberian timber wolf which has been incorporated in the breeding programme – the first experiment being with a German shepherd bitch.

Israel
Rottweilers first appeared in Israel in the early 1970s and the Israeli Rottweiler Club was formed in 1976. Although numbers of the breed are very small, those that do own them are very enthusiastic. The club works within the framework of the Israel Kennel Club, its direct influence being accepted voluntarily by breeders. The breed warden system, along German lines, was instituted soon after the club was formed and should ensure that the breed develops on strong foundations. Dogs and bitches are tested for character before matings take place and Rottweilers under the age of two years may not be bred from; bitches are mated only once per year. Most imports are from Germany and Scandinavia. The first Rottweiler to appear in the IKC breed register was Falk v Horster Dreieck, owned by Mr Arrael Aviner Givatayim; Falk was also the first champion of the breed.

The club organises three limited shows each year and these are well supported, given the small breed numbers in the country. Training classes are popular and are along German lines. Although one or two dogs have attained SchH1 standard, none of these have been Rottweilers, but this is surely only a question of time.

Italy

The wheel turned full circle when, in 1950, Ondra v Zabergam crossed the Alps in the opposite direction to that taken by the Roman legions and their herding dogs some 2,000 years earlier. The reason he was imported to Italy goes back to the war years. Two doctors, Armando Colombo and Gustavo Sala, were the guests of the German military in a PoW camp during the latter part of the war. Always hungry, they took to raiding nearby farms when the opportunity came – depriving both the farmer and his dogs of any scraps left lying around. It was during this phase that they made the acquaintance of a Rottweiler – not to their advantage at that time!

Developing a very healthy respect for the breed, they determined to acquire one for themselves, but it was to be five years before this became a reality. They imported four Rottweilers before being granted the now-famous Rotargus prefix. This, out of interest, is composed as follows: Rot(weiler) Ar(mando) Gus(tavo).

Their first import was, as stated, Ondra, a dog who was graded excellent. Next was the bitch Norma v Luisenhohe, bred by Reisinger and imported in 1951. She was also graded excellent and was awarded a CAC – one leg towards her Italian championship. The third dog came from the famous Martinsberg kennel and was Alex v Martinsberg, bred by Meyer, and also imported in 1951. He later became an Italian champion. In 1953, the kennel imported Alice v Forchenköpf, and in 1955 the dog Int Ch Ero v Hackerbrücke, bred by Englert. These latter imports were mated to produce Arko Di Rotargus – the first Italian-born champion – owned by Ellie Luigi. A litter brother, Crack Di Rotargus, went to Romanelli Ferdinando who is the father of our good friend, Dr Carla Lensi, president of the Italian Rottweiler Club. Over the next four years the Rotargus kennel imported a number of fine Rottweilers, including Rita v Kohlwald and Ch Ero v Butzensee, and the breed seemed to be developing very steadily. However, Ch Ero was to be the last import of the kennel, in 1959. Dr Colombo continued on his own and imported about four more Rottweilers, but sold the last two to Mr Locatelli. Interest in the breed then seemed to wane, and it was to be a few years before the next major kennel was established.

The Italian Kennel Club admitted Mrs Lensi as a breeder, with the prefix della Riva Petrosa, in 1974, and a new line of Rottweilers was underway. The brother and sister imports, Nick and Nelly v Kallenberg, both became international champions, whilst a bitch, Diana vd Hofreite, proved to be of outstanding merit. She was accepted as an Italian Champion for Reproduction, and to gain this honour a bitch (or dog) must have produced six champions from at least two different matings to dogs graded excellent.

Carlo v Liebersbacher was imported by Giancarlo Tosi and mated to Diana to produce Int Ch Kranz della Riva Petrosa. To the same dog Diana then whelped Jessica della Riva Petrosa who became world champion in Verona in 1980. Next, Diana went to the German dog Fetz vd Waldachquelle and from that mating came Ital Ch Ives della Riva Petrosa who gained a third at the ninth *Klubsieger* show. The success of the Lensis has continued, with numerous champions, and the growth of the breed in Italy, as in most other countries, progresses steadily.

The Italian KC (known as the ENCI) is controlled by the Ministry of Agriculture and retains a fairly strict hold on breeding and exhibiting. At this time it recognises only three breeders. The Italian Rottweiler Club was formed in 1979 under the presidency of Dr Lensi. The club has studied the example of the ADRK and has close associations with it. Italian exhibitors attend German shows and vice versa. They take a very serious interest in the breed and, although their numbers are still very small by European standards, the future looks very rosy for that country – and why not? It was the reforms of Caesar, all those years ago, that resulted in the magnificent Rottweiler we have today.

The European Show Scene

Europe, in the context of dog shows, may be divided conveniently into three sectors. Geography, and its influence on quarantine barriers, is the determinant. The first sector is the British Isles, which stage the great dog shows of the world including Crufts. The premier British Rottweiler show is The Rottweiler Club Championship Show staged in the London area. It was held in the autumn but the date was changed in 1981 to spring. The British Isles are guarded by a quarantine barrier and every dog, regardless of the country from which it comes, must be cleansed by quarantine; this period is not forty days but one hundred and eighty! This is a powerful constraint on exhibits and every dog shown is a resident of the country.

The mainland of Europe, excluding Finland and Scandinavia, is the second sector. It has no restriction, and dogs move freely from Italy to Denmark and from Spain to Hungary. Denmark, except for the island on which Copenhagen is situated, is part of mainland Europe and Danish dogs take part in all shows on the mainland.

The third sector includes the three countries, Finland, Sweden and Norway, and they impose a four month quarantine on all dogs except those coming from the British Isles. Finland and Sweden have stringent qualifications for dogs entering championship shows and Norwegian shows are generally restricted to Norwegian dogs.

The premier Rottweiler show is the Polar Sieger held alternately each year in Sweden and Finland. The atmosphere of the Polar show is one of happy involvement with dogs, exhibitors and spectators all making a joyous contribution. Dogs are well socialised and move freely around. The show is held over two days the first being devoted to working trials. Dogs compete for conformation, working and obedience titles. A tally of placings is kept on a large board divided into a number of squares; each is numbered with the catalogue number of the exhibits. A coloured ribbon, indicating the grade awarded to the dog, is attached to the dog's collar; the same ribbon is placed on the square on the board. Different coloured ribbons are awarded for each grade; ribbons awarded for obedience are worn in the show ring.

In the last show that we attended in 1981, was a splendid specimen who would have compared favourably with his German counterpart. His parents were Swedish but his grandsire was a German import. Two hundred and thirty dogs were exhibited and only four were German born; eighteen dogs were sired by German imports. The show was conducted in the best sporting spirit and the general impression given was that the exhibitors took part rather than competed.

In the same year Mrs Gerd Hyden, the Swedish specialist, judged ninety-four Rottweilers in the Swedish Championship show. A month later the Swedish Kennel Club conducted its annual all-breeds show. The Rottweiler entry was restricted to thirty-eight.

Mainland exhibitors travel enormous distances to compete. The Group winner at the all-breeds show, held in September 1981 by the Danish Kennel Club, set off for Hungary to compete in a show the following day. He was Dux, sired by the German dog Astor v Fuisse der Eifel, who was placed V 3 at the *Klub Sieger* in 1985. Danish all-breed shows follow the same pattern as the British and Australian shows; the only difference is that they have eight groups. CACIBs and Reserve CACIBs, when available, are awarded to each best of sex winner provided that they are over fifteen months and meet the breed standard. The two premier all-breed shows in the Low Countries are the Amsterdam Winners' Show and the Belgian Eurodog Show both held in a complex of halls in the late autumn.

The accent, in Germany, is on breed judging and this is obvious even to the novice. Judging, in an all-breed show, generally concludes with breed classes. There is no group judging and males and females, except in the *Klub Sieger* show, do not compete against each other. Champions are selected from the senior classes where all exhibits have working qualifications. Prior to 1971, when the ADRK introduced its specialty, the *Klubsieger-Zuchtschau*, the premier Rottweiler show was the *Bundessieger Zuchtschau*. It is staged in late autumn under the umbrella of the VDH; the venue, generally, is Dortmund. The total all-breed entry is about four thousand. The Rottweiler entry is around eighty with a record of one hundred and three in 1969.

Two other all-breed shows of distinction are the *Weltsieger*, held in March, and the *Europasieger Zuchtschau*, held a month later. CACIBs are awarded at these shows but the Rottweiler entry does not exceed one hundred. Breeds seldom compete against each other and one gets the impression that breed shows are being run independently of groups with little relation to each other.

The most important event in the show calendar is the ADRK speciality conducted in early autumn. This was the brain-child of the Chief Breed Warden, the late Friedrich Berger. The first show, appropriately, was held in Rottweil. It is held over two days with the senior classes being judged on the second day. If the venue is suitable the *Leistungssieger Prüfung* (working trial) is conducted at the same show. The chief restraint placed on the working class, the class that produces the *Sieger*, is the working qualification required. There are five classes generally and entries are received for the junior classes from Denmark, Holland, Belgium, Switzerland and Italy. Entries are around one hundred and fifty with the record being established at Borken-Burlo of two hundred in 1978.

'The breeding of Rottweilers is the breeding of working dogs' so runs the motto of the ADRK, and more Rottweilers are trained for *Schutzhund* than for the show ring. The *Leistungssieger* is keenly contested with qualifying trials being held months before in various districts. Dogs must have the Sch H 3 qualification and very few bitches enter. In 1985 forty-four entered the competition. The winner was Erasmus v Mägdeberg with a score of 295; he was second the previous year. The record number of wins is held by Axel v Rhein-Elbe-Park who, incidentally, is trained by one of the very few women trainers, Petra Pelz.

Strangely enough Italy stages more shows than any other country in mainland Europe and has more CACIBs awarded for its championship shows than any other country. The Rottweiler Club conducts its speciality show, inviting judges from other countries in Europe. Rottweilers also enter the all-breeds show organised by The Kennel Club. The average entry is thirty-five Rottweilers. The last speciality was judged by Mary Macphail of England when fifty-two appeared. The top international judges, Willi Fausner, Adolf Ringer, Ludwig Schatz, Paul Schaefer, and the top Rottweilers from Germany have appeared in Italian rings.

8 The Standard and Its Interpretation

History

The first standard was compiled by Albert Kull in 1901, being a joint one for Leonberger and Rottweiler dogs. The two Rottweiler clubs that were formed later both issued separate standards – the IRK in 1913, and the DRK in 1914. The IRK, with its concern for conformation, concentrated on anatomical detail; the DRK was concerned with character and working ability. The clubs merged in 1921, issuing one standard which synthesised the two existing ones. This standard was revised after the Second World War. The major change was that faults were divided between those affecting beauty and those which would reduce working ability. In 1960, the ADRK made a further revision, emphasising that the country of origin, Germany, was responsible for all matters relating to breeding and judging, and that all countries associated with the FCI were obliged to observe this. A third category of faults was added – six in all – any one of which excluded a dog absolutely from being shown or bred from. This category concluded with a full description of ideal dentition.

The standard was discussed at the first IFR conference in 1969, and a revised version issued in 1970. The additions were a paragraph on gait and one on character; specific mention was made of anterior and posterior angulation. Two disqualifying faults were added – hip abnormality, and dogs with yellow eyes, hawk eyes, multi-coloured eyes, or a staring expression.

The current standard was issued in 1981. This gave greater detail, a sixth page being added. A concession was also made with regard to bite; a level bite is acceptable, but it lowers the grading by one. Attention was directed to the imponderables in judging a living creature, which requires a trained eye to assess the whole animal within the framework of the standard.

It is important to remember that the first standard emphasised the importance of temperament. The Rottweiler possesses courage, has a good nature, and is a pleasant companion with an incorruptible image. In every revision this message has come through loud and clear.

UK and Australia

The first standard in the UK was adopted in 1936 and was taken from the ADRK standard of 1921. It was later revised, in 1965. Australia also uses the British standard. This standard follows the national pattern of understatement, allowing the individual to judge by personal interpretation. It has been maintained by objective application, rather than by functional requirement.

USA

The AKC used British standards from the time of the first dog show, in 1874, to 1929; after this date it issued its own. The AKC approved a standard for the breed in 1935. The present Rottweiler standard was drafted by a committee appointed by the ARC in 1974. It was approved by the AKC on 20 September 1979. The standard was the first, from a country not affiliated with the FCI, to enumerate teeth and to list a missing tooth as a fault. The paragraph on the head, apart from preserving the anomaly of proportion, and particularly the description of the muzzle, is excellent. New ground was broken on colour, with the statement limiting quantity of rust markings to 10 per cent of body colour.

FCI (*Fédération Cynologique Internationale*)

The subject countries of the FCI are: all countries in Europe, except the UK, Morocco, USA, Canada, Mexico and all South American countries. The FCI was formed in 1911, the founder countries being Austria, Belgium, Holland and Germany. The policy of the FCI is to accept breed standards from the country of origin. Through an oversight on the part of the ADRK, the 1960 standard was not forwarded to the FCI, but the 1970 version was accepted on 25 March 1970. In a footnote to the 1981 standard, the ADRK points out that any errors in translation must be referred to the ADRK for determination.

It is not possible for any book attempting to take an international view of a breed to cite only that standard relating to the country in which the book is published. For this reason the standard quoted in this chapter is that of the FCI which adopts the ADRK standard, but is much more detailed and therefore beneficial to both breeders and serious students of the Rottweiler. Any standard is only of value if it is considered within a framework of criteria which affects both evaluation of the breed at any one point in time and the way in which the standard is interpreted. The many aspects that both breeder and judge must consider are discussed immediately following the standard; it is on the conclusions of such people that the future of the breed will rest.

The FCI Rottweiler Standard 1981

CONFORMATION

General Appearance

The Rottweiler is a sturdy dog, <u>medium-sized to slightly larger than medium-sized</u>, neither too coarse nor too light, neither leggy nor spindly. Its conformation is well proportioned, compact and powerful indicating great strength, agility and stamina. Its appearance is down to earth. Its behaviour is self-assured, strong-nerved, and without fear. Its calm mein shows good demeanour. Very attentively it responds to its surroundings.

<u>Size</u>

Height at withers in dogs – 61–68cm (24.01 inches–26.77 inches)

   61–62cm – small (24.01–24.4 inches)
   63–64cm – medium (24.8–25.10 inches)
   65–66cm – tall (<u>desired height</u>) (24.19–25.59 inches)
   67–68cm – very <u>tall (26.37–26.77</u> inches)

Height at withers in bitches – 56–63cm (22.04 inches–24.8 inches)

   56–57cm – small (22.04–22.44inches)
   58–59cm – medium (22.83–23.22 inches)
   60–61cm – tall (<u>desired height</u>) (23.62–24.01 inches)
   62–63cm – very <u>tall (24.4–24.8</u> inches)

The length of the trunk, measured from the breastbone (sternum) to the ischial protuberance, should not exceed the height at withers by more than 15% at the highest.

<u>Head</u>

Of medium length, the skull is broad between the ears, the line of the forehead is moderately arched when seen from the side. The occipital bone is well developed without protruding excessively. <u>Strong broad upper and lower jaw!</u> <u>Stop and zygomatic arch are well developed. The proportions of the measurements from the end of the nose to the inner corner of the eye should be 40% related to 60% from the inner corner of the eye to the occipital bone.</u>

<u>Desired measurements:</u>

   <u>9.5cm–15cm (3.74 inches–5.90 inches) in dogs</u>
   <u>8.5cm–13cm (3.34 inches–5.11 inches) in bitches</u>

<u>Skin of the head:</u>

Fitting tightly everywhere and may form slight wrinkles when the dog is extremely alert. A head without wrinkled skin is desired.

---

*Masculine pronouns are used generically throughout this article. The underlined parts, except for the subtitles, are new or changed words, phrases or sentences.

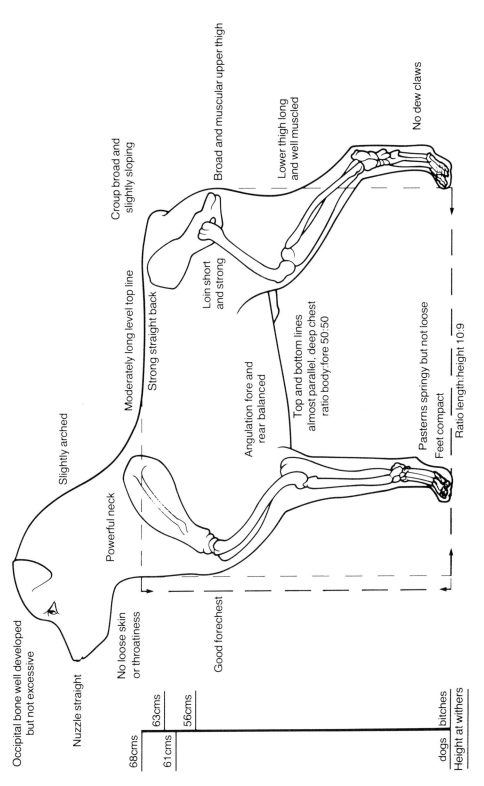

Occipital bone well developed but not excessive

Nuzzle straight

Slightly arched

Powerful neck

No loose skin or throatiness

Good forechest

Moderately long level top line

Strong straight back

Croup broad and slightly sloping

Loin short and strong

Angulation fore and rear balanced

Top and bottom lines almost parallel, deep chest ratio body:fore 50:50

Broad and muscular upper thigh

Lower thigh long and well muscled

No dew claws

Pasterns springy but not loose

Feet compact

Ratio length:height 10:9

68cms
63cms
61cms
56cms

dogs   bitches
Height at withers

Fig 1 The structure of a typical male Rottweiler

Lips
Are black and fit tightly; the corner of the mouth is closed. The jaws are dark; there is less pigment in older animals only.

Nose
The bridge of the muzzle is straight, broad at the base, and slightly tapered towards the tip. The tip of the nose is well-shaped, broad rather than round; the nostrils are comparatively large and always coloured black.

Eyes
Medium sized, almond shaped and of dark brown colour; the lids are well fitting.

Ears
Ought to be comparatively small, pendant, triangular, set high, and well apart from each other. The upper part of the head seems broader when the ears are turned forward with the inner edge carried tightly against the cheek.

Teeth
Dentition must be strong and complete (42 teeth); the upper incisors grasp like a scissors over those of the lower jaw.

Neck
Powerful, moderately long, well muscled, rising from the shoulders in a slightly arched line of the back of the neck with tightly fitting skin without dewlaps or loose skin.

Body
Roomy, broad and deep chest, with well-developed front part and well sprung ribs. The topline is straight; the back strong and sturdy. The loins are short, strong and deep. The flanks are not drawn up. The croup is broad, slightly curved from the middle part onwards, neither straight nor dropping strongly.

Tail
The tail is docked short, close to the body.
   'Angeborenor Mutzschwanz muss, wenn zu lang, nachkupiert werden', eliminated, ie, the hereditary bobtail must be docked if it is too long.

Forequarters
Shows a long, well-placed shoulder. The upper arm is well set against the body but not too tightly. The lower arm is strongly developed and well muscled. Pasterns slightly springy, strong, not steep. Feet round, very compact, and arched. Pads hard; nails short, black and strong.
The front legs as seen from the front are straight and not set closely together. Seen from the side, the lower arms stand straight. The angle the shoulder blade and the horizontal form measures about 45 degrees; shoulder blade and upper arm show an angle of about 115 degrees.

Hindquarters
Thigh moderately long, broad and very muscular. Lower thigh long, powerful, and extensively muscled, forming a wiry transition to a powerful hock joint, well angulated, not steep.
Feet are somewhat longer than front feet, equally compact, arched with strong toes and without dew claws.

Seen from behind, the hind legs are straight, not set closely together. Standing unrestrained, an obtuse angle is formed by the hipbone and upper thigh, likewise by upper thigh and lower thigh, and again lower thigh and metatarsus. The angle of the hipbone is about 20–30 degrees.

Coat

The coat consists of outer coat and undercoat. The outer coat is of medium length, coarse, dense, keeping flat to the body; the undercoat must not show through the outer part. The hind legs have a slightly longer coat. ('Vorderlaute' eliminated from the statement about slightly longer hairs.) The colour is black with well-defined markings of red(dish) brown (mahogany) on cheeks, mouth, throat, breast, and legs as well as a spot over each eye and under the tail.

Gait

The Rottweiler is a trotter. Moving in this way it creates the impression of strength, stamina and determination.

The back remains firm and comparatively quiet. The sequence of motion is harmonious, sure, powerful and unhindered, showing good length of pace.

Character

The character of the Rottweiler consists of the combination of all the innate and acquired physical and mental attributes, qualities, and abilities that determine and control its behaviour concerning its environment.

Due to its mental disposition, it is of a basically friendly and peaceable nature, very devoted, well trainable and willing to work. Temperament, the inclination for moving and acting are on a medium level. It is tough, fearless, and self-controlled when faced with disagreeable circumstances. Its sensory organs are appropriately developed. Its reactions are quick and it has an excellent capacity for learning. It represents the strong, well-balanced type. Being unsuspicious, of moderate sharpness, and high self-confidence, it responds quietly and without haste to influences of its environment. Being threatened, its fitness to fight, based on a highly developed instinct for fighting and protection, gets obvious at once. It puts up with painful experiences without being afraid or shocked. Once it is no longer threatened, the tendency to fight vanishes comparatively fast and changes to a peaceful disposition.

Its additional merits are: strong attachment to its house and homestead, forceful watchfulness, and a good capacity for tracking. ('Er ist apportier-freudig' eliminated from the statement, ie, happy retriever and tracker.) Its stamina is high; it likes the water, and is fond of children. It is not especially zealous to chase. In detail, the following traits of character and instincts are considered desirable:

(a) in daily life:

self-confidence	high
fearlessness	high
temperament	medium
stamina	high
mobility and activity	medium
alertness	high
tractability	medium-high
mistrust	low-medium
sharpness	low-medium

(b) as companion, guard, and working dog:
   all qualities mentioned in (a) as well as:

courage (fearlessness)	high – very high
fighting instinct	high – very high
instinct for protecting	high – very high
hardness	high
retrieving ability*	medium-high

*Moved from (d) to (b)

(c) guarding characteristics:

watchfulness	medium
threshold of excitability	medium-high

(d) scenting ability:

searching instinct	medium
tracking instinct	high

It should be taken into consideration that these instincts and qualities prevail in different degrees of intensity, often merge into one another and correlate with one another. They must be at least as much present and highly developed as is necessary for working efficiently.

Appearance and Working Faults

Appearance faults are noticeable deviations from the features described in the standard. They diminish the working value of the dog to a limited degree only, but may obscure and distort the image typical for the breed. According to the standard of the ADRK the following are considered appearance faults:

Light, leggy, spindly general appearance; too long, too short, too narrow body; prominent occipital bone; houndlike head and houndlike expression; narrow, light, too short, long, or coarse head; flat forehead; missing or too little stop; narrow lower jaw; long or pointed muzzle; strong protruding cheeks; ram's or split nose; bridge of nose dished or sloping; tip of nose light-coloured or spotted; open, pink, or speckled lips; corners of mouth open; distemper teeth; wrinkled skin on head; ears too deep set, heavy, long, floppy, turned back, sticking out, or irregularly carried; light (yellow) or one light and one dark eye, open, deep-set, too fully rounded eyes; goggle-eyes, piercing eyes; neck too long, thin, weak-muscled, dewlaps, or throatiness; forelegs narrow set or not straight; light-coloured nails; tail set too high, or too low; coat soft, too short, or too long; curly coat; absence of undercoat; markings of the wrong colour, poorly defined or too extensive; white spots; hind dewclaws.

More serious than the faults mentioned above are those deviations from the ideal that affect both the appearance of the dog and its working abilities. They are called working faults, and are listed in the standard of the Rottweiler as follows:

Weak bones and muscles; steep shoulder; missing or deficient juncture between elbow and body; upper arm too long, too short or too steep; weak or steep pasterns; spreading feet, too flat or excessively arched toes, stunted toes; flat rib cage, barrelshaped or pigeon chest; back too long, weak, 'dip' or roach; croup too long, too short, too straight, or too steep; bloated, unwieldy body; hind legs flatshanked; sicklehocked, cowhocked or bowlegged legs; joints too narrow or too widely angled.

Fig 2 Too long in neck

Fig 3 Too high in rear

Fig 4 Roach back

Fig 5 Short in leg

Fig 6 Long in body

Fig 7 Long in leg

(pages 119-20) *Figs 2–10 Conformation faults*

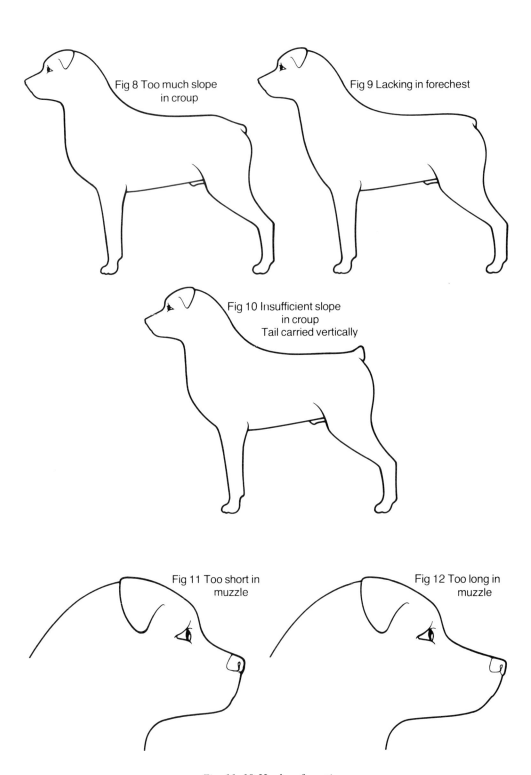

Fig 8 Too much slope in croup

Fig 9 Lacking in forechest

Fig 10 Insufficient slope in croup
Tail carried vertically

Fig 11 Too short in muzzle

Fig 12 Too long in muzzle

Figs 11–19 Head conformation

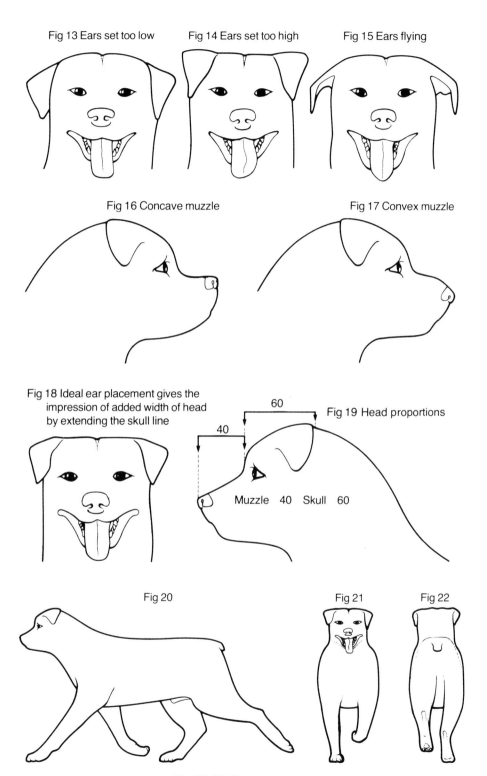

Fig 13 Ears set too low   Fig 14 Ears set too high   Fig 15 Ears flying

Fig 16 Concave muzzle   Fig 17 Convex muzzle

Fig 18 Ideal ear placement gives the impression of added width of head by extending the skull line

Fig 19 Head proportions

60

40

Muzzle   40   Skull   60

Fig 20

Fig 21   Fig 22

Figs 20–22 Correct movement

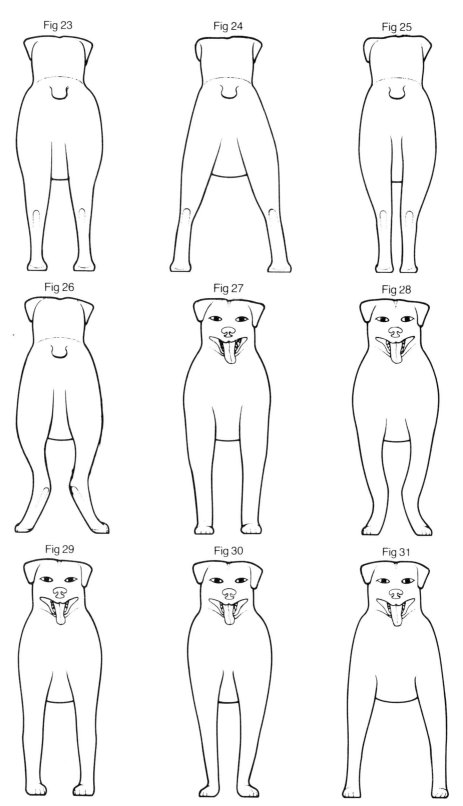

Figs 23–31 Stance: Fig 23, correct; Fig 24, too wide; Fig 25, too narrow; Fig 26, cow hocks; Fig 27, correct, front view; Fig 28, fiddle fronted; Fig 29, toeing in; Fig 30, toeing out and too narrow; Fig 31, toeing out and too wide

The following must not be used for breeding and have to be disqualified:

1. Dogs lacking one or both testicles. Both must be well developed and clearly visible in the scrotum;
2. All Rottweilers showing an anomaly in the hip-joints. The breeding committee decides on the action that has to be taken concerning breeding according to the severity of the symptoms;
3. All Rottweilers showing faulty dentition, ie, over-shot, under-shot, dogs with missing premolars and molars (x-ray pictures are not accepted as proof of complete dentition;
4. All Rottweilers with eyelids that are loose or turned inwards (entropion) as well as all Rottweilers with open eyelids (ectropion). Veterinary examination in case of doubt is recommended when a dog with eye trouble is presented at a breed show or a test for breeding suitability. The report on the affliction of the dog is given by the judge of the studbook office. In case the dog being ill when it is shown again or the lids have been operated on, this dog is finally excluded from breeding. If an eyelid operation is concealed, this is condemned as a deceitful practice and is punished according to the show regulations;
5. All Rottweilers with yellow eyes, a piercing look resembling that of a bird of prey, and with eyes of different colours.
6. All Rottweilers with distinctly obvious reversal of sexual characteristics (dogs that look like typical bitches and vice versa);
7. All timid, cowardly, shy, gunshy, vicious, excessively mistrustful, nervous Rottweilers as well as those of stupid expression and behaviour. Dogs showing conspicuous reluctance to move, are unusually slow to react, or convey extreme one-sidedness of character ought to be watched and examined with particular care before they are used for breeding (the possibility of deafness should be considered).
8. All Rottweilers with definitely long or curly coats. Smooth-coated or short coated dogs with missing under-coat are only eligible for breeding with the approval of the committee of the breed wardens (this is a change from 'chief breed warden').

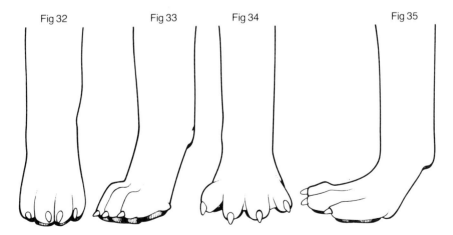

Figs 32–35 Feet: Fig 32, correct, front view; Fig 33, correct, side view; Fig 34, splayed; Fig 35, flat feet

DENTITION OF THE DOG

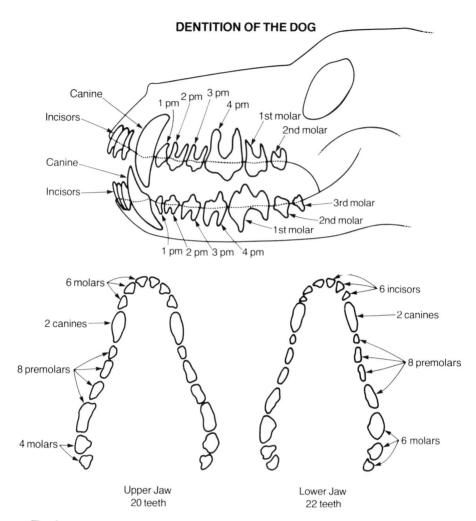

Upper Jaw
20 teeth

Lower Jaw
22 teeth

Teeth

The adult dog has 42 teeth: 12 incisors, 4 canines, 16 premolars, and 10 molars.

Dentition is of highest vital significance to the dog. No Rottweiler is allowed to be judged and used for breeding unless it has well developed, flawless, and complete dentition.

The so-called scissors-bite teeth are demanded (apart from a few exceptions due to a special shape of head) for all breeds of dogs. It is the dentition of the dog, in which the upper incisors grasp slightly grinding over the lower ones. In case this grinding touch does not exist, in case there is consequently a marked interval between the incisors of the upper jaw gripping over those of the lower jaw, then one defines this as an overshot bite. In case the lower jaw overlaps the front teeth of the upper jaw, this is called undershot. Both types of bite are disqualifying and result in the prohibition of breeding this dog. Pincer bite (level bite), which means exact meeting of both rows of incisors, is tolerated but degrades the qualification of the dog by one step. Irregular position of the incisors is considered likewise.

Moving apparatus and types of gait
The hindquarters are the means of support and act as a leverage for locomotion. In every type of action, the forward thrust proceeds from the hindquarters which are more strongly angulated and have more powerful and complex muscles than the forequarters. Due to more intense strain, the forequarters show a less strongly angled leverage system for support and braking. The propulsive forces are transmitted to the forequarters through the body. The back plays an essential part in the forward movement. In moving forward the powerful extensor muscles of back and neck cooperate with the muscles of the lower neck, the inside loin and stomach. Extremely strong and well developed back muscles are the prerequisite for a good and enduring gait.
The types of gait in the Rottweiler are walking, trotting, ambling and galloping; ('und der Sprung' was eliminated, ie, the leap.)
In the trot, the forequarters and hindquarters are mutually synchronised (brace, lift, float support). The back remains relatively stable. While walking, the back movements are more visible; while ambling (simultaneous advance of the hind and front limbs on one side) they are more pronounced; and strongest of all when galloping, then the back is bent like a spring and throws the body forward.

Defective types of gait are
Stiff, restricted, moving feet too high or dragging over the ground, short-paced, swaying, swaying to the side, rolling.

General points concerning external appearance
Defects in harmony and firmness of the physical structure detract from the appearance of the dog and diminish its working capacity.
The ability for working in a dog depends essentially on its account in judging conformation and character. In the standard there are several references stressing the importance of length and power of the limbs, back and shoulder, as well as of the angulation of the joints and the strength of the muscles.
In judging a living thing, many imponderable factors also play a part that can only be appreciated correctly in the total context by the trained eye of an experienced judge.

Some figures may be mentioned for guidance
A Rottweiler with 65cm (25.19 inches) should measure about 75cm (29.5 inches) from the breastbone to the ischial protuberance. The circumference around the chest should be about equal to the height at withers plus 20cm (7.8 inches). The depth of the chest should be neither more nor very much less than 58–59% of the height at the withers.

Comparison of Judging Criteria

It is interesting to compare the attitude of judges in the countries where the breed is shown. The main discrepancy lies in the area of character, the definition of the word 'aggression' and the consequent appraisal of behaviour when dogs are handled in the ring. In Germany they are not handled as they are in other countries, and aggression is encouraged, often openly. The aetiology of ring behaviour is clearly evidenced in the German attitude and the encouragement of this trait in all phases of a dog's upbringing. Dogs are submitted to many breed tests, and, looking at the proforma test sheet, it is easy to see the importance that is placed on aggression. Of the thirteen separate characteristics that are tested, six are associated with an extremely confident and outgoing nature. No dog coming from this sort of background can behave like a cocker spaniel!

The Germans are ruthless with anything approaching nervousness and dogs are subjected to searching tests so that nervous animals can be weeded out. Most European countries will not tolerate nervousness and Austria and Switzerland follow the German method of character testing. Nervousness is not a problem in Britain, the United States and Australia, although the odd nervous animal is encountered. Viciousness is severely penalized in these countries and in some European ones, although, in Sweden, a judge must be bitten before the dog is disqualified! The judge in these countries is required to handle exhibits. German judges have been bitten, but they usually keep well clear and are practised in taking evasive action. Aggression towards other dogs is not penalized in any country and the American standard makes a point of saying this. The Australian attitude is that no person should be placed at risk and no dog should be upset by uncontrolled aggression on the part of another.

The attitude to size varies. The Germans have not been consistent and parameters have changed with each revision. The present standard sets these at 61–68cm for dogs and 56–63cm for bitches. Anything outside these is not permitted, and dogs are measured when they appear for testing. The Scandinavians prefer animals in the middle register. The British standard clearly states that height should always be considered in relation to general conformation, and judges are seldom influenced by height alone.

There is a noticeable discrepancy in the attitude to teeth. These are counted in Germany, usually by a trainee judge. (The dog may be restrained by two or more handlers.) In Britain, the USA and Australia, the bite is examined by the judge; this must be shown by the handler and a refusal will cost the dog a place. Teeth are not counted, except in America where a missing tooth is penalized and four missing teeth earn disqualification. In other European countries excepting Austria and Switzerland, condition of bite, and not its completeness, is important; a missing tooth is only one of a number of faults to be weighed in the framework of the whole evaluation.

Insight

Most Australian judges' perceptive acquaintance with the Rottweiler commences with the standard; discernment relates not so much to the dog, but to its description on paper. His German counterpart, on the other hand, grows up with the breed – acquiring his knowledge by long exposure to all related activities. Judges, and most breeders, in Germany are associated with the warden system. It is mandatory for them to see litters when they are no more than three days of age. They examine dogs during the growing stage, when they appear for the initial breeding test, for the *Körung*, and when partners are considered for breeding. Recognition of type and character are practical accomplishments obtained with little reference to the standard. The Australian judge concentrates on the standard, seldom losing sight of his goal, a group licence which may cover twenty or thirty breeds. The German cares little for examinations; his knowledge is tested practically. The Australian judging system is far more structured, but the attitude to education is open to question. The thrust of curricular processes is towards a demonstrable acquisition of knowledge, rather than its use in solving life's problems.

German judging philosophy is well illustrated by the comments of two leading judges after the judging of the annual speciality. At the second *Klubsieger* Show, held in Cologne in 1972, Dr Schmitz selected four dogs in the champion class, placing them as follows: V1 Bulli v Hungerbühl; V2 Elko v Kaiserberg; V3 Falco v Grunsfeld; V4 Berno v Abtal. He commented on the last three's outstanding qualities, but placed them behind Bulli because of his character and record at stud. In a purely conformation rating, the placings would have been 2, 3, 1, 4. Breeding worth can only be recognised by in-depth knowledge, and is separated from mere form.

In the eleventh speciality, held in Bensheim in 1981, Herr Freiberg placed the bitch Nike v Kupferdach V2 in the champion class. She was obviously a good bitch, but I thought her a little plain and rather fortunate to obtain this high rating. In the following year, at Stadthagen, Miss Bruns placed this bitch V3 in a very strong class. I enquired why. The judge explained, at some length, that the bitch had qualities of balance, size, robustness and other essentials necessary to the breed. These qualities, moreover, were being lost to the breed. The exhibits placed behind her, though very good, had produced undesirable qualities in some litters. Faults that are likely to be handed down should be recognised, while show points that have been taught, or are of an environmental nature, are not important when the breed's future is considered. The key to judging, she said, was to be tolerant of small faults so long as the breed essentials were there. Herr Berger, the late Chief Breed Warden, once told me that Miss Bruns knew more about the Rottweiler bitch than anyone in the world. Having corresponded regularly with her for fifteen years, I have no doubts about this statement.

It is quite unfair to compare Australian judges, some of whom are required to judge a hundred different breeds, with German judges who concentrate on a single breed and spend a lifetime doing so. We have little more than a minute to evaluate each exhibit and it is not possible for our judges to have any extra knowledge of all the dogs presented. They can only do their best with what is placed before them. Much can be done, however, to sharpen the image of the Rottweiler and to promote a more uniform interpretation of type.

Recognising Type

How accurately does any breed standard describe type? How much can we learn from the Rottweiler standard? What image comes to mind when we read the paragraph on the head and skull? What is medium length or moderately arched? Could an artist paint a picture from the description in the standard? It says nothing about the taper of the muzzle or the influence of the shape of head on bite. The statement 'muzzle length no longer than the length from stop to occiput' is incorrect and misleading. These matters were the subject of a special meeting of wardens called by the Chief Breed Warden, Jacob Köpf, in 1957. As a result of discussions held, the shape of the actual head altered dramatically within a period of four years, but the ratio of muzzle to skull was not changed to 40:60 until the 1981 standard was issued. It has yet to be altered in the KC and AKC standards.

What exactly is meant by 'long and excessively wavy coat'? How is undercoat affected by long exposure to warm climates? Unless breeders and judges see and handle typical dogs and discuss the effect of climate on various specimens, these matters must be left to individual interpretation. We have found, in Australia, that climate has a marked effect on both density of outer coat and the presence of undercoat. This does not apply to length of hair. It is widely held that length of coat is a genetic fault not affected by climate. I have examined dogs in Trondheim, where the temperature often falls well below 0°C, and found that while the coat was dense, the length was only moderate. We have had dogs that have experienced successive winters in Britain and Australia; in these cases the coats have been dense, with a profuse undercoat; coats have thinned out in later years. Judges in Australia are inclined to frown on dense coats, preferring those that are very short and thin. This Dobermann-type coat is a fault that appears without being penalized. Most countries outside Germany are liberal in their attitude, but the Germans allow no deviation.

Judges with whom I have spoken have varying attitudes to anterior angulation. Most favour the conventional layback of 45°. The AKC stipulates this, but the KC wisely refrains from explicit comment. Authorities also differ. Rachel Page Elliot, *Dog Steps: illustrated gait at a glance*, and Smythe, *Conformation of the Dog*, favour 45° and produce convincing evidence in support. Dr Carla Lensi, president of the Italian club, with eminent qualifications both academically and in the Rottweiler context, is unequivocal on the matter. Commenting on the standard in *Il Mio Amico Cane*, she has this to say:

> The anterior joints must be constructed in such a fashion that permits the subject to exploit, in the most advantageous way, the impulse that travels across the back. Consequently the construction of the bony radius must follow the best canons for obtaining ideal anterior articulation of a trotter: shoulder long, arm slightly longer, angle of the scapula/humerus between 95°/100°.
>
> Unfortunately the dictates of the standard are consistent only in part to these specifications; in fact, while rightly expecting a shoulder to be long and well inclined nothing is said on the length of the arm. But what is more stupid is the contemplated angle of the scapula/humerus.
>
> If one attempts to construct a Rottweiler with the shoulder correctly inclined at 45° to the horizontal, but with an inclined arm always at an angle of 70° to the horizontal (the standard provides for a scapula/humerus of 115° and for that reason 115°−45° = 70° of inclination of the arm to the horizontal), no such thing could be obtained. A subject that has a high thorax (to permit the correction of a tendency to the perpendicular), or a subject off the perpendicular, above all else, cannot trot! I cannot explain this incongruity in the standard; however, it is useful to perceive, and, above all else, underline, that the physical laws of statics and dynamics seem, at least in this case, to be more valid than the standard. It is my deep conviction that the scapula/humerus angle of a Rottweiler must clearly be smaller than that envisaged in the standard. It is necessary for the anterior articulation complex to be lean and endowed with strong and toned musculature.

Dr Quentin Laham, Professor of Biology at Ottawa University, is of the opinion that 45° is excessive for shoulder layback: 30° in sight hounds could be good angulation; even a rectangular dog, like a dachshund, would have good angulation with 39°. He says, with eminent good sense, that moderately angulated dogs, with balance between front and back angulation, are the best movers.

My observation is that a layback of 45° simply does not occur in a Rottweiler. Problems with movement occur when one end is more angulated than the other. Technicalities apart, I feel that the eye is the only tool available in the evaluation of a dog, and it cannot measure to the degree of accuracy required by some experts. Some statements, although technically correct, lie in the area of theory, far removed from the arena of judging. Machines and mechanical parts can be measured precisely within a fraction of a centimetre. Precise measurement in living things is not possible, and more important factors must be considered in evaluation. A living creature can compensate for minor structural defects. A machine cannot do so and an imperfect part must eventually fracture under stress. There are many examples, particularly in the world of athletics and horse racing, when world champions have overcome obvious structural failings. We all agree that balance is essential in the dog; we should extend this to our canine philosophy.

Recognition of type is the first essential in the appreciation of the Rottweiler. How is this acquired? A child growing up with Rottweilers, while not able to explain what is meant by type, will recognise a typical specimen instantly because of an intimate association. An adult not familiar with the breed, on the other hand, may not recognise one, but, having benefited from a few lectures, will explain the meaning of the word and even recite the standard. In one case the image of the dog conveyed by the eye is matched easily and instantly to the image stored in the brain, in the other the image has to be matched by abstraction to the words contained in the standard, knowledge, in this case, being built up, bit by bit, with attention being focused on individual parts. The value of the written word, in the judging curriculum, must be placed in perspective.

Judging Discipline

Each country has its own particular discipline, applying both in the ring and in the education of judges. Every system has its weaknesses, but before criticisms are levelled we should appreciate the conditions that prevail and how each country makes the best use of them. No system is perfect, but we should address our minds to improvement rather than replacement. The weakness in Australia lies at the breed level when judges are confronted by a new breed. My statements are based solely on my experience with Rottweilers, but other breeds coming into the country could be similarly affected – Neapolitan mastiffs, giant Munsterlanders, akitas, shar peis and Alaskan malemutes to name a few.

Judging is based purely on the standard, image has to be acquired without perhaps seeing top specimens of the breed and there is room for considerable variation. Having spent some twenty years gaining no more than peripheral knowledge, and having looked at thousands of dogs, some of them the best in the world, I admire the man who can evaluate a hundred different breeds. I am also aware, however, of the chinks in a judge's armour and offer no more than the analytical threads from which a constructive garment may be woven.

Recognition of type is essential so that uniform interpretation is possible. Our judges are conversant with ring procedures, regulations, general principles of conformation and what may be called the arithmetic of judging. In a Rottweiler context, analysis is quantitative; in the placing of exhibits the judge is influenced by such palpable facts as size, colour, feet, pasterns and any obvious, though minor, deviations. He looks for details that will downgrade a dog, rather than the quality that distinguishes an animal from the rest of the class. Demerits may be the result of a dog's environment rather than the results of a genetic base. One judge told me that she would never place a dog with slightly flat feet. Another, because the dog stood with feet slightly east-west. Yet flat feet may be the legacy of diet, exercise, weight or the surface on which a pup is raised. Again, a dog will sometimes stand with feet pointing outwards because it is more comfortable; this is corrected on the move. The same applies to a man. The Germans, and they are the best Rottweiler judges in the world, always look for the breed worthiness that distinguishes an exhibit, and, with a judge unfamiliar with type, this is not possible. How can the situation be improved?

Encouraging Interest in the Breed

State breed clubs conduct an annual speciality, and this show, and its associated activities, could be a focal point for the sort of activity that prompts interest in the breed. Specialist judges are invited because of a special interest in the breed. They should provide a critique on the dogs placed in each class. Critiques lose credibility when publication is delayed, so these should be dictated at the show and circulated within two weeks. A postmortem discussion, attended by all interested parties, should be held – if possible with the subjects of critiques present – shortly after. If the judge is a specialist from another country, a workshop, attended by all parties, would be of benefit. Live models, films, etc, should be discussed in an informal atmosphere. A Rottweiler lecture is currently scheduled each year, the lecturer being a prominent canine personality. This could be extended to four per year, run by the breed club, with greater input from breeders, and closer liaison with the

KCC. Prospective judges should have the opportunity of evaluating and discussing dogs of all ages. The key to success is an informal atmosphere. This would encourage general participation and help to promote the object of the exercise.

Rottweiler Judges

In his address to the IFR conference in 1972, Friedrich Berger, Chief Breed Warden of the ADRK, used these words:

> Sometimes one nearly gets a fright to find out in discussion how little is known of the standard in England and America . . . It is apparent to the practised eye of the specialist judge that the conformation and breed worthiness of these animals – English and American – have been quite inconsistent with the championship labels so inappropriately applied and that, as a result, the judges – who should be the most important element in safeguarding the breed – have had a far-reaching negative effect on the Rottweiler.

The standard of judging in most countries outside Germany is very poor. This does not mean that competent judges are found only in that country; there are many excellent judges in Austria, Denmark, Britain, Holland, Finland, Sweden, Switzerland and the United States, and the top judges from these countries are invited to judge in Germany on a regular basis. However, these judges have emerged in spite of the system and not because of it. In every case two common factors have been present: individuals have had a special interest in the breed, and they have enjoyed a close and privileged association with German judges and German dogs. The reason is obvious. Judges in Germany are exposed to conditions that do not occur elsewhere. They are familiar with every facet of the breed; they are closely involved with breeding, training, testing and discussing Rottweilers for most of their lives. Most of our judges, especially the all-rounders, only see Rottweilers when they are presented to them in the show ring.

British judges, especially the specialists, and some all-rounders, are far better acquainted with type than their Australian counterparts. This is to be expected when we look at prevailing conditions. There are twenty-eight British specialists, most of whom have bred Rottweilers for twenty-five years and more. Seven of these have judged Rottweiler specialities in countries outside Britain; one is qualified to judge in Germany. There are only fourteen British all-rounders and only one is qualified to award tickets to all breeds.

In Victoria alone there are ninety-eight judges qualified to judge group 6 – and therefore Rottweilers – and thirty-seven of these are qualified to award challenges to all breeds. Of all these qualified judges,

Austrian dogs at a Vienna show. Note the use of muzzles. By law a dog trained for Schutzhund *must wear a muzzle in public* (courtesy Adolf Ringer)

only one has bred a litter. There are nineteen names on the British 'B' list – not qualified to allot challenges – and most of these have been breeding for twenty years; two have been breeding for twenty-five years. There are five judges in America who are all breeders, and all highly qualified, and who have been breeding for some forty years and who have judged abroad. Three of these judge in Germany on a regular basis and are highly regarded.

Attitude to Standards

Before embarking on a study of the standard, we should understand the history and purpose of the breed. We can then appreciate the origin of the standard, the purpose of revisions and, particularly, the changes that have been made. The standard is there to be discussed, analysed and criticised, but it must always be the firm base from which advances are made. No standard is immutable and we can see, from the changes that were made to the German standard, what progress has been made over the last seventy-five years. The standard has always been retrospective, codifying changes that have already taken place. It has been flexible enough to admit individual interpretation and yet firm enough to preserve the essence of type. The specialist and the all-rounder will always differ in certain aspects of interpretation; both are necessary to maintain the breed. All-rounders cannot have the penetrative approach of the dedicated specialist, but a wider approach does provide balance without which the broader essentials may be lost. The specialist is better able to recognise type, but this could lead to the overemphasis of particular facets, which could defeat the purpose of the standard. A far greater risk of the emasculation of breed type lies in the increasing glamour in which in-group and in-show winners are enshrined. Another factor is the inordinate attention that is paid to handling and presentation. These tendencies could lead to a subversion of breed essentials. In Germany little attention is paid to group or even best of sex. After all, we do not judge the best cricketer against the best footballer, or compare the performance of the field athlete with that of the sprinter. Best in Show seems no more than a lottery, although I must confess to a certain excitement when personally involved, and think our shows would lose a great deal of their glamour and attraction if the lottery was abolished.

Falko vd Tente Ksgr Bsgr, bred by Hans-Adolf Ackerman, with his owner Herr Palm

Ch Auslese Galileo CD

(above) Rottweilers on the author's farm; (below) Ch Auslese Iago Rabe (whelped 1977), at nine years of age

(above right) International and Italian Rip Ch, Dick Zur Klamm, bred by Peter Stephan, owned by Frederico Lensi; (below right) Dual Ch Auslese Bold Gammon, the only dual champion Rottweiler in Australia, litter sister to Auslese Galileo. Trained by Mrs Read (courtesy Mrs Read)

Felix v Mägdeberg being introduced to a kitten (Photo: Alan Hutchison)

9 Kennelling, General Care and Exercise

There is no doubt that geography is the most influential factor in determining the environmental effect on a dog's upbringing. Having lived both in the city and the country, and having inspected many kennels, I am convinced that country people have a great advantage when it comes to the rearing of dogs. We lived for some fifteen years on a small farm overlooking the sea. The whole area in which we lived was devoted to pasture, except for two stands of timber. The dogs had access to a dozen paddocks and, apart from the aspect of exercise, this meant that pups were brought up with farm animals, and their natural herding and tracking instincts were developed.

We now live on 40 acres of mountain forest. The dogs are exercised over the whole area at least twice a day and they can be taken by car to other parts of the forest without much trouble. City people are greatly restricted, and, although parks and playing fields are most attractive to dogs, they are reserved for other uses and most municipalities discourage dogs. Training schools offer an opportunity for dogs to meet and socialize but this is generally confined to weekends and the area is not usually conducive to exercise.

Dogs that are free to exercise in large areas are healthier and happier than dogs kept in kennels for long periods and restricted to exercise on a lead. Happiness is one important attribute that people often overlook when considering the wellbeing of their dogs. We notice a dramatic change in a dog's bearing when he is allowed access to free range after a long period of incarceration in quarantine kennels.

A kennel is an essential piece of equipment, but it should not be regarded merely as providing confinement. In addition to providing sleeping quarters that are comfortable, kennels should instil discipline and give a dog a sense of territorial ownership. This means a warm, dry, draught-free area with a clean and cosy bed. We find that the best area is one some 2.2 sq m (24 sq ft) that is almost totally enclosed, with a door 61 × 183cm (2 × 6ft) giving access to the sleeping kennel for cleaning purposes. The dog has access through a small opening in the lower half of the door. Within the sleeping area is a platform 122 × 92cm (4 × 3ft), surrounded on three sides with lining boards and insulation is packed between these boards and the brick walls. A removable roof at 92cm (3ft) prevents down-draughts in the winter, and, when removed for the

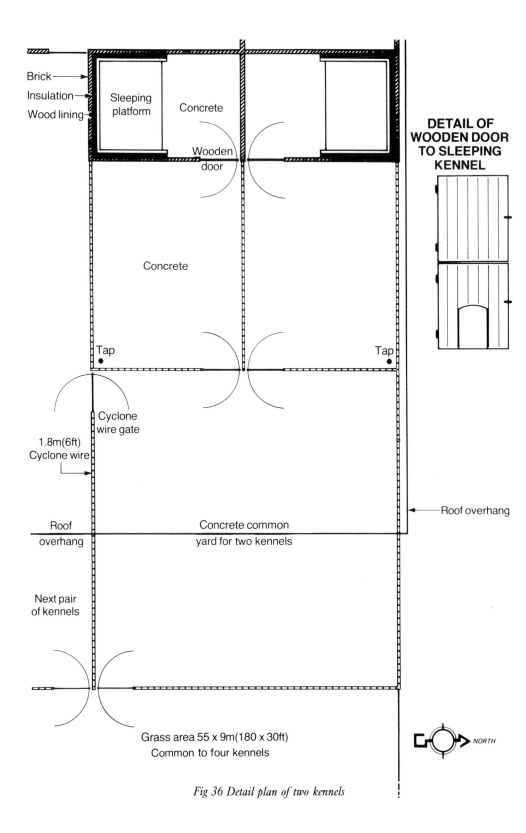

Brick

Insulation

Wood lining

Sleeping platform

Concrete

DETAIL OF WOODEN DOOR TO SLEEPING KENNEL

Wooden door

Concrete

Tap

Tap

Cyclone wire gate

1.8m(6ft) Cyclone wire

Roof overhang

Roof overhang

Concrete common yard for two kennels

Next pair of kennels

Grass area 55 x 9m(180 x 30ft) Common to four kennels

NORTH

Fig 36 Detail plan of two kennels

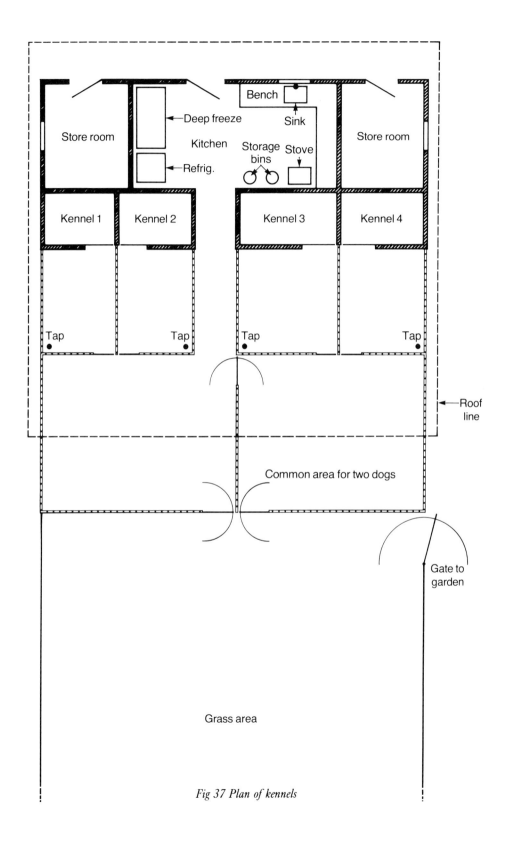

Fig 37 Plan of kennels

summer, the natural 3m (10ft) ceiling makes the kennel cool and airy. The area immediately outside the sleeping quarters is fenced with 1.8m (6ft) of galvanised mesh, with a door that can be locked; this 2.4 × 1.8m (8 × 6ft) area is private to each kennel; each pair of kennels then has a common 4.8 × 3.6m (16 × 12ft) area with a door to an outside, grassed run of 55 × 9m (180 × 30ft). The floor of the entire kennel area is of concrete and is roofed with a 2.4m (8ft) overhang. A dog must learn to stay in this area without developing a feeling of being punished. This is his home, to which he can retire when he wishes to chew a bone, or when he wants to rest, or just be alone.

The layout, shown in the plan of the general area, allows some flexibility in separating dogs, and the yard is an area where dogs can run unattended. The kennel complex is self-contained and all food is stored and prepared on site.

Our previous home allowed a much larger kennel area with several enclosed paddocks in which dogs could be left unattended. The facilities for rearing pups were excellent with a great deal of alternative accommodation for bitches in season, visitors, etc.

Hygiene and Prophylactic Care

The Rottweiler being a tough, shortcoated, working dog requires little if any cosmetic attention. The accent, in this context, is on minimum but regular attention. Passing reference only is made to a few matters of general care.

Teeth are often neglected. It is quite simple to prevent problems with the mouth, but extremely difficult to eradicate them after they have become established. The dog has forty-two teeth, twenty in each jaw, with an extra pair of molars in the lower jaw. A puppy will start to cut his early teeth when he is about three weeks old. These will sharpen, wear down and fall out when he is about five months. Permanent teeth will erupt alongside baby teeth which they will loosen; as a rule these fall or are pulled out in the normal course of chewing and playing. Sometimes, however, a baby tooth will not be dislodged and the permanent replacement may grow out of alignment. Mouths should be inspected almost daily when permanent teeth are erupting. We have found that the trouble occurs mainly with the top canine. Here the milk canine can cause its replacement, and the neighbouring incisor, to grow crookedly. We know of one case where the mouth was neglected for several weeks and these three teeth formed a triangle, with all three out of alignment. When it does not dislodge easily, the milk tooth should be extracted before any damage is done. If the matter is neglected, the bite will be affected permanently. The least painful method of helping in the removal of milk teeth is to give the pup a bone or a sock; it may be necessary to play a game of tug-of-war using the sock as an extractor. Removal should be incidental so that the puppy does not associate pain with the examination of teeth. On one occasion I was showing a puppy which was in the process of acquiring its permanent teeth – this was very foolish of me – when the judge noticed the condition of the mouth. Being a friend he offered very kindly to remove a loose baby tooth. This procedure is most inadvisable as, by association, a pup might refuse to show his bite when being shown in later years. On another occasion, a little bitch of ours proved most recalcitrant when it came to showing her bite. The judge, a novice, reproved her for showing poor temperament. In fact, the pup had some teeth which had 'doubled up' and her lip was split. Teething can be painful and no pup should be shown during this phase of life.

We make a game of examining the bite. The baby is cajoled into showing its bite, then praised and given a tit-bit. Showing a bite voluntarily is not done in a German ring as the judge does not handle exhibits; sometimes a dog is restrained by several handlers and even held in a prone position. Our system requires a dog actually to 'show' its bite and remain perfectly steady while the judge examines it. Like everything else in the show ring, a dog must be trained to accept handling by strangers and the best time that one can start is with a young pup.

Strong healthy teeth are a gift from parents but, when neglected, the best set of teeth can fall into decay. Hard food is the best method of keeping teeth clean and is also a natural method. Bones are a good cleaning agent, but care must be taken to feed the right sort. Brisket bones are excellent and large marrow bones will give pleasure for hours. Dogs can digest the raw bones they eat, but gastric juices will not act on cooked bones. I have seen many sheepdogs fed whole rabbits, but being over-cautious, we avoid all small bones, particularly poultry. Bones will prevent tartar forming, but once tartar gains a hold, scaling by a veterinary surgeon is the only course open. I brush the teeth with an ordinary toothbrush and paste when any discoloration shows, but if dogs are allowed to chew bones and hard biscuits, their teeth should be clean and their gums healthy.

Feet and nails require periodic inspection. Grass seeds can lodge in between toes, but these are easily removed if seen in time. A pup's nails should be cut regularly from one week to three or four months. If this is done, providing the dog is exercised on hard ground, no further attention should be necessary. We used to remove all dew claws but now follow the German custom and remove only the rear.

Rottweilers have a tendency to develop a callus on the elbow. These look ugly and can sometimes grow quite large, with fluid forming inside. The callus is caused by the dog dropping its weight on its elbows on hard surfaces. The natural bodily reaction is to develop some protection so that bones are not damaged, thus the callus forms. This can be prevented by the provision of suitable bedding. We have found that a trampoline type of bed not only provides comfort, but helps to prevent this condition.

Every dog will require veterinary attention at some stage of its life. A mature dog introduced to the vet without previous conditioning will always be a problem. We had two bitches that were never subjected (unfortunately!) to this handling and, as a consequence, vaccination, swabs, and so on, had to be performed by me. Every pup should be trained to allow these liberties to be taken so that, when the occasion arises, it is not upset.

Authorities disagree with regard to the advisability of bathing dogs. Some say that natural oils are removed, leaving a dry skin that can become flaky. Others state that natural oils are replaced very quickly if the diet is correct. Dogs, particularly puppies, have a bad habit of rolling in unhygienic places, and so bathing is often necessary. This, also, is a matter of training and a dog that is accustomed to a bath will accept the procedure as normal. The most important aspect with small puppies is that they should never be allowed to get cold. Warm water, a draught-free room and thorough drying are essential. I fill a laundry trough with 5–8cm (2–3in) of warm water, stand the pup in it and wet it thoroughly. Dog shampoo, mixed in a cup of warm water, is then applied. Care is taken not to allow soap to enter the eyes or ears and only a mild shampoo is used. The bath becomes a game and pups will accept this without much fuss. All traces of soap should be rinsed out and the pup dried thoroughly. A hand-held hair dryer is useful in removing the last traces of dampness.

Bedding and sleeping quarters should be kept scrupulously clean. We put flea powder under the sleeping platforms where the fumes will discourage parasites. Sunlight and fresh air are useful allies in this operation, and mats and rugs are left out in the sun and air as long as possible. It is essential, when constructing kennels, to slope the concrete so that water drains away rapidly. This is a point that should be checked carefully.

Kennels should be disinfected once a week. There are many chemical agents on the market; we find halamid a useful preparation. If dogs are exercised last thing at night and first thing in the morning, the necessity to clean kennels is reduced, as the dogs will develop the habit of evacuating during these periods. Faeces give a good indication of a dog's health and it is wise to check this when possible, so that any tendency towards diarrhoea or constipation can be noted and early action taken to correct the condition.

Diarrhoea is not a disease, but a symptom of one. It can be caused by a number of agents, eg bacteria like salmonella, or a virus like parvo or coronna. Generally, however, it is something far more simple and easily remedied, such as too rich a diet or food that has turned sour or rancid. The withholding of food for twenty-four hours is useful and some kennels starve dogs on certain days, generally once a week, as a matter of routine.

No milk should be given when the bowels are upset. Kaomagma is a useful medicine and small quantities of food, such as cooked white meat, potatoes and rice, well cooked, should be fed. Severe diarrhoea can cause dehydration, especially in pups under six months, and these cases should be treated as serious.

The use of powerful antibiotics on your pups will reduce the total bacteria population of the gut; this causes the loss of useful bacteria which must be replaced. A simple measure to restore the balance is a tablespoon of *live* natural, unsweetened yoghourt, made from unpasturised milk, without preservatives. This is made with lacto-baccillus acidophillus and is distributed only by health-food shops. A more stringent measure is a teaspoon of droppings from a healthy dog, mixed with water and douched into the patient via the mouth. Sometimes we come across the 'disgusting' behaviour that dogs exhibit, of eating the droppings of cattle, horses, koala bears and wallabies. This may sound revolting, but it is nature's method of restoring the balance of useful bacteria.

We have never had the misfortune of having a dog poisoned, but many dogs do succumb to poison, sometimes deliberately administered. This is another field where prevention is better than cure and some thought should be devoted to the subject. The safest measure is not to purchase toxic materials, but if this is unavoidable, they should be kept in very safe custody. If a dog appears to have been poisoned, the first step is to identify the material or discover what access the dog had to poison. Baits usually contain strychnine, and, in country areas, the more toxic, 1080. Immediate veterinary attention is vital and it would help the surgeon to know what he is treating. If the dog has vomited, a specimen should be given to the surgeon.

The following chart outlines some of the more likely poisons and the immediate action that should be taken. Cats are seldom induced to eat toxic material and grown dogs will only eat something that has been made palatable.

Pups, however, will chew the most unlikely materials and the incidence of accidental poisoning is far higher in young stock.

Poison	Symptoms	Treatment	Remarks
Arsenic	Vomiting, abdominal pains	Emetic to induce vomiting	Contained in rat poisons and herbicides
Phosphorous	Vomiting	Emetic. No milk or fatty liquids	Contained in rat poison, matchstick heads
Lead	Vomiting, pains in stomach	Emetic. Milk and honey	Chewing or licking surface with lead-based paints. Has cumulative property
Metaldehyde	Convulsions, drooling	Emetic	Slug and snail baits become more toxic with age
Ratsac (Warfarin)	Blood does not coagulate, haemorrhaging weak pulse, staggers	Do not aggravate bleeding by handling	Puppies will eat this bait in sufficient quantities to be lethal very quickly
Strychnine	Convulsions caused by great pain	Emetic. Collect evidence for examination	Usually used as a bait
Solvents and cleaning fluids	Abdominal pain, vomiting	Do not induce vomiting as this will cause more burns	Pups will play with plastic bottles taken from the cleaning cupboard and these could puncture
Alkali-based	Burns on mouth and tongue	Neutralise by giving water and citrus juice	
Small balls, bottle tops, bones, etc	Lodgement in mouth or trachea	Try to hook obstruction out by crooking fore finger, ensure no damage to mouth or throat	Ensure that the dog cannot bite by using a small plug of wood. Keep windpipe free so that he can breathe

In all these cases urgent veterinary attention is essential. The vet should be alerted at once so that there is no delay. Do not spend too much time on first aid, although this is useful if administered by experienced persons. In all cases keep the dog warm so that the chances of shock are reduced. Cover with a blanket and avoid rough handling.

Separating Fighting Dogs

The most vicious fight is between two dogs or bitches that know each other well and hate each other more. Bitches are worse than dogs. These enemies will fight to the bitter end unless separated. Once separated they must be kept apart, otherwise they will return immediately and carry on the battle. An owner knows which dogs are antagonistic, therefore precautions can be taken to keep such assailants apart. Accidents, however, will happen.

There are many surefire recommended ways to stop a fight. Pressure hoses, fire extinguishers, pepper in the eyes are all effective, but seldom available on the battlefield. Over the years we have found that the best way to stop fighting dogs is to cut off their air supply. We never exercise dogs without carrying leads and a piece of nylon cord. Should trouble start and the dogs have a good hold of each other, the lead can be passed round the neck of a dog and the long end slipped through the holding piece, so forming a noose. The dogs are usually so intent on their grip that this is not too difficult. When the noose is tightened and the dog feels the pressure on his throat he will let go his hold. This is fairly easy when there are two people available, but it is almost impossible for one person to stop a fight. When only one person is present, one of the dogs must be anchored to a tree, fence or other strong fixture. It is quite useless separating the dogs if both are then free to return and start the next round. Dogs should never be dragged apart; this will cause excessive tearing of the skin. A dog should not be pulled away, when it has a hold, by lifting its rear legs; this can cause severe back injuries. Beating is quite useless unless the aim is to knock a dog unconscious! When adrenaline is flowing, no amount of punishment will achieve the desired result. A temporary shock can be administered by squeezing paws or testicles, or by throwing a bucket of water on the head. If this induces a dog to release his hold then he must be anchored immediately. A choke chain is not an effective tool as the loop cannot be placed around the neck when the dog has a hold on another dog.

Two suspect fighters should not be kennelled together and any two that have had an argument should always be kept separate. A very good young bitch that we bred was resented by the senior lady of the kennel; the bitches were left unattended one day and the young bitch was killed.

Dogs will argue over a bone even when they are of the opposite sex. A fight may ensue over some object, or be caused by jealousy when one dog receives preferential treatment. These squabbles can be stopped quite easily, but dogs that hate each other will fight with the object of killing. We have not witnessed a serious fight of opposite sexes, although this does occur with other breeds. Trumler reports one occasion when a bitch killed her mate, but I have not heard of this happening with Rottweilers.

Show Preparation

Of the work required to present a dog in the show ring, 90 per cent is done before the entry is made. Before leaving the kennel on the morning of the show, we exercise dogs lightly, giving them an opportunity to evacuate. The dogs are given their usual daily brushing, teeth and paws are checked and then the dogs, with associated show equipment, are loaded in the station wagon. On arrival at the showground, depending on the time available, the dogs are walked and watered and placed in the shade. More grooming, at this time, is quite unnecessary and does nothing for a Rottweiler. Coat sprays, vaseline and other preparations are a waste of time and money. In the ring the dog is part of a team; the other half, the handler, encourages the dog to move well on a loose lead; to fall into a show pose without assistance, and to take a lively interest in the surroundings. If the dog will react to conversation, exhibiting this by its expression, then it is more likely to attract attention. The show ring, or rather handlers with an obsessive desire to win, have done little for the Rottweiler character. Some handlers follow a routine which is copied and repeated without purpose. A Rottweiler propped up in the ring with a hand or knee under the chest, and the other hand holding the chin at the desired angle, looks foolish. Vaseline on the nails, spray on the coat and the scissoring of flanks are unbecoming and no breed judge of experience is influenced by these antics. Aggressive males look good,

Aus Ch Auslese Bold Galileo and his daughter Aus Ch Bold Kristy seen winning the challenges at Western Suburbs show under Mrs Henbest of England. Kristy, owned by Mr and Mrs Young, also won the bitch challenge at the Rottweiler Ch Show under Mrs Freeman (Photo: Max Neilson)

A typical show stance is exhibited here by Faunus Demon, owned by Georg Stenbacka (Photo: courtesy Mrs Hyden)

provided they do not upset other handlers or dogs and are kept under strict control; Rottweilers should not be required to behave like lap dogs.

Peak condition can only be obtained by regular attention to diet, exercise, discipline, grooming and the rapport between the two members of the team which is built up over a period. If these things are neglected, the situation cannot be rectified by a flurry of activity on the day of the show.

Life Span of Rottweilers and the Old Dog

What is the average life span of a Rottweiler? This depends on many things. The genetic factor influences the foundation on which a dog builds its life. Added to this are early upbringing and freedom from debilitating diseases, the sort of life that it has led, including nutrition, exercise, accidents, a happy home life and the care that is taken of it in later years to minimise the progressive inroads that are a part of the natural process of ageing. In our experience, between eight and ten years is the time span. We have had dogs live a little longer; only this year three of our breeding died within a period of two weeks and each had passed his tenth birthday. Benno v Allgaüer Tor died within a week of his twelfth birthday. A number of British Rottweilers have celebrated their thirteenth birthdays: Anouk from Black Forest, Argolis Garaint, Chloe of Mallion, and Alberich of Mallion. The first dog to gain an American UD, Gero v Rabenhorst, completed the exercises at a show in Wheaton in 1948 – he was whelped in 1937.

The French veterinary surgeon Dr Lebeau provides the following equation, comparing the equivalent ages of man and dog.

Dog	1	2	3	4	8	12	15	20
Man	15	24	28	32	48	64	76	96

The period of a dog's life being one-seventh of that of a man is pure myth. A dog of our breeding sired a litter from a German shepherd bitch before he was six months; no one had taken notice of him when the resident bitch came into season, except, of course, the bitch. This would be quite beyond the capacity of a boy aged three and a half years! Small dogs live much longer than dogs of the larger breeds. One of my terriers lived for twenty-three years.

A dog that has worked all his life will continue to do so at seven without any sign of age. Galileo, rising eight, can go through the obedience routine as well as any young dog, and is quicker in agility work. Obesity is the villain and the calorie intake of *all* dogs must be controlled at *all* times. The condition of the older dog depends on the care and treatment that it gets and nutrition is a vital consideration. Calorie intake must be reduced to conform with reduced exercise. Fat and cholesterol levels in old dogs will increase and nutrition must be tailored accordingly. It will be more prone to illness and take longer to convalesce. It will feel the cold, the heat and the wet more with each advancing year. Its senses will gradually decline and the onset of old age will become more apparent in the look of its eye, coat, limbs and muscle tone. Its kidneys may become less efficient and it may become arthritic, taking longer to warm up. The owner's attitude, and this embraces much more than physical care, plays a large part in the maintenance of health and well-being in the old dog. The joy of living does not diminish with age; the accent merely shifts to other things.

My ideal Rottweiler would live a full life, with his abilities kept at their fullest stretch, and he would finish like a river cascading in full body into the sea over a Niagara-like waterfall, rather than struggle to a miserable close in some stagnant delta. Such a life and fitting end came to Dimitie of Mallion. She lived for ten riotous years and died of heart failure in full flight after an errant hen.

Some owners are faced with the agonising decision of putting their pets down. Some owners do so because a dog has outlived its usefulness. We have often been faced with the problem of 'when'. We feel that if a dog enjoys living, if the zest for life is strong enough to overcome low-grade pain, then no action is necessary. Sometimes the dog himself will indicate what should be done. Beaujolais, aged ten, lost his footing on an icy slope, pinching a nerve in the region of the croup. He was paralysed in the hindquarters. The vet thought that careful nursing might restore him in four to six weeks. I sat by his bed to comfort him. Beau reached out with both forelegs telling me very clearly that he wished to stay. He was unable to move for over a month and developed a bed sore as big as a saucer on one hip. The will to live was strong and we persevered, in spite of the well-intentioned people who advised putting him to sleep. He eventually recovered and lived happily for ten months. He was knocked over by another dog while exercising on the mountain and had a relapse. We nursed him again for a week but the spark had gone out of his life. On the way to the vet on the final journey I drove him past the scenes he knew so well. I drew attention to some landmarks and birds but he was not interested.

The Final Chapter

We get a good idea about an owner's feeling for his dog by watching him play with his pup, discipline his dog, and particularly, care for him in the twilight years. We can gauge this feeling very well when the dog dies. How does one dispose of an old friend after years of faithful companionship. We lost our first Rottweiler bitch when she was four years old. She was buried on the fringe of the garden. She knew this spot. She would come up each day from the paddock, turn, survey the landscape and retire to her quarters. She always stopped at this spot. We replaced the turf and there is no mark but we know where she lies and she is surrounded by friends in our dogs' graveyard.

We have a similar area set aside in our new home. The first grave belongs to a bitch owned by an old friend. The bitch had to be put down, our friend was very upset and we felt that we helped at this sad time. The grave was prepared and all was ready when she arrived.

Sir Walter Scott thought a great deal of his bull terrier, Camp. The old fellow had lost most of his senses, but retained enough to thump out a recognition with his tail whenever his master arrived. When he died, he was buried in the garden. Scott's son-in-law described the brief lantern-lit ceremony. Scott was committed to a dinner date that night, but he begged to be excused 'because of the death of an old friend'.

10 Nutrition

A great deal has been written about how dogs should be fed. The impression often conveyed to novice owners is that, in addition to proteins, carbohydrates and fats, the dog requires additives, such as vitamins and minerals, in order to keep it in top condition. Some owners feel that if a certain amount of an additive is beneficial, then twice as much is even better! One can be carried away by science and analysis. How does one recognise the elements in an additive, weigh out .05mg of an essential mineral, or measure 2,000 international units of a vitamin? The same common sense that one uses when feeding a child should be used when feeding a dog – it must be understood that the general advice on feeding relates to normal healthy animals.

The amount of food is calculated in calories which form the basis for measuring energy, or heat-producing units. The metabolic process that converts food into energy differs in its rate and effect from one dog to another. The success of a feeding programme may be judged by the general deportment and health of the dog. If it is full of beans, bright-eyed, glossy-coated and with healthy gums, teeth and nails, then the diet is perfectly satisfactory. An early warning sign may be seen in the faeces. These should be firm, without much smell, and, if the diet is balanced, the dog should excrete one quarter of its intake. A greater proportional intake of protein will reduce this, just as extra carbohydrate will increase it. Loose or blackish-coloured droppings indicate that something disagrees with the dog – possibly an excess of minerals. It is not a cause for worry unless it continues for some time. Grey, constipated droppings are caused by too much cooked bone in the diet. The author does not feed cooked bone, except softened large bones to start very young pups off. Some animals do not absorb all the nutrients in their diet; this has been shown by experiments using cow droppings as food. Eberhard Trumler, in *Understanding Your Dog*, quotes a case where a litter of four ten-week old pug puppies strayed away from their owner while out in the forest. This was in the middle of winter when the temperature was −10°C (16°F). Two of the pups were lost for nine days and one bitch for fourteen. When found, they were none the worse for their adventure, having lived on deer and rabbit droppings.

One should be practical in implementing diet. One cannot suggest 1kg (2lb) of beef in a country where no cattle exist, or fish in an area where this is difficult to obtain. It is useful, however, to have a general idea of how a dog functions, the best sources of nutrition, how these are utilised, and what amounts are necessary, for example in the case of a growing puppy or a lactating bitch, as compared to a maintenance ration. We know a great deal more today about a dog's requirements, and more time and money are apparently spent on this research than the equivalent for human nutrition in many parts of the world. Research has shown that a dog's diet is made up of some forty-three different nutrients, the whole being presented in balance, with each element being in a specific ratio to the others. However, one should not become preoccupied with technicalities, or be too conscious of vitamins and additives. The necessity for these is almost impossible for the layman to detect, and, more often than not, the results of excessive doses – the symptoms of which appear exactly the same as for deficiencies – are treated as deficiencies. A healthy dog derives no benefit from being given additives. The vitamins it needs are readily available in good-quality food from which it extracts its requirements and preserves a natural balance. Balanced diet is a subject that is poorly understood by the average pet owner: pets are more likely to be affected by imbalances than deficiencies. The danger of obesity, excessive amounts of vitamins and over-feeding are far more common in show kennels than malnutrition and vitamin deficiencies.

The important constituents of the diet are easily understood and are as follows:

Protein

Protein comes from the Greek word meaning to come first and this illustrates its importance. Protein provides the amino acids that the body needs to build and repair itself; it is especially important during the growth phase. In combination with other elements, protein helps with other bodily functions, such as the secretion of hormones and enzymes. It is associated with all the normal processes of the body. The sources should be as wide as possible, as the nine amino acids vital to growth are converted from a mixture of foods. Chief sources of protein are meat, fish, milk, cereals, egg yolk, yoghurt and cheese. Raw egg white contains a substance called avidin which destroys biotin in vitamin B. Some say, therefore, that egg white should not be fed raw; however, it is not an important factor if only one or two eggs are fed weekly.

Protein, like many other sources of food, loses some of its value when cooked and over-cooking should be avoided with all foods. A healthy dog can tolerate excess protein. Some of it is expelled in the urine, after being broken down into nitrogen, and some excess, converted to energy, can be stored. Excess protein is not recommended for the older dog as the liver function is sometimes impaired with age. The dog will then find it difficult to excrete excesses and this leads to a build-up of nitrogen. It is always advisable to check on a dog's progress as it advances in age, and some changes in diet will be necessary, either in the elements or their preparation.

The best source of protein available for dogs (19 per cent) may be found in beef cheek. Poultry meat contains approximately the same calorific value, while mutton is about 17 per cent. One should not depend on analyses as figures can be misleading; for example, dried peas contain some 25 per cent protein, but this is a vegetable protein. Lucerne meal is an excellent source of protein, but this applies only to herbivorous animals. Carnivorous species cannot extract protein from vegetable matter as efficiently as cattle and sheep.

The best source of protein is meat, but it has been found that soya beans make an excellent substitute, and 'boneless meat' was used extensively during the last war as a substitute for meat. Other non-meat sources of good-quality protein are wheat, wheat germ and nuts; dried beans, corn and rye also provide nutrients that can be combined with first-quality protein. The following table is provided only as a guide.

Quantity	Source	Protein (gm)
113gm (¼lb)	lean beef	20
"	chicken	23
"	beef heart	19
"	liver	21
"	fish	21
"	potatoes	4
1lb	egg	6
32 fl oz (1 quart)	milk	34
" "	yoghurt	33
½ cup	soya beans	36
"	lentils	9
"	cooked barley	8
"	oatmeal	3
"	wheat germ	9
1 tablespoon	brewers yeast	5

Protein should make up about one-fifth of the dog's daily intake and while excesses can be tolerated, it is better to feed a little less than a little more.

Carbohydrates

Slightly more than half the dog's total intake should be made up of carbohydrates. They provide an inexpensive source of energy and help to maintain body temperature. Carbohydrates are starches that are broken down into sugars in the digestive system. A diet deficient in this element will cause the dog to use the more expensive protein to provide warmth and energy. Stable owners often use a blanket or other covering over their horses in cold weather, to keep the animals warm. This allows the food eaten to be used for growth and repair of muscle, rather than being consumed as a fuel to keep the animal warm.

Carbohydrates are found in the fibrous part of the ration. Vegetables and cereals, particularly cooked whole-grain cereals, are the best source. Anything prepared from refined flour – bread for example – has little value. A number of kibbled dog biscuits are on the market and they are useful for both dogs and pups. Roughage contains very little food value, but it is an essential part of the diet, stimulating and cleaning the digestive system and preventing constipation. Many vitamins and minerals are found in carbohydrates and dogs should be encouraged to eat a wide variety of vegetables and even fruit.

Most of these, potatoes being the exception, should be fed raw or semi-cooked. We find that grated carrot and spinach cooked with soup are particularly good. All our dogs are encouraged to eat vegetables and some relish such fruit as grapes, apple, pear, melons and similar items; Catja, our German bitch, will eat any fruit that is offered. An older dog would benefit from an increased intake of roughage which, if it does not extend its life, at least will make it healthier and happier.

Fats

A misconception exists about the feeding of fats, many people believing that dogs become obese when fed on fat. Too much animal fat should be avoided, although the diet should include about 8 per cent. Fats are a concentrated source of energy and an equal amount will provide more than twice the energy of any other food. A tablespoon of butter provides 100 calories and a tablespoon of vegetable oil 125. Fats from vegetable sources are superior to those coming from animal sources and they do not become rancid as easily. Vegetable fats have low melting points, 37°C (98°F), are easily digestible, contain both vitamins and minerals, and cut down on cholesterol.

Fats are broken down in the digestive system to fatty acids, glycerol and glycerin. These acids help the action of vitamin D in mobilising calcium. The best sources of unsaturated acids are found in corn oil, safflower oil, peanut oil, soya bean oil, and olive oil. A tablespoon of any of these will help to maintain general health and, in particular, the dog's coat. Signs of fat deficiency show up in a harsh coat, skin irritation, loss of hair and cracked pads. Fats are palatable and most prepared foods are sprayed with fat. Fat also has an attractive smell and this is a big factor in improving palatability. The ability to digest fat is helped by an enzyme secreted by the pancreas, and thus dogs with pancreatic damage have difficulty in digesting fat. A tablespoon of corn oil will help, particularly if animal fats are omitted from the diet.

Sugars

Sugar is an element that is seldom discussed in the context of a dog's diet. In the production of energy, however, fats burn more efficiently when combined with sugar. The two most important sugars are glucose and fructrose and these are found in a wide variety of fruits and vegetables. Milk contains a sugar called lactose, but we have found that some dogs, particularly older ones, do not digest milk easily. Milk is essential for growing dogs, however, and our brood bitches are given at least two pints a day, mixed with water, in the first two weeks of lactation; this is gradually reduced and stopped after some four weeks.

Most of the sugar-producing vegetables and fruits are easily and cheaply obtained, depending on where one lives, and this table may help as a guide:

Producing 20 per cent	15 per cent	10 per cent	5 per cent
bananas	apples	celery roots	beet greens
cereals	apricots	squash	carrots
sweet corn	grapes	turnips	lettuce
sweet potatoes	green peas	canned peas	pumpkin
	parsnips		spinach
			milk (lactose)

Vitamins

Bobby Riggs, the American tennis player, increased the sales of vitamins tenfold by advertising the vast number of pills that he swallowed. While this benefited the manufacturers, it is doubtful if it had any effect on the health of the people thus influenced. In the show world people use additives, hoping these will turn their show winners into champions. Vitamins and additives will never replace good food or care and affection, and a great deal more harm is done by their indiscriminate use than the corresponding benefits. Vitamins are essential, but they need only be present in minute quantities, and they must be supplied in perfect balance. Unless prescribed by a veterinarian, they should not come out of a bottle or a packet, but should be found mainly in the diet, as the dog has the ability to synthesize some vitamins and extract others from its food diet. In special cases, their use may be necessary, particularly vitamin B, but the need for such supplements must be diagnosed and the correct dosage prescribed. A point to remember is that vitamins have no food value.

Vitamins play a vital role in every function of the body, but one should bear in mind that tablets and powders can be harmful. Vitamin therapy has its own uses but it must be confined to sick animals and must be prescribed by a veterinarian. New vitamins are being discovered, and, in the case of vitamin B, new members are added to the family each year. All vitamins existed in various food sources long before the word was even invented; some are yet to be identified. A and D are fashionable and are packaged under various labels. Spreads like Marmite and Vegemite contain the B family and, while these are palatable and safe, the expense when feeding a kennel can be high.

Vitamin A
Medical authorities state that this vitamin can be manufactured in the human liver from a substance known as carotene – denoted by the reddish-yellow colouring found in carrots. Dogs, however, cannot manufacture it and therefore it must be supplied in their diet. It is available in most animal sources, such as meat, kidney, egg yolk, milk or cheese, to give the best examples. The richest source is liver, but liver should only be fed in small quantities, say 226–282gm (8–10oz) per week. Fish liver oils are an excellent source but, like most concentrated sources, overdosing can occur very easily. The best vegetable source is carrot. A deficiency of this vitamin is due more often to the dog's inability to extract it from its food, because of a metabolic defect, rather than the absence of it in the food. The symptoms of deficiency are dry skin, skin lesions, loss of hair and a swelling of the joints. The same symptoms also occur when too much is given. Being a fat-soluble vitamin, it can be stored in the body.

The following table is provided as a guide

113gm (4oz) liver provide	20,000 units	not more than 226–282gm (8–10oz) week
113gm (4oz) heart/kidney	1,200	up to 1kg (2lb) week
113gm (4oz) fish	150–200	more when canned in oil
1 egg yolk	500–800	dependent on fowl's diet
32 fl oz (1 quart) milk	2,300	can drop to 700 when green feed is not available to cows
113gm (4oz) cheese	1,600	

By comparison, concentrated amounts of up to 50,000 units are sold in capsules or tablets. Vegetable sources are not rich in vitamin A or minerals, but they are of great benefit and vital to the dog's health.

Carotene, in vegetable sources, is contained in cellulose which is not readily digestible unless the plant stems are broken down mechanically. Humans do this by chewing, and juices in the saliva start the digestive process. Herbivores secrete an enzyme that dissolves cellulose and the process, known in ruminants as 'chewing the cud', completes digestion; carnivores are not proficient in digesting cellulose. Dogs swallow their food without chewing and the digestive process starts in the stomach. Only 1 per cent carotene is absorbed from raw carrot; the equivalent in cooked carrot is 30 per cent. These factors should be borne in mind when preparing a dog's diet.

Vitamin B

This is a vitamin complex and no less than fourteen parts have been identified in the family so far; twelve of these can be manufactured synthetically and are sold under various labels and in a variety of foods. The best known members of the B family arc sold in combination with two or more of thiamine chloride (B1), riboflavine (B2), pyridoxine (B6), niacin and pantothenic acid. Some of the remainder, such as folic acid – destroyed by heat – inositol, biotin, choline, para-aminobenzoic acid and cyniocobalamin (B12) are found only in natural sources like liver, brewers yeast, brown rice, wheat germ, milk, unrefined grains, nuts and soya beans. The lactic acid bacteria in sour milk and yoghurt synthesizes thiamine and riboflavin. The entire complex is vital to health and, unlike A, B cannot be stored in the body. A deficiency will cause a lowering of resistance to disease and infection. Vitamin B is an important aid to digestion and some of it is destroyed by the administration of sulpha drugs and antibiotics, especially penicillin. We feel that the fading puppy syndrome is closely related to the loss of this vitamin in the bitch's stomach. Many puppies have faded after the mother was treated with these drugs, and puppies left on the mother after being delivered by caesarean section usually suffer from this complaint. This could be related to an inability to digest milk because the aids to digestion have been destroyed. Little has been recorded about hypervitaminosis and dogs can tolerate excess, particularly of thiamine. Owners of sled dogs have been known to inject B12 to increase a dog's performance before Arctic races, and it is prescribed for dogs suffering blood loss. A brood bitch making a slow recovery after the birth of a litter could benefit from small doses, and yeast, wheat germ and liver are ideal supplements in the circumstances.

Food	Quantity	Thiamine (mg)	Riboflavin (mg)
brewers yeast	2 tablespoons	3.5	0.7
dried soya beans	½ cup	1.13	0.38
liver	113gm (4oz)	0.30	4.50
wheat germ	½ cup	0.7	0.28
lamb	113gm (4oz)	0.16	0.28
milk	1 cup	0.09	0.42
oatmeal	1 cup, cooked	0.22	0.05
brown rice	1 cup, cooked	0.10	0.02

Vitamin C

This vitamin plays a useful, though minor, part in the dog's diet, helping in the utilization of amino acids. It also helps to form the dentine of the teeth, although poorly formed teeth, or loss of enamel, is rare in our breed. It is found in the fresh fruits of the citrus family, in peppers and cabbage. It cannot be stored and is lost in drying. Cooking destroys it completely. There is a theory that ascorbic acid – vitamin C – given to pregnant bitches prevents hip dysplasia, but no conclusive evidence has been provided in this context.

Vitamin D

The importance of this vitamin lies in its catalytic influence and its close relationship with calcium and phosphorus in the production of bone. It is one vitamin that cannot be extracted from food in sufficient quantities. However, adequate supplies can be produced from the action of the sun on the skin of both humans and dogs. In theory, a grown Rottweiler requires approximately 1,000 international units per day, and two hours of direct sunlight will produce this amount. Vitamin D capsules, or tablets containing concentrated amounts, are readily available; the labels will indicate the amount of units per capsule. In countries where there is little sunlight in winter, fish oil concentrates, especially from cod, may be given, but it is inadvisable to give more than 1,000 units per day. There is a condition, called osteomalacia, that occurs in humans and is known as malabsorption syndrome. Here abnormalities of vitamin metabolism occur where the kidneys are not functioning properly. Vitamin D therapy is used and massive doses given. It was once used in some 25 per cent of post-gastrectomy cases; modern treatment has reduced the incidence of these cases. This inefficient function of the kidneys may occur in dogs, and no doubt the veterinarian will indicate the treatment that is necessary.

The interaction of vitamin D, calcium and phosphorus is of vital importance in the study of canine nutrition and some aspects of this are discussed later in this chapter.

Vitamin E

Vitamin E is regarded as being vital to bodily functions, particularly those of reproduction, and it is sometimes called the anti-sterility vitamin. Vitamin E deficiency may be seen in animals that have been given excess cod liver oil, or unsaturated fats that have become rancid. The former upsets the balance of vitamins, and the latter destroys the vitamin E content in food. Wheat germ oil, olive oil, oatmeal, whole wheat, butter, eggs, and such vegetables as spinach, carrots, kale, parsley and brussels sprouts are the best natural sources. We have used tablets in cases of bitches that have had difficulty in conceiving, but we cannot comment on any positive result. This vitamin should be readily available as there is a sufficient variety of foods to provide it without recourse to tablets or capsules.

Minerals: especially Calcium and Phosphorus

The importance of minerals in the development and general health of a dog is seldom appreciated. They help to maintain the amount of water that is necessary to the life process and in the deposition and reabsorption of matter in bones and cells. They also help with the secretion of hormones and enzymes. By far the most important are calcium and phosphorus and they are required in far larger quantities than all the other minerals combined.

Calcium and phosphorus are deposited in bones and teeth in chemical combination with vitamin D and there is very little margin for error in the ratio of these three. If the requirement of phosphorus or vitamin D is exceeded, the system will restore the ratio by drawing calcium from the bones. The result can be disastrous, particularly with growing animals. Rickets is a well-known disease in the young infant child or animal. The symptom is a softening of the bone because of a lack of calcium. The incidence of the disease in modern western countries is negligible and it seldom occurs in puppies. The disease that is common to dogs and which results in the weakening of the bones is called *nutritional secondary hyperparathyrodism* and it is induced by an imbalance of calcium and phosphorus.

Too much phosphorus is added when a predominantly meat diet is fed. Meat contains approximately .01 per cent calcium and .18 per cent phosphorus. The calcium/phosphorus ratio should be 1.2:1.00.

I am often asked, 'How much calcium should I feed my pup?' If the owner appreciated the matter correctly he would ask himself, 'What calcium/phosphorus am I feeding in the ration and what should I add to maintain the balance?'

A healthy adult fed on a balanced diet requires no additives; it finds these in its diet and the natural intake preserves the vital balance. If the ration contains much meat, a good rule of thumb is to add 1 teaspoon of calcium carbonate to each 500gm (1lb) of meat. Prepared foods have the correct amounts included. If the ration is 50 per cent meat and 50 per cent prepared food, some calcium is necessary. However, this is available naturally, for example in milk or milk derivatives. Phosphorus is available in a great many more foods than calcium and growing animals do require minute additional amounts of the latter. A pregnant or lactating bitch will provide calcium for her puppies and, if this is not added to her feed, she will get it initially from her blood and, in the longer term, from her bones. If the blood calcium is low, and this may well occur between the second and third week of lactation, when demand from her litter is highest, she may develop milk fever.

An imbalance of calcium/phosphorus/vitamin D can have disastrous results, particularly to a heavy dog like a Rottweiler, and owners should study this aspect of nutrition with particular care.

Most diseases of the bone are associated with two phases of a Rottweiler's life. The first is the period when cartilage is being transformed into bone – up to the age of about twelve months – and the second some time after the change has taken place – about the age of four to five years. Both are caused by imbalances in calcium/phosphorus/vitamin D and both are exacerbated by the stress placed on joints, in the first stage by too rapid development, and in the second by too much weight and the onset of arthritis.

A pup is born with cartilage containing minute traces of calcium; this cartilage assumes the shape that the bone will eventually take. The form and shape of cartilage is probably influenced by genetic factors; this is the message conveyed by the genes of both parents. Whether the potential is developed or not depends on environmental factors. Initially, this is influenced by the condition and feeding of the bitch prior to the birth of the litter. Secondly, it is influenced by the provision of amino acids which provide the pup with the energy to grow, the reinforcing material, in the shape of minerals, chiefly calcium and phosphorus mobilised by vitamin D, and the amount of pressure placed on growing joints by the exercise the pup receives. Hence the saying, 'The breeder (or breeding) makes the pup; the owner (or feeding) makes the dog.'

If the pup is allowed to go through the gradual process of growth without this growth being forced, and if the calcium/phosphorus/vitamin D balance is maintained, then the structure of the bones – their shape, size, thickness and strength – will be sound. If this is denied then the dog will run into trouble with shoulders, elbows and hips because too much pressure was placed on joints that were not strong enough, and the change from cartilage to bone has been faulty. Cartilage may become inflamed, or, in some cases, pieces will chip away. Bones may be too soft because of insufficient reinforcing material, or too brittle because of too much. Many a proud Rottweiler owner has run into bone problems with a yearling that won handsomely in the show ring at the age of six months, in company far beyond its years.

The basis for this statement is partly empirical and partly conclusions reached by various authorities, some in research centres, and others in private veterinary practice. We found, in twenty years of breeding, that some pups went through a stage when a limp was noticeable. The cause, generally, was not located and the treatment – rest – invariably cured the condition.

The results of an experiment conducted on twenty-four Great Dane puppies, at the department of Animal Science at Cornell University, are revealing. The pups were divided into two groups of twelve. The first group was fed unlimited amounts of beef, dry food and evaporated milk, combined with the necessary additives. The second group was restricted to two-thirds of the amount. A pattern emerged after a few days which showed that the first group nibbled at their food continuously while the second devoured two meals a day within two minutes of being served. The unlimited group played very little, spending their day eating and sleeping. The restricted group raced about energetically running up and down a platform that had been placed in the yard; the unlimited group could only manage the platform with assistance. Clinical changes in this group were the sinking of the pasterns, weak feet, saddle backs, cow hocks, and arthritic front legs. It was concluded that unlimited feeding caused maximal growth early in life and had an adverse effect on skeletal development and body co-ordination, inducing some bone diseases.

The degree of subluxation in the hip joint may be detected by palpation by an experienced veterinarian as early as four weeks. Conformation of the hip joint, therefore, is present at this early age. As the pup grows, cartilage is transformed into bone and the hip status of the grown dog is influenced by several factors. Evidence of change may be seen in X-rays taken at intervals of two to three months.

Remodelling may occur because of genetic influence, over-feeding, over-exercising, an imbalance of calcium/phosphorus/vitamin D, or a combination of two or more of these. Our attitude to HD, and the tools that we fashion to combat this disease, should bear all these factors in mind. Puppy owners should check the rate of growth, the exercise the pup receives and the amount of calcium that is added to preserve the balance.

Most owners assume that bone, once formed, becomes inert and static, but bone is a dynamic material, constantly changing. Mineral is both deposited and reabsorbed in bone and osteoid tissue, and, if soundness is to be maintained, both these processes must be kept in balance and the rate of growth must be steady. If sufficient minerals are not available in the diet, the system will draw them from within the body. A classic example of this is related to the old saying of the eighteenth century, 'two teeth per pregnancy!' In the latter stages of pregnancy the baby draws its mineral requirements from the mother. If her own bodily needs are not met, she will be deprived of the amount taken by her baby. The diet of pregnant women in the twentieth century is supplemented and the mother should, therefore, be able to retain her own teeth!

Injections of calcium should be avoided, the only exception being when a bitch has milk fever in which case a veterinary surgeon should be called. The lactating bitch should draw her own requirement of calcium from milk intake, supplemented by small quantities of calcium, the composition of which must be dictated by her diet. Balance is the key and prevention is better than cure.

The Remaining Minerals
In addition to calcium and phosphorus, the dog requires minute quantities of a number of other minerals. These are magnesium – a lack of which may cause flat feet in puppies – manganese and iron – which helps in the transport of oxygen in the blood and removes carbon dioxide from the tissues. It is prescribed for anaemia in humans and is therefore of assistance to dogs suffering loss of blood. It is found in meat, but the absorption rate is low; heart 80 per cent, liver 70 per cent and muscle meat 50 per cent. Copper, cobalt, trace elements and iodine are other minerals needed. Iodine, in minute quantities, is an important ingredient in the human diet also. Together with the secretion put out by the thyroid gland, it produces thyroxine which is essential to the system. Food sources contain very little, if any, iodine although it is found in cabbage and seaweed (kelp). An iodised vegetable salt can be a useful additive. Our current practice is to add one teaspoon of iodised salt to the dogs' soup once a week and, although raw meat is fed occasionally, the incidence of skin irritation is remarkably low in our kennels.

Practical Aspects of Feeding

How much should I feed my dog? How often? What is best? Cooked or raw? An owner should be sufficiently aware of the subject to make his own decision. An analytical explanation allows one to appreciate the position before making a judgement. A simple concise answer, while being positive and constructive, merely helps one to carry out a function without understanding.

Some dogs eat a great deal more than others and will eat still more if permitted. This is not necessary and is not good for the dog. The dog's digestive capacity, compared pound for pound, is far less than that of a herbivore. Brandy (Rintelna the General) once consumed about 3.5kg (8lb) of semi-frozen beef. The vet ordered a tablespoon of brandy and castor oil, and he did vomit the meal immediately after. The basic ration for an adult Rottweiler should be about 1.1kg (2½lb) per day. We have had the most satisfactory results from feeding amounts slightly below those recommended by most authorities.

Dogs vary in their approach to food. Some are voracious eaters while others simply pick at their food. Some dogs extract more from their food, and metabolism varies from dog to dog. Working dogs, and those exercising a great deal, burn more energy and therefore require more food. Growing pups require more than mature dogs and will eat more than twice as much. The same applies to a pregnant bitch. She should not be allowed to get fat, however, as excessive quantities of food do more harm than good. The total quantity fed should not increase in the first month, although protein content could be increased. She should be exercised quite normally in the first six weeks. Exercise can be reduced gradually, with the bitch setting her own pace. She should not be allowed to exercise with other dogs, or jump or twist.

With regard to quantity, the dog himself will tell you whether his diet is adequate. Indicators will be weight, muscle condition, not being fat and general deportment; he will always be on the look-out for food, but this is quite normal. Grown dogs are generally fed once a day. In theory, they would benefit from a division of the amount into two meals a day. Weaned pups may be fed up to five times a day, but only two of these meals are solids. A pregnant bitch should be fed twice a day when she shows obvious signs of carrying a litter and, in the last week or so, meals could be divided into three. Immediately after whelping, she should receive plenty of liquid nourishment with some soft meat – chicken, rabbit, tongue, or such. After two or three days, normal diet should be resumed, with plenty of good fat-free beef. The peak demand from the litter will come at two to three weeks; she should not be allowed to get fat.

Feeding time depends on personal circumstances. Dogs are creatures of habit and expect their food about the same time each day. We feed in the early evening, after exercise. One British kennel that we visited fed in the morning and the dogs were in excellent condition. Morning feeding gives a better opportunity to observe dogs after feeding; we have lost three bitches through bloat, and, feeding late, before shutting dogs in for the night, gives the owner no opportunity to take action if the condition occurs and is not noticed.

Dogs, being carnivorous, should thrive on raw flesh. Their teeth and digestive systems are designed to cope with this. The comparatively short digestive tract – they evacuate twice daily at least – prevents putrefaction in the system. Civilisation, however, has weaned them away from their wild environment and, although we have made no change to their internal anatomy, we have changed their eating habits and diet. They no longer have access to bones, hair, skin and the stomach contents of their kill, and so we must provide adequate substitutes. Wild animals in captivity are fed flesh with some additives that are concentrated. The effect may be seen in the difference between a zoo tiger and his jungle counterpart. In addition to meat, dogs must be given carbohydrates, roughage, vitamins and minerals if they are to function effectively.

We cook a pot of soup (the container was made to our specifications with a wire insert that holds such unwanted items as chicken bones), using bones, cereals, vegetables, vegetable peelings, rice water and the water in which household vegetables have been boiled. Two or three cloves of garlic are added. Liver, when added, is cooked with the soup. Organ meats and paunches, when used, are put in after an hour. Meat, preferably beef cheek, is added last and the heat turned off. In winter the soup will last a week; in summer there is a danger of it turning sour and this must be avoided at all costs. Two double handfuls of dry food are put in each dish, covered with soup and allowed to soak for a few minutes. The meat, in large chunks, is then added, together with a sprinkling of wheat germ. Cooked meat is easier to digest, but this is no kindness as the digestive system is not exercised. Large chunks force dogs to exercise the muscles in their jaws. Skull measurements – wolves versus dogs of comparative size – show that the former have larger skulls, with heavier bone. This is the result of eating hard food. We notice that dogs with obviously strong jaws will demolish a large piece of meat, quickly tearing and crushing it sufficiently to swallow.

Our dogs have access to pasture and the city dweller would be surprised to see how much grass is eaten. Fresh vegetables are most important and kennels and a garden are compatible. Water used for washing kennels provides both moisture and nourishment for the adjacent vegetables. Uneaten food is not left in kennels and plates are removed after ten minutes. We use large stainless steel basins that are standard equipment for washing patients in hospitals. These are hygienic, easily cleaned and they look as good as the day they were purchased, fifteen years ago.

Prepared Foods

There are many brands sold in convenient-sized packages, weighing 10, 15 and 20kg (22, 33 and 44lb); some brands are more suitable than others. The ingredients may not be of the same quality as we use, particularly the meat content, but a great deal of research has gone into the manufacture of pet foods and the result is a balanced ration with all the necessary elements in the correct proportions. We feed a quarter to a third of this food, mixed with meat and soup. Many kennels use this food alone with good results. Some feed only this food on an *ad lib* basis. Dry food is certainly more convenient to feed and requires no preparation; also the kennels are easier to keep clean. Packets of dry food must be protected from the atmosphere as the slightest moisture will cause mildew.

Canned Foods

Again, this type of food is sold under many brands and all are highly palatable. Boiling an opened tin to see how the food reacted to heat, we found that it turned to liquid. When used, these foods should be fed cold.

Meat

A great deal has been written about the superiority of fresh meat to the frozen variety. There is no doubt that this is true, both in palatability and food value. Our dogs show the most obvious enjoyment in disposing of beef cheek freshly killed, unwashed, bloody and slimy. The practical aspect, however, must be considered, and when journeys of a hundred miles or so have to be made to get meat, the frozen variety is the only alternative. Thawing is important and meat should be taken out of the freezing chamber and allowed to thaw gradually in the refrigerator. When fed raw, or cooked, it must be completely soft. Beef, we find, is the best source and cheek the best cut. Liver, heart and tongue are used in small quantities, always cooked. Paunches are excellent and should be fed green. The contents are a good natural food, but messy to handle. Mutton cheek, head and neck pieces are excellent with tongue and organ meats. Sheep paunches are easier to handle. Sheep heads make good soup. Some kennels use mutton flaps, but we feel that they contain too much fat. Rabbits, in Australia, are fed to working sheepdogs complete with skin, but we prefer to cook the flesh lightly. The meat is excellent for young puppies and for bitches that have just whelped. Beef and mutton bones are fed occasionally, always raw, and brisket bones are the best. Cooked marrow bones are good for starting young puppies off and all our puppies have bones of one sort or another each day. Older dogs may suffer teeth damage and bones should never be left in kennels.

We cook vegetables of all varieties in the soup. The best appear to be carrots, spinach, green beans, lentils, squash, pumpkin, marrows and turnip. Most dogs will not eat peas; dishes will be licked clean with peas pushed neatly into a corner. Cereals are of great benefit and we cook them after crushing or flaking. In the wild, carnivorous animals extract their nourishment from cereals that are already semi-digested in the intestines of the animals that they have killed. Brown, or dogs', rice – unpolished rice – is used extensively in dogs' diet in countries where meat is difficult to get; protein can be extracted when the rice is cooked. Barley, maize or corn can be treated similarly. Milk is essential for puppies and goat's milk is richer than cow's. Eggs are a rich source of protein and may be fed two or three times a week. We once lived near a poultry farm and had a plentiful supply of cracked and blood-spot eggs. Most of our dogs eat shells with relish. Brewers yeast and wheat germ are two foods that we use regularly in our household and the dogs enjoy it as much as we do. It is especially good for puppies and pregnant bitches. Fresh water is essential and we are fortunate to have a spring on the property. Water in the kennels is changed two or three times a day and more frequently in summer. Buckets are always placed in the shade.

Fasting

Much has been written about the benefit of fasting one day in the week. This is not a custom that is observed ritually in the wild, but carnivores may fast involuntarily, sometimes for more than one day, when the hunt has been unproductive. One of the kennels owning dogs of our breeding observes this rule and the dogs are both healthy and happy. There is no doubt that it is better to withhold food when dogs are ill, especially with intestinal disorders. A rest day, we feel, could be of some benefit and there should be no ill effects.

Food Allergies

We often receive a call saying, 'Our dog is scratching. What should we do?' Individual dogs may be allergic to a number of things, generally resulting in some form of skin irritation. They may be allergic to organic material, either in the food or by contact. Allergies sometimes may also be the result of something inorganic, like mental or physical stress. Generally, scratching is caused by internal or external parasites and these should be checked for first.

Food allergies are difficult to detect and novice owners are not always conscious of this possibility. Dogs may be allergic to milk, eggs, raw meat or many other foods, and a high protein diet, or an excess of some vitamin could be the cause of skin irritation. Experienced breeders have stated that this is caused by heat in the food! Explanations may seem illogical, but there is some truth in them and a sensible owner will learn from another's mistake. An observant owner may notice a change that coincided with either the omission or inclusion of some item of diet. If this is not possible then one should experiment by adding something, taking care to see that only one item is added at any one time.

A Sensible Balance

Some owners tend to move from one extreme to another, going overboard for some fad or fashion, particularly in feeding or in the rearing of puppies. Our reaction to advice is to consider it and, if acceptable, to introduce change gradually. A pup, like a child, should enjoy all the phases of growth, and play is essential. The development of a young child is based on play and while guidance and discipline are always present, their constraints should not be evident. No one expects a child to earn its living, so why then should a young Rottweiler be pushed into achieving a title and perhaps a CD before it is a year old? It must enjoy its puppyhood and growth, both mental and physical, should be in keeping with its age. It should not be mollycoddled or pampered if it is to grow up into a robust and powerful dog. In its historical role it had to withstand the kick of a cow and have the capacity to negotiate the toughest country and keep going all day. A pup must be exercised, but exercise should be limited to a rough and tumble with pups of its own age, and it must set its own pace. In the early, and most important, stage of its development, a young Rottweiler must have proper food and exercise and, most important, affection and company. These things, like nutrition, must be supplied in the correct balance.

11 Common Ailments

Skin and Coat

Coat, particularly in the context of the show ring, is of primary importance to all dogs. Show quality in the Rottweiler is easily maintained. Two or three minutes' vigorous brushing, morning and evening, a balanced diet to which the dog responds, reasonable exercise and clean quarters are the simple ingredients required. Our Rottweilers shed their coats and replace them continuously. As the weather gets cold, the coat thickens. When it gets warm, excess coat is shed. The weather, in our environment, changes several times a day, so we have a great deal of hair about the kennels! Regular brushing will remove dead hair and discourage the dog from scratching. A diet lacking some form of fat will cause dryness in the coat and the skin will become flaky.

Skin problems, we find, are generally caused by parasites. External parasites are fleas, lice, ticks, mites, flies, sand flies and so on. When these parasites bite or sting, they leave saliva in the wound which irritates dogs, some much more than others. Secondary infection, caused by the dog's reaction to bites, is generally more serious than the initial trouble. Some dogs ignore parasites, while others will be driven mad and tear at themselves in an effort to be rid of the irritation. We find that the dogs that are sensitive to brushing are sensitive to bites. Sensitivity is not related to the amount or density of the coat.

Fleas

The flea population is influenced not by the dog itself or its coat, but by the state of its sleeping quarters. These must be made and kept clean before any measures are taken to bathe or disinfect the dog. Fleas lay their eggs in cracks and crevices, coating them with blood; this provides the young fleas with immediate nourishment. The blood is washed off by using plenty of water. This deprives young fleas of their first meal, thereby reducing the population. Sunshine and disinfectants are useful in creating a hostile environment. An attack on the habitat is a more effective way of controlling fleas than direct measures to find and kill them individually. Flea dirt, deposited at the root of the tail, is the easiest method of finding infestation on a dog. The dirt forms a shape like a grain of sand, the size of a large pin head. A steel comb, run through the coat in the reverse direction, will reveal the evidence. The sand fly, although more confined in habitat than the flea, is a worse problem in some climates. Kennels sited near the sea are not ideal for dogs with sensitive skins.

Ringworm
Ringworm can present problems with regard to diagnosis. To start with the trouble is not caused by a worm; it is a fungal infection spread by contact, and it can be passed to humans. Hair falls out in a circular patch in the form of a ring. It is not irritable to start with and, if treated quickly, may be no problem. The problem is to diagnose it correctly so that the correct treatment is given before the dog starts to scratch. Crushed garlic, rubbed into the spot, will contain and eventually cure the infection. However, a dog could be more sensitive to the treatment than the fungus.

Mange
Mange is the generic term used to describe many skin irritations, but is better applied to two types of mange. *Demodectic mange* is caused by tiny mites which attach themselves to the hair follicles. In small quantities these can be tolerated by most dogs and are kept in check by brushing, bathing and general cleanliness. Dogs debilitated by disease are less resistant to demodectic mange mites and these can multiply, causing a serious skin condition. *Sarcoptic mange* is also caused by a mite but these burrow into the skin. The mite, *Sarcoptes scabei*, can be identified when skin scrapings are placed under a microscope. Your veterinary surgeon will recommend the best treatment, depending on the extent and severity of the infection. In early cases, a mild sheep dip and sulphur ointment will give good results. The same mite causes scabies in humans.

We have two problems peculiar to the mountain forest where ferns grow in profusion, or to pasture grazed by sheep and cattle. Dogs collect ticks which attach themselves to legs and faces. These are small brown creatures resembling minute crabs; certain species can cause paralysis. They can also attach themselves surreptitiously to humans, bringing little reaction. These can be removed with a pair of tweezers taking care to crush the head so that the whole creature is removed. If the head is left embedded, minor infection can result. Another way to remove ticks is to smear the tick with white spirit and wait for it to drop off.

In Australia ferns are also inhabited by leeches which fasten onto both humans and dogs without giving much indication of their presence. They get into the webbing of the toes and, unless dogs are examined each day, the first sign of a leech is a tell-tale spot of blood on the floor of the kennel. Leeches will drop off if covered by a pinch of salt.

Peggi v Mummler (bred by Ingeborg Krämer, owned by Frederico Lensi) nursing her litter
(courtesy Dr Lensi/Photo: Alan Hutchison)

Paul Narik with Auslese Esparte and Ch Auslese Bold Banner CD, trying their sea legs
(courtesy John Duffin)

Skin irritations

Eczema is a generic term for all skin problems. There are a number of agents that cause irritation and, apart from parasites, dogs may suffer an allergic reaction to food, chemicals, drugs, pollens and even an irritant like sunburn. It is important to diagnose the complaint.

Skin irritations can also be caused by allergic reactions. Dogs are sensitive to exactly the same number of allergens as humans, and they must be diagnosed and treated in the same way. Correct diagnosis is important, so that the correct treatment can be administered. Three years ago my best show prospect showed signs of skin irritation. The Royal Melbourne Show was one month away, so I took the dog to the local surgery. The surgeon tried the routine medication without success. Some months later another veterinary surgeon diagnosed the cause. We had just moved into our new mountain home and the wattle bloomed in August. The dog was sensitive to wattle pollen.

My first Rottweiler suffered a chronic skin irritation. His skin was dry and flaky, hair fell out and he scratched incessantly. Different surgeons tried to find the cause but to no avail. An old lady asked me about his diet. Did I cook his meat? I said 'No'. She told me that cooking would cure the irritation, by removing the acid! I had just read an article describing the effect of a lack of iodine in the diet and its action on the skin. Chab's meat was cooked and a pinch of iodised salt was added. The eczema cleared up in a fortnight. Had I adopted a more scientific approach I would have been in a position to say which, the iodine or the cooking, was responsible.

Occasionally we have skin problems caused by an allergy to a particular food and when this occurs all items of diet are checked to discover the culprit. All dogs are not subject to the same allergy! Milk, raw meat, cooked meat, eggs, a certain type of dry food and all additives are eliminated *one at a time*. We generally find the culprit within a couple of weeks.

I left for an overseas trip in 1968, leaving my wife with four dogs. She decided to put flea collars on all the dogs late one evening. One of them reacted violently to the chemical in the collar. By morning he had torn much of the skin on his neck and chest. An area some 15cm (6in) square was raw and bleeding. Secondary infection set in and it took many weeks of medication and nursing to get him well.

In all cases of skin irritation, it is important to diagnose what causes it and to stop the dog scratching. Scratching is generally followed by secondary infection which is long-lasting and much worse than the original bite or irritation.

International Ch Ives Eulenspiegel Sch H3 Eur Sgr (courtesy M. Bruns)

Grass seeds, particularly those of barley grass, can enter the dogs' ears, paws and loose skin. On one occasion Chab had a lump which caused us concern. It showed up in his groin and the prognosis was not good. We sat anxiously in the waiting room while the surgeon performed an operation to explore the growth. We were greatly relieved when he presented us with a grass seed reclining in a bed of cotton wool. After this incident feet were examined regularly and many a grass seed removed with a pair of tweezers.

A healthy dog, correctly fed and exercised, will withstand most attacks by the agents described. External parasites are successfully contained by ensuring that dogs inhabit an environment which is unfavourable to parasites. If food allergies are suspected it is important to isolate each ingredient so that the offending item can be identified. This can only be done one at a time.

Worms

Roundworm

The most common internal parasite is the roundworm, *Toxocara canis*, and we have found, almost without exception, that all litters are born with this infestation to some degree. Adult worms remain in the intestinal walls and muscles, undetected and immune to anthelmintics, emerging in the last days of pregnancy to infest pups in the uterus. Young worms can grow 5–7½cm (2–3in) a week and can attain a size of 15–20cm (6–8in). Clinical signs of infestation are emaciation, pot bellies, poor coats and diarrhoea, but it is criminally negligent to allow a dog to get these symptoms. The age at which pups can be successfully wormed depends on the time when larvae are passed to them by the bitch before they are born. We worm pups at two weeks, but find that a second dose, given ten days later, produces more worms. Worming is continued at ten-day intervals until pups are free. The first two doses of Antoban syrup – piperazine citrate – is given with a pipette; subsequent doses, which may be in tablet form, crushed, are mixed with food. All pups should be eating and lapping by this time; each pup should be weighed and fed separately. Veterinary advice is to worm the bitch before mating. We do this regularly, but find that it has no effect. Some bitches are free of worms all their lives; we add garlic to the diet and this could be a factor.

Older pups and dogs may acquire the infection by ingestion. A small sample of droppings put under a microscope will show whether eggs exist. These eggs are also detected by flotation tests. Human beings can be affected and children can easily pick up eggs through contact with infected animals.

Our latest German bitch, Echo v Mägdeburg, was wormed a day or so before being mated. Her subsequent litter of eight was heavily infested with roundworms. When the litter was five weeks old, Echo's droppings were tested; there was no sign of worms or eggs. Isobella, the daughter of our older German bitch, Catja, has been given garlic regularly ever since she came out of quarantine. She has no worms nor does she pass them to her puppies.

Hookworm

Hookworm, *Ancylostoma caninum*, a small blood-sucking worm, is far more dangerous. Dogs, and especially pups, can be infected, resulting in severe malnutrition and anaemia. The worm can be ingested, but it is also passed to the unborn young or via the colostrum. Positive diagnosis is possible only by testing droppings. We have not encountered this worm in our kennels. Good hygiene and cleanliness are the best methods of preventing infestation.

Whipworm

Whipworm, *Trichuris vulpis*, is smaller than the hookworm but acts in much the same way. Identification and eradication are exactly the same. This is a more dangerous parasite because eggs are far more resistant, living in the soil for several months. Infected dogs require repeated treatments. Pfizer has recently manufactured three anthelmintics which effectively combat all the worms referred to, excepting tapeworm: Canex and Canex 2.5 (pyrantel pamoate) are most effective against round- and hookworm while Canex plus (pyrantel pamoate + oxantel pamoate) is effective against all three. Consult your veterinarian for correct treatment and advice.

Tapeworm

Tapeworm, *Dipylidium caninum*, is another parasite which infects dogs, particularly those that live near farms. Tapeworm cannot be transmitted to any animal except via an intermediate host. Fleas are the most common host, followed by sheep and rabbits. Tapeworms can grow to a length of 61cm (2ft), but they are not dangerous to humans, as we are not infected by the ordinary tapeworm. Hydatid tapeworm, however, is extremely dangerous to humans and therefore all tapeworms should be attacked whenever signs appear. The most common sign of infestation is the appearance of segments in the droppings. These look like flat, slimy grains of rice and are seen in the droppings or on the flanks of infected animals. Close inspection will show the segments moving by lifting the front portion and dropping it down again, somewhat like a caterpillar.

New Zealand has eliminated tapeworms by the use of strict laws regarding imports and by the regular worming of all dogs by law. The life cycle of the worm is broken by the removal of the intermediate host. A precaution that we take against tapeworm is the cooking of all offal, particularly from sheep.

There are numerous proprietary medications available for eradicating these worms and your veterinary surgeon will advise the best ones to use.

Digestive Problems

Gastric Dilation
Acute gastric dilation is generally fatal because owners have little, if any, warning of an impending attack. In most cases the animal is found dead, usually in the morning, with a greatly distended stomach and all the evidence of having died in agony. The conclusion drawn is that a blockage has occurred somewhere in the intestines or stomach and the consequent fermentation of food produced gasses which could not escape. This is what occurs, although authorities do not agree on the exact cause or causes.

The stomach is like a sack into which food and water are ingested. The inlet is the oesophagus and the outlet, to the small intestine, is a valve called the pyloric sphyncter. Digestion starts in the stomach where hydrochloric acid is secreted. Food is mixed with digestive juices and broken down for absorption by the blood and lymph streams. Most of this occurs in the small intestine where food is mixed with bile and pancreatic juices.

Food passes from the stomach to the small intestine soon after eating, the process continuing for about four hours. During this time food can be vomited or gas belched back out. This means that one or both ends of the sack are open. When the openings are blocked, the condition of gastric tortion, aptly described as bloat, takes place. Initially gas is given off when trapped food begins to ferment. The stomach distends, occupying more and more space in the peritoneal cavity. Pressure is exerted on internal organs. Circulation is impeded, breathing restricted and the return flow of blood to the heart is cut off. The stomach, being a sack that is filled and emptied regularly, is not attached to the rib cage. Being unstable it can move on its axis and turn over. This happens in severe cases, sealing off both exit and inlet valves. Twisting or turning violently, especially on a full stomach, could cause the condition, or it may be triggered when the dog makes violent attempts to vomit.

Gastric juices secreted in the digestive system speed up the breaking down of food, restricting bacterial fermentation. Secretion of juices can be impaired by the type of food that is eaten; it can also be reduced by the failure of the system due to stress or genetic inability. Food eaten in large chunks may not be exposed sufficiently to the action of digestive juices. Fermentation of carbohydrates produces carbon dioxide and hydrogen and if carbohydrates are fed as dry matter, and the dog then given access to water, swelling could exacerbate distention.

Immediate treatment is to reduce pressure. This can be done, if the oesophagus is open, by giving the dog some anti-acid emulsifier, causing it to belch.

A tube can also be introduced into the stomach, to enable gasses to escape. In more urgent cases, an aperture may have to be made in the wall of the stomach. This is done surgically, by tapping the stomach with a large diameter needle, or by inserting a knife point into the stomach. I have seen this done successfully with cows. An incision is made with a knife in the side of the animal, causing an exodus not only of gas, but a great deal of green food. The recommended area for incision in the dog is in the middle of the stomach a couple of inches above the umbilicus. This action would delay the process of death and should only be undertaken by the breeder as a last resort. The dog would be in urgent need of medical attention and the surgeon would probably have a case of acute peritonitis to deal with, as well as shock.

Authorities do not agree on the cause and indeed there seems to be no definite one. A dog that bloats can only be saved by early recognition of the symptoms and the only effective treatment must be administered by a veterinary surgeon. Prevention is better than cure, but can a definite course of action be recommended? We have known of many fatal cases in several breeds, but only three in our own dogs. The first occurred with a six-year old bitch who was in excellent condition. Jimnam Magdaline was exercised late in the afternoon and fed about sunset. She was alive and well at 6.30 pm. We found on our return from dinner, about 10.30 pm, that she was beyond assistance. An autopsy confirmed what the distended stomach so clearly indicated.

The second fatality was our champion bitch Auslese Heidsieck who was seven years of age and in perfect health. Exercised and fed at the usual time, she was well at bedtime, but was found dead in the morning; there was no mistaking the cause. Her kennel abutted a paddock in which a flock of sheep grazed. She was apt to react violently when the sheep came close to her kennel. We had the impression that violent exercise caused her stomach to turn on its axis.

The third bitch was a six-year-old, Ch Auslese Claret, who survived the first attack simply because the symptoms were recognised early enough for veterinary attention. She died some months later after a second attack of distention.

Symptoms of distention are obvious discomfort, drooling, unsuccessful attempts to vomit and general restlessness, followed by an obvious swelling of the stomach. Generally, the attack occurs at night with symptoms going unobserved. We do not believe that ordinary exercise could cause the stomach to turn over. Exercise after a meal, however, especially a large one, should be avoided. A dog could consume five or six times its normal ration, and dogs should still be hungry after a meal. Dry food followed by water are a bad combination; we soak all dry food before feeding. A kennel in England feeds in the morning; this owner has not experienced a single case of bloat. Some kennels feed minced meat or meat fed in small portions. We feel that large pieces encourage a dog to exercise his jaw muscles, thus keeping teeth and gums healthy.

Bloat in cattle is always associated with food . . . either too much, too rich, or both. Cattle, however, eat for a large portion of the time, while a dog's meal time can be measured in seconds and therefore easily supervised. Common sense, care in feeding, a varied diet with roughage and a last check before bedtime are the only steps that can be recommended. A surgical precaution, which has been successful with large deep-chested dogs, such as great Danes, is to anchor the stomach to the rib cage; this would prevent the stomach turning. A more simple and practical step would be to feed twice daily.

The Eye

Entropion
This condition was the subject of much discussion in Germany during the 1950s and 1960s. Two Chief Breed Wardens, Miss Marieanne Bruns and the late Mr Friedrich Berger, examined the subject closely and wrote about it in detail. Miss Bruns's kennel, Eulenspiegel, was affected by it in the early 1950s, but I have not read any authoritative account of its origin. Very few dogs with entropion are seen in Germany today and none in the show ring. I have seen a number of dogs in Miss Bruns's kennel and a great many more of her stock; there is no suspicion of entropion. One of her dogs, Int Ch Ives Eulenspiegel SchH3, was, without doubt, one of the best sires of the 1970s. The breed warden system, with its close and continuous inspection, and the breeding tests to which dogs are subjected ensure that serious faults are soon eliminated from the breed. I have not discussed the matter in the American context and would be surprised if this was a serious problem in that country. I saw no evidence of it in Scandinavia or in the European mainland. Carriers of entropion, however, were imported into Britain from Germany, and the resulting evidence is recognisable in Britain today. All Australian imports, save seven, came from the UK and the early dogs were carriers. Our kennel was alerted to it in 1967 and we

were conscious of carriers in our bloodlines. Our efforts to breed it out appear to be successful, although the odd case can occur, even after five generations of breeding clear stock.

Herr Berger stressed very clearly the danger of labelling entropion too hastily. Many reported cases in Germany were later diagnosed as *conjunctivitis* and not entropion. Entropion causes the eyelid to turn inwards. When the lid is inverted, the lashes brush against the cornea and the irritation produces an excess of fluid which flows from the corner of the eye. If the irritation is not arrested, severe eye damage, and even blindness, can result and the dog is in constant discomfort. A tendency to entropion may be seen when the eyeball does not fit the socket properly. Combining lines with this tendency can lead to entropion. Treatment is by simple surgery which not only corrects the trouble, but, when performed by an expert, leaves no trace. An animal that has been altered is not eligible for showing, however, and it should obviously not be used for breeding. There is no need to destroy a dog that has entropion.

A film of moisture keeps the eyeball lubricated and free of dust and debris which would otherwise scrape the cornea. Excess liquid, which trickles out of the eye – dogs' tears – does not have a psychological trigger, but is caused by foreign bodies or some other form of irritation. The term used for temporary irritation to the conjunctiva (connective membranes) is *conjunctivitis*; it is the least serious of eye diseases. Foreign bodies or a draught of air may be the cause. A more serious form, *follicular conjunctivitis*, occurs when eyelids are granulated. The third eyelid is inflamed and small nodules form on the inside of the lid, giving it a raspberry look. If not treated, this could lead to developmental entropion. It can be cured without surgery if treated early. When irritation is caused by the eyelids being inverted, the irritation is permanent, the trouble is of genetic origin and relief can only be given by surgery.

If recognised, entropion tendencies can be prevented from developing in later generations. Breeds that are prone to it have too much skin around the eyes, giving them a wrinkly effect, sockets are too large, not allowing the ball to fit snugly, and the cranium lacks a sculptured look. Deep-set eyes and ill-fitting lids always lead to trouble. Dobermanns, with their tight-fitting skin and sculptured heads, are relatively free of the disease.

A study of pedigrees and careful selection of partners will enable a breeder to avoid pitfalls. Congenital entropion comes through the bloodline. It could show up in offspring or miss a generation or two, the symptoms appearing in later generations. If the sire and dam, although appearing normal, are carriers, then half the litter would carry the gene and some pups may show signs. Our policy is not to breed two animals, regardless of whether they have symptoms or not, if they carry the gene. In case any pup shows symptoms later in life, prospective purchasers are contracted not to use such pups for breeding.

Research into German pedigrees, about the time the condition was causing concern, produced some interesting, but conflicting, evidence. Manfred Schanzle, author of *Studies of the Breed History*, in his in-depth study of the various faults that prohibited breeding of individual dogs, stated that only four animals were rejected because of entropion between 1958 and 1962. Hans Bressen, in *Rottweiler*, states that Clou Eulenspiegel, imported into Denmark by the Ostjyden kennel in 1960, was destroyed after having two litters, because of entropion. A study of Eulenspiegel breeding shows that the sire, Asso von der Wakenitzburg 31674 SchHI, used on several bitches in the early 1950s, produced the first cases reported in that kennel. His first litter, 'M', out of Ena Eulenspiegel, produced at least one pup with entropion. His next litter, 'P', by the same bitch, produced some pups with deep set eyes and loose eyelids. His third litter, 'S', to Ena, produced that lovely bitch, Sonne, who was mated to the outstanding sire Sieger Arros vd Kappenberger-heide; some of the pups had deep-set eyes. Sonne was then mated to Kamp von Hook and the pup Clou went to Denmark and was later put down as stated above. Asso was mated on three occasions to the 1954 *Bundessiegerin*, Blanka vd Eppendorfer Baum SchH3; some pups had deep-set eyes and one in the 'U' litter had entropion. One of the bitches in the 'Q' litter, Quinta Eulenspiegel 34311, was imported into Britain by Mrs Chadwick where she exercised considerable influence, through the Mallion 'A' and 'B' litters. Sonne's daughter to Arras vd Kappenbergerheide, Bim Eulenspiegel, also went to Britain, but she had only one litter.

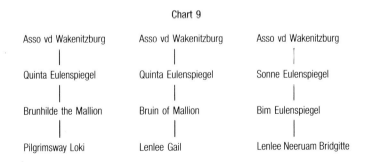

Chart 9

Asso vd Wakenitzburg	Asso vd Wakenitzburg	Asso vd Wakenitzburg
Quinta Eulenspiegel	Quinta Eulenspiegel	Sonne Eulenspiegel
Brunhilde the Mallion	Bruin of Mallion	Bim Eulenspiegel
Pilgrimsway Loki	Lenlee Gail	Lenlee Neeruam Bridgitte

These two bitches had an effect on Australian bloodlines in the 1960s; Pilgrimsway Loki and Lenlee Gail, two early imports, both have Asso in their pedigrees.

I saw both Loki and Gail on many occasions and neither had any sign of entropion. Several of the progeny and second-generation pups, however, were affected and one daughter, used extensively for breeding, was badly affected in both eyes.

Ectropion

The eyelid turns outwards, allowing too much of the eye to be exposed. The eyeball is not properly protected and is susceptible to dust, debris and draughts. This leads to conjunctivitis, and surgical correction to the lid may be necessary. Sometimes the lower lid is slack, lacking muscular tone, and this aggravates the condition. Rottweilers are not affected by ectropion to any great extent.

Blue Eye

When the cornea is affected by injury or infection, an opaque whitish-blue film spreads across the eye; the whole of the cornea can be covered. There are many causes, but blue eye resulting from live hepatitis vaccine is one that must be watched. Post-vaccination blue eye occurs when the vaccine moves through the circulatory system, collecting in the capillaries of the eye. Antibodies in the system are alerted and move in to 'attack' the enemy. Too great a concentration of the virus and antibody causes a spill into the cornea, resulting in the opaque blue film being formed. Live hepatitis vaccine has a tendency to migrate to the eye and some veterinarians prefer to use killed vaccine; there are advantages and disadvantages to this, and, providing the breeder has been alerted, the risk of using live vaccine is a calculated one.

We experienced two cases in the same litter. A bitch was sent to another state and after four days the new owner informed us of the trouble. Unfortunately, it was diagnosed and treated as congenital glaucoma. The bitch was returned to us immediately and a specialist diagnosed blue eye; this was a result of using live vaccine. A male pup showed the same symptoms. Fortunately, this time it was recognised immediately and treated correctly. The eye cleared in thirty-six hours.

Glaucoma

Glaucoma is caused by pressure within the eye. The eye is filled with a clear transparent liquid, called the acqueous humour, which flows continuously through the eye. One may liken the eye to a tank, with water coming in at one end and going out the other end at a constant rate. When the outlet is blocked, pressure builds up. When this happens, the optic nerve is damaged. The nerve is like a telephone cable with a number of wires all carrying messages to the brain. As each wire is damaged, the cable is impaired and some portion of vision reduced. If the entire cable is impaired then total blindness results. Glaucoma can be an hereditary complaint and a pup may be born with the defect, or it may develop it later. In the case of congenital glaucoma, the pup is born with defective openings, the outlet being smaller than the inlet. The trouble may also be caused by the outlet becoming blocked by debris collected during its life. This is *secondary glaucoma*, and when blockage occurs gradually, it is referred to as *chronic*; it can be treated by medication if discovered early. If the blockage occurs suddenly, then the condition is *acute*. The condition must be corrected surgically. Pressure cannot be seen and can only be measured by a tonometer. The damage to the nerve can only be detected by an opthalmoscope and diagnosed by a specialist.

Ear Problems

Problems associated with Rottweiler ears are more common than with dogs whose ears are pricked. Incidence of the problems increases when ears are thick and hair grows prolifically inside. A narrow ear canal, which restricts air flow and encourages fungi and bacteria, adds to the severity. When all these conditions occur, ears will require a great deal of attention; a point to watch when choosing breeding partners. All dogs get a build-up of wax which requires periodic removal. A little warm oil – olive, baby or mineral – will soften the wax which can be removed by wrapping some cotton wool round a finger and gently easing the wax out. Cotton buds are more efficient, but care must be taken not to damage the ear. No implement, match sticks, orange sticks, or so on, should be inserted into the ear, as irreparable damage can be done when ears are treated roughly. Water should not enter the ear which must be thoroughly dried after cleaning. Alcohol-based drops are useful, but they can sting sensitive ears. Hydrogen peroxide is a good cleaning agent that vapourises, but sensitive dogs may resent the fizzing that accompanies the cleaning process.

Mites

Mites are sometimes a problem and infection can lead to a blackish discharge. When infection becomes chronic, the dog will be in a state of constant discomfort. It will scratch, trying to insert a paw into the ear, shake its head or drop it on one side. When the air flow inside the ear is impeded, discomfort is increased. The only cure is surgical; a piece of cartilage is removed to straighten the bend in the canal. Two of our dogs were subjected to this operation; both had thick heavy ears and narrow canals. Much nursing care was required to get them well. The main problem was to prevent them removing the stitches by scratching their ears. The answer is the use of an Elizabethan collar. Both dogs made a complete recovery and neither was bothered with ear irritation for the rest of its life. It is advisable to consult expert opinion if ears discharge, smell, or irritate dogs, causing them acute discomfort.

Canine Brucellosis

This is not a disease that has troubled the dog family in Australia, although the bacterium, *Brucella abortis*, which infects cattle, was the prime concern of dairy and cattle owners some years ago. *Brucella*, the cause of the infection, is a bacterium that has been present for over a hundred years. It once caused a fever in humans, known as Malta fever, being transmitted through milk that came from goats inhabiting the island of the same name. A researcher named Bruce located the bacterium in 1886, giving it his name. It was found later in the reproductive tracts of cattle and called *Brucella abortis*. It was not until 1966 that the infection, *Brucella canis*, was identified in dogs.

Clinical signs are a heavy vaginal discharge and abnormalities of the sex organs, but these are not readily discernible. It causes damage to breeding stock through abortions and infertility. It is transmitted by venereal contact or by the mucous membranes. Infected dogs can be checked very easily by a test called the rapid slide test; this will indicate whether the dog is free. If the test proves positive, another and more complicated test, the agglutination test, is required. Some dogs, tested positive by the first test, may be cleared by the second which gives more accurate results.

There is no vaccine that can be used to immunise dogs and the infection cannot be cured. Infected kennels can only carry out a massive culling of infected stock. Australian breeders are not troubled by the infection, and, to my knowledge, no cases have been reported.

Clinical Lameness

Rottweilers sometimes go through stages of lameness, generally of the fore end; these often correct themselves without veterinary treatment. The surgeon may advise the breeder to delay treatment until the growing pains stage has been passed. This is usually between the ages of five and ten months. We do not allow young puppies to play with grown dogs without strict supervision. Rough play with heavier animals can lead to muscle injury and hair-line fractures.

A cause of serious lameness in the hind legs is a *ruptured cruciate ligament.* We have had three cases. In one case a second rupture of the repaired ligament occurred. Weakness to the cruciate could be hereditary. Our three affected bitches were grandmother, daughter and grand daughter. All three have recovered completely. The eldest, Catja, is in her tenth year. Although dogs are not in pain when the ligament ruptures, clinical symptoms are immediate and obvious. The dog is unable to place any weight on the limb. Surgical treatment is the only remedy and it should be done immediately to avoid arthritic complications. Ruptures are more common in grown dogs; fractures are more common in pups.

Osteochondrosis

Osteochondrosis is a condition that affects the normal conversion of cartilage to bone. The process of ossification is retarded causing portions of the cartilage to flake off and enter the joint cavity causing lesions and inflammation. Confusion exists regarding the terms osteochondrosis and osteochondritis dessicans also known as OCD. The former is the condition that affects normal ossification of the cartilage. The latter is the symptoms that result, ie lesions and inflammation.

Animals may have an hereditary predisposition to the condition which is exacerbated by incorrect feeding. Experiments with pigs have clearly established a close link between the condition and rapid growth. Experience with dogs has shown that excess calcium could contribute to the condition but this was not proved with pigs. The condition affects most joints particularly elbows and shoulders. It is detected more readily in the shoulder but occurs more frequently in the elbow. It affects males more than females. If the condition is not treated osteochondritis will set in getting progressively worse. Surgery is recommended but complete rest, in less serious cases, may help.

Canine Hip Dysplasia (HD)

This subject is deep and extensive enough to warrant its own book. It has been, and will continue to be, covered by a body of experts, so I shall not enter into discussion on subluxation, metabolic changes, the influence of the pectineous muscle or the genotypical component of the condition. There is little doubt that some conditions have a genetic base and that bloodlines are predisposed one way or another. A combination of an unfavourable environment and predisposition will cause the severity and incidence of the condition to increase. This is the case with HD. It is always dangerous to diagnose the condition by looking at dogs. The only positive means of establishing the status of hips is by expert interpretation of X-rays. A promising sign in a young pup is when it is able to lie flat on its tummy, with rear legs extended like a frog, and regain its feet quickly and easily. A pup should not carry too much weight, grow too quickly, or be subjected to rigorous exertion during the developmental phase of its life. Vitamins and minerals absorbed through natural foods are far more beneficial and safer than powders and tablets. Additives, administered carelessly, can cause far more harm than any of the benefits expected from them. Calcium should be given only to preserve a balance between calcium/phosphorus/vitamin D. Pressure placed on the hip joint – too much weight or too much exercise – during ossification, may cause a remodelling of the joint. Pups should be allowed to grow gradually, enjoying the various stages of development and not brought to peak condition to satisfy some short-term goal in the show ring. When appreciating the condition, in the context of breeding, one should remember that hip status is only one of the many factors involved in the selection of partners.

Immunisation

The dog, like all warm-blooded animals, is susceptible to disease introduced by viruses, bacteria and parasites. The more dangerous are due to viral infections like *distemper, canine hepatitis* and, after 1978, to *parvovirus*; these do not respond to treatment by antibiotics. *Leptospirosis* is the worst of the infections caused by a bacterium and there are a number of others, *staph, spirella*, and so on, which attack the intestines and to which pups are especially susceptible. *Tetanus* is also caused by bacterial infection, but dogs are not nearly as vulnerable as humans. All viruses produce a toxin that causes destructive changes in blood cells. Not all bacteria, however, are dangerous; indeed some are useful and even necessary in the dog and human digestive system. It appears, therefore, that the various types should be recognised so that suitable counter-measures can be mounted. Nature has provided the body with a defence mechanism and it is important to understand how this applies to your dog.

My early lessons in physiology taught me that red and white corpuscles were the main components of blood. Red nourished and revitalised the tissues, while white were soldiers that defended the body from attacks by disease-carrying invaders. Pus, collecting in a wound, is caused by dead white blood cells, together with viruses or bacteria that they have killed. White blood cells are helped in their fight against viral or bacterial attacks by antibodies and antitoxins. What is necessary is the ability of the system to recognise and identify a particular enemy quickly so that the defence system can destroy it or render it harmless. This ability is the body's natural immunity, the level of which is determined by the action we take to immunise the dog against specific diseases.

There are two types of immunity, passive and active. Passive immunity is the protection that the pup receives from the mother; this is acquired partly in the later stages of placental development, but mostly via the colostrum in the thirty-six hours after birth. Active immunity is the antibodies the pup itself creates when it is vaccinated and exposed to infection. If the young pup is exposed to the 'real' viruses or bacteria, before its defences have been built up, then generally it is not able to repel the invader. The defence or immune response can be improved by exposing the pup to 'fake' attacks made by bacteria or viruses that have been killed or rendered harmless. The emasculated enemy is introduced, allowing the system to identify it but without it being able to do any damage. When the 'real' attack comes, at a later stage, the defence is prepared to repel it.

The principle of using the body's immune system was discovered by Jenner when he used a vaccine from cowpox in 1795; the vaccine that he produced protected people from the dreaded smallpox disease. Using the same principle, Pasteur produced a vaccine to protect people against rabies. The science of immunology has advanced enormously since then, and, as each new disease is discovered, a suitable vaccine is produced to combat it. Vaccines or antigens are introduced into the system to build immunity to specific diseases. Resistance occurs when the system, alerted by the memory of the previous attack, prepares to destroy the virus or bacterium. The enemy is identified and despatched and information stored in the memory bank. Should the disease reappear memory alerts the system to the attack by that particular enemy. Memory may weaken or become hazy with time and so a jolt, by way of boosters, is given to keep it alert.

The immune system is contained in the white blood corpuscles, consisting of two-part cells called lymphocytes; T and B. A pup is born with its share of T-lymphocytes; B-lymphocytes are produced continuously in bone marrow. The interaction of these two, stimulated by specific antigens, produces specific immune responses. As soon as the enemy is identified B-lymphocytes are alerted. The order goes out and cells multiply furiously, producing specific immunoglobins which attack the invader.

The attitude to immunising puppies changed with increasing knowledge of how lymphocytes work. Puppies are born with T-cells that produce immunoglobins – passive resistance. The level of resistance in individual pups is determined by many factors: the dam's antibody level (this depends on her own exposure to the infection); the production of colostrum in the first thirty-six hours after whelping (bitches may lactate before or after the actual time of birth, and weak pups may be deprived of their share of colostrum). The level of protection that each pup receives, and the timing, determines the response to vaccination. Immunoglobins, providing passive immunity, reduce by half every 8.3 days. If a pup has a sufficiently high level of passive immunity when vaccinated, no immune response will be stimulated, and this pup may succumb to an attack by the real disease at a later stage because it has no protection. Levels of passive immunity may remain sufficiently high even at eight, ten, or twelve weeks. Antigens, therefore, should only be introduced into the system when the level of passive immunity is no longer high enough to neutralise the vaccine. One method of ensuring this is by taking a titre from the bitch, prior to whelping, and subsequently of the pups, up to the age immediately prior to vaccination.

The level of protection afforded by maternal antibodies against *parvovirus* generally declines by the eighth week, after which a successful response to antigens can be evoked. Recent studies, however, conducted at Glasgow University, showed that the Rottweiler bitch possesses a high level of parvovirus antibodies; these are passed on to pups via the colostrum. Cases of Rottweilers dying between the ages of five to ten months, after being vaccinated at eight and ten weeks, have been reported; seven of our pups died at the age of five to six months after these vaccinations. This indicated that either the vaccine had an inherent defect or that the pups' immune system failed to produce the required response.

Individual breeders should have an objective approach to an immunising programme and it is wise to consult your local veterinary surgeon. Immediate environmental factors and the endemic state of the disease will influence a decision, and the veterinary surgeon is well placed to advise.

Puppies exposed to stress, particularly cold, are always at risk and are an easy prey to whatever infection challenges them. Stress and hygiene/ cleanliness factors are vital considerations that cannot be overlooked.

Canine Parvovirus Enteritis (CPE)

This disease struck the canine world in August–October 1978. Symptoms were similar to panleucopaenia in cats and the virus was identified as a mutant of feline parvovirus. The disease reached epidemic proportions simultaneously in countries as widely spaced as Europe, North America and Australia. Symptoms were the rapid onset of a foul-smelling, greyish-coloured diarrhoea, sometimes streaked with blood, vomiting, listlessness, fever, an inability to eat or drink and consequent dehydration. Most affected young pups died within seventy-two hours. The virus was thought to have originated from a wild strain of

CANINE PARVOVIRUS HI ANTIBODY TITRES		CANINE DISTEMPER SN ANTIBODY TITRES	
TITRE	INTERPRETATION	TITRE	INTERPRETATION
<4	Not protected Susceptible to infection. Generally responsive to vaccination.	<4	Not protected
4 — 32	Doubtful protection Low vaccine response. Maternal antibody in young pups.	4 — 32	Doubtful protection
64 — 512	Good protection Good vaccine response. Maternal antibody in very young pups.	64 — 128	Good protection
1024 — 4096	Very good protection Excellent (but rare) vaccine response. Earlier active infection (most likely).	≥256	Excellent protection
≥8192	Life-long protection Recent active infection (diagnostic).		

Fig 39

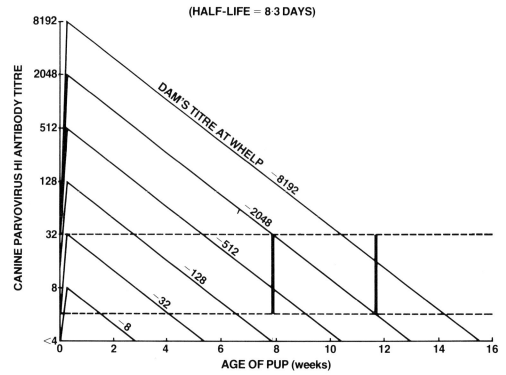

DECLINE OF MATERNAL ANTIBODY TO CANINE PARVOVIRUS
(HALF-LIFE = 8·3 DAYS)

the feline virus prototype: another explanation was that the origin may have been biological, occurring when a vaccine was manufactured in a laboratory. Neither explanation accounts for its simultaneous appearance and it is also difficult to accept either in the scenario of strict quarantine requirements applying in the UK and Australia.

A variant of the prototype affects dogs, mice and racoons. The virus affects pups in two ways; it attacks the mucous membrane of the intestine, causing symptoms of enteritis, or it affects the cell growth of the heart.

Young pups are more susceptible to *myocarditis* because the virus multiplies at a greater rate in rapidly dividing cells; the rate of cell division decreases with age. Pups under the age of three weeks are more susceptible to myocarditis because heart cells stop dividing after three weeks and pups are sometimes even infected in the uterus. Clinical symptoms depend on the amount of damage to the heart; cardiac irregularities and sudden collapse generally occur. Damage to the heart, after pups show an apparent recovery, is irreparable and collapse and death can occur many months after.

In the case of *enteritis*, susceptibility is increased by subjection to stress, or hookworm or bacterial infestation. Stress, mental as well as physical, are factors, and reaction to other vaccinations could predispose a pup to an attack. I have known of pups recovering after massive infection, and it is possible that both pups and dogs have been attacked by the virus without exhibiting clinical symptoms. Serious cases require immediate veterinary attention and careful nursing. Fluid therapy, administered intravenously, is generally prescribed, with antibiotics to counteract secondary infection and diarrhoea.

When the virus first struck, the canine world was quite unprepared with regard to immunity measures, and the disease, striking when dogs had no natural resistance, reached epidemic proportions. Whole kennels of young pups, particularly greyhounds, were wiped out dramatically. The first vaccine, used tentatively, was killed feline parvo. It produced a measure of immunity, due to cross-infection, but results were not as good as those associated with cats. Modified live feline vaccine was then used, but although veterinarians refused to accept responsibility for side effects none were reported. The first canine vaccine used was killed virus. Cornell University then produced a modified live canine parvovirus vaccine which appears to be very satisfactory.

The object was to produce a vaccine that had no side effects, that gave rapid and long-lasting protection, and that could be used within the framework of kennel immunisation procedures. These procedures, unfortunately, are mechanical and functional. Pups are given a temporary shot of distemper antiserum at the age of six to eight weeks, with a permanent shot, for distemper/hepatitis, at three months. With the threat of parvo, pups may receive three shots of parvo vaccine before reaching the age of four months. Some kennels continue shots at three-month intervals, without checking antibody status. If passive immunity still exists in pups, parvo shots are unnecessary. More pertinently, when this immunity is retained at certain levels, because of the high level of antibodies in the bitch, antigens introduced into the system will not produce the desired reaction. Pups vaccinated during this period, therefore, are not protected; this could account for pups dying at five to six months after receiving three shots.

This aspect of immunisation has received much attention over the last four years at the James Cook University of North Queensland. The veterinary faculty has produced a graph showing antibody titres in bitches prior to whelping, with the decline of the antibody in pups; this allows prediction of the times when successful vaccination is possible. I am most grateful to Dr Jan Smith who sent me a copy of the graph shown on p. 188 and kindly allowed its publication.

Parvovirus is highly infectious and most resistant to attempts to eliminate it from kennels. Bleach, or a 5 per cent formalin solution, is recommended as a disinfectant. Examining the scourge more optimistically, it appears that the threat to dogs in Australia is not now as great as it was two or three years ago. Dogs have built up an immunity, especially those that have recovered from an attack. Bitches that have been affected pass on high levels of passive immunity to pups. The problem, unless a new strain evolves, should resolve itself. Kennels will probably be contaminated with a low-grade virus and the endemic situation should actually help to keep the disease in check.

The commonsense approach is to check the antibody status of the whelping bitch, so that by following the graph the breeder can predict when vaccination of pups would offer the best chances of protection. It appears, from results, that of the vaccines currently available in Australia – CSL and Websters manufacture this range – live canine appears to be the most effective method of providing the longest and safest protection.

12 Breeding

Mating

Rottweiler bitches come into season between seven and nine months of age; thereafter, they will continue to come in twice a year, at roughly six-month intervals. While this applies to the average bitch, there are some that do not follow the pattern. One of ours did not come in until she was nineteen months of age! She came in again at twenty-five months, was mated successfully and continued with the normal pattern. In a kennel situation, males will alert the breeder by their interest in the bitch. The owner of a single female could miss the early signs and what he thinks to be the first day may well be the third or fourth.

The normal oestrus cycle may conveniently be divided into three stages: pro-oestrus, oestrus and metoestrus. The first sign of stage one is a reddish discharge with a swelling of the vulva. The bitch is flighty and encourages males, but will not allow a mating; this stage may last for seven to ten days. The second stage is signalled by a change in the colour of the discharge, from red to straw-coloured, by a softening of the vulva, by the bitch moving her tail from side to side and lifting it when prodded around the vulva and by a change in behaviour; the bitch will now stand for the dog. This stage generally lasts for just under a week. The third stage is reached when the bitch starts to lose interest. She will still be attractive to dogs, but will not allow a mating. Some bitches may take ten days before the third stage has been completed, while others return to normal three to four days after mating. It is unwise to schedule bitches as not all of them behave in the same manner, and the same bitch may act differently in a later season. The vulva of some bitches will remain swollen if they have conceived, but a return to normal does not indicate that bitches have missed.

There is a fourth stage in the cycle known as anoestrus. This is the period between seasons. A bitch may not follow a regular pattern and departures must be expected.

The breeder's chief concern is the date on which the bitch should be mated. The answer is simple – when ova have reached the optimal moment for fertilisation by the sperm. An experienced stud dog will indicate when this moment has arrived. There is also, however, a method of predicting it. Vaginal smears may be used to predict the date, although such prediction may not always be accurate. A smear should be taken immediately the bitch shows the first sign of discharge – which can be confirmed by brushing a piece of white tissue against the vulva. The smear should be examined to ensure that no infection is present, otherwise she will not conceive. A mild infection can be cleared up prior to the bitch being mated, but a more serious one, or one that is difficult to identify quickly, may mean mating the bitch at her next season. Any infection, however, must be cleared up and the earlier this is done the better. Some breeders have had success by mating the bitch on the eighth day, some on the eleventh. Consequently, they insist that this is 'the' date. This rule-of-thumb method is generally successful, but there are many exceptions.

One of my early bitches, Dark Impression, was mated on the eighth and tenth day of her third season, producing fifteen pups. Two years later, having failed to conceive during two seasons, she was mated on the nineteenth day of her seventh season, producing eight pups. Catja von der Flugschneise was mated on the eleventh day of her sixth season, producing thirteen pups. Her last tie took place on the twenty-fifth day, although she failed to conceive. Echo von Mägdeberg was mated on the thirteenth and fifteenth days of her sixth season; the following season she was mated on the seventh and tenth days.

If the stud dog is close at hand, a mating can be tried any time after the sixth day. However, if a bitch is to be transported some distance each day timing may be critical. A vaginal smear and examination of the cell pattern may predict the most suitable date.

Cells in the bitch's reproductive system change in pattern as they respond to various ovarian hormones. These changes can be seen under the microscope. A vaginal smear contains white and red blood cells, epithelial cells and bacteria. As the cycle advances, white blood cells disappear and changes in the epithelial cells indicate when stage two, oestrus, is reached. Epithelial cells can be divided roughly into non-cornified – parabasal – and cornified – superficial; between these two stages there is an intermediate stage, marked, appropriately, by the preponderance of intermediate cells. Cells have different shapes. They also have two distinct colours – shown clearly when treated with a reagent. Non-cornified (parabasal) stain green, and cornified (superficial) stain orange. The cells can be identified by two different tests, using two different reagents, one by the pattern and the other by the colour. When the pattern shows a 90 per cent dominance of orange-coloured superficial cells, mating should be successful.

The optimum time for mating may be predicted as indicated in the chart opposite:

Stage 1 Pro-oestrus	Marked by a preponderance of parabasal cells, staining green, with white and red blood cells.	Parabasal cells are round with a relatively large nucleus.
	As the season advances intermediate cells replace parabasal and green changes to orange.	Intermediate cells are the same shape, only twice as large; nucleus about the same size.
Stage 2 Oestrus	White blood cells disappear. If present, at this stage, they are a sign of infection. 90 per cent of the pattern dominated by this cell. Colour orange. Bitch will now ovulate shedding eggs for some seventy-two hours; these will mature in twenty-four hours. A mating now should be successful.	Largest of the cells, outline irregular. Nucleus small and deep red before disappearing.
Stage 3 Metoestrus	White blood cells begin to reappear. Superficial cells rapidly decline. Parabasal cells may take up 50 per cent of pattern as season advances.	
Stage 4 Anoestrus	White blood cells now make up some 80 per cent of the pattern. The stage will last four to six months until the bitch comes into season again.	

(I am indebted to Mrs Catherine Inkster for showing me these patterns.)

Some authorities are of the opinion that sperm will live in the reproductory tract of the bitch for eleven days; others state eight days. This length of time, from a practical point of view, is open to considerable doubt. It is preferable to mate a bitch earlier rather than later, if she will stand. The time of ovulation, in some bitches, is short, being restricted to twenty-four hours; the time of mating can be critical. Eggs remain alive for about twenty-four hours after shedding, so fertilisation will not occur if mating is delayed.

Generally, when a bitch refuses to mate and is artificially insemi-nated, conception will not result. If both dog and bitch live close to each other, a mating may be attempted about the seventh day. If this is unsuccessful, then further attempts can be made on alternate days, and this can be continued until a tie results. The Germans favour one tie when the bitch will stand and this generally results in a litter. Both dog and bitch should be exercised lightly; neither should be fed before mating. Some animals will play for several minutes. Some breeders recommend muzzling the bitch, but we have not experienced any problem with a bitch becoming nasty. A firm hold of collar and muzzle by the owner are sufficient to keep the bitch under control.

A good stud dog will manage without assistance. Indeed, he will resent it and our best stud dog will discontinue operations immediately he is handled, walking away in disgust. A young dog may need help and guidance and it is advisable to keep some pressure on the dog's rear as soon as it mates, in order to keep him in the bitch. Some bitches will not tie, but if the dog is held in position for a minute or so, enough sperm will be deposited. I know of one famous beagle who sired a number of litters, but refused to tie. One of our earlier studs, Auslese Pedro Ximines, failed to tie when first mated to a bitch, yet she produced eleven pups. Some breeders recommend additives like vitamin E or meals of milk or egg yolk and glucose to help the dog, but we find that the Rottweiler stud requires none of these things. Each time a car enters our drive all the stud dogs prepare for action, thinking that a bitch has arrived for their particular attention. We have never resorted to artificial insemination, although the sperm of one of our dogs was used in this manner because of a deformity in the bitch's vulva. The owner of one Pyrenean mountain dog fashioned a cradle which assisted the dog to mate. We feel, however, that if a dog is unable to perform this natural function, he should not be used, to avoid perpetuating a weakness.

Some owners, wishing to avoid the inconvenience of a bitch in season, put her on the pill. Later the bitch may take two seasons before she is rid of this influence, yet I have known a bitch conceive within months of being taken off the pill and produce nine puppies. Some bitches, particularly maidens of two to three years of age, will have a phantom pregnancy without mating nine weeks after oestrus; they will show every sign of pregnancy, including milk production. Other bitches will have a false pregnancy – the difference being that in a false pregnancy mating has actually taken place.

Whelping and Early Care

Sixty-three days is generally regarded as being the term of a bitch's pregnancy, the date being calculated from the time of service. In order to predict the date of whelping, the breeder can either count the days, using a diary, or consult a gestation table. The correct date, however, is from the time when the eggs mature and fertilisation takes place. We can never be certain of this, but sixty-three days from mating is a sufficiently accurate guide. After mating, the bitch should be treated normally in all respects – feeding, exercising and training. Increasing the amount of food and reducing exercise is one way of making the process of whelping difficult. When the bitch is obviously in whelp, food intake may be slightly increased and the total amount divided and fed twice daily. A week or two before the date of whelping, give another slight increase and then three meals are advisable. A pint of milk and an egg yolk three or four times a week will help, together with fresh vegetables, particularly carrot and spinach; these are better than extra meat in the diet. Seaweed and raspberry leaf tablets may help with the birth and assist in providing a good supply of milk.

Puppies can sometimes be felt about a month after mating if one is experienced. Some bitches will thicken in the rib cage about this time, whilst others will keep their secret until a fortnight before the birth. Behaviour may signal the happy event to be; bitches will be more affectionate, demanding more attention. An X-ray is the only certain way of knowing, but we prefer to wait for nature to take its course.

After the eighth week, the puppies will begin to move and slight ripples may be seen when the bitch lies in a relaxed position. When the time of whelping is near she will be uncomfortable and restless, the vulva will soften and swell and she may be reluctant to exercise. Each bitch approaches her confinement with characteristic individuality. The temperature should be taken early to establish what is normal; this will be around 38°C (101°F) and it will drop by 2–4° a day or so before she whelps. Some bitches have a clear discharge a week, or even two weeks, before whelping.

The bitch should be introduced to her whelping box and she should be familiar with her quarters some time before whelping. These should be in a quiet, draught-free room, out of direct sunlight, with the temperature around 27°C (80°F); this could be increased slightly when whelping starts. In cold climates, a heated whelping box is necessary, but if it is too warm the bitch will not stay. She may try to make her own nest in an area that she regards as suitable though the midwife may not agree, in which case she should be returned gently to her box. We place the box on several thicknesses of newspaper, lining it with the same material. This is easily removed and replaced two or three times a day. A small square of carpet is placed in the middle. We have several squares of this material which are changed and washed daily.

Immediately prior to whelping, a bitch may tear up the newspaper in her box, getting in and out and generally showing signs of restlessness and apprehension which may continue for some hours. Deciding whether to leave her or to stay becomes a problem. I offer the bitch some meat; if she eats it then I get some sleep! This does not always work. Isobella once ate meat which I offered her about midnight. I went to bed for three hours only to find that she had delivered three puppies by 3 am. On another occasion Tatachilla, a bitch that we had left with friends while we were in Europe, ate a large meal, played with the dogs and was left unattended during the night. By 6 am the next morning thirteen pups were cleaned and ready for inspection.

The water bag generally bursts an hour or so before the first whelp appears. Then the bitch will push, arch her back and give every indication that a pup is about to be expelled. The first pup could arrive while the bitch is standing outside the whelping box! She should be encouraged to return and if one is able to place the pup in the box, she will follow.

Some bitches prefer company and appreciate assistance; others, particularly those not long out of quarantine, will not allow a hand on the box and certainly will object to any handling of pups. These bitches will allow us to handle pups after a day or so and all our old bitches prefer us to be close.

Equipment in the whelping room should include the whelping diary, scales, a pair of scissors in antiseptic solution, a bottle of disinfectant, a rough towel and several squares of 30cm (12in) towelling; the latter will help to hold a new-born pup. We did have a lot of paraphernalia years ago, but found that many items were unnecessary. Rottweilers give birth very easily and a healthy bitch will shed pups like peas.

Entry into the world is not a recognised drill. Pups will be born in a sack, or out of it, and breech births are not uncommon. Although sixty-three days is the prescribed term, a small litter may be late in arriving. Chesara Dark Impression produced her last pup, named Solo, without warning while we were at dinner. This was quite unexpected, as she had been mated seventy-three days before.

Once the pup is separated from the dam, the most urgent requirement is oxygen. The pup will generally arrive in an envelope of slimy membranes, attached by the umbilical cord to the placenta. A bitch will generally bite or chew the cord and pull the membranes from the whelp. If she does not do so, you must clear the pup's mouth immediately. Mucus and liquid may be cleared by holding the pup upside down. Bitches generally attend to new-born pups, but a maiden bitch, left unattended, may panic and leave the pup untouched. Our introduction to breeding was made at 3 am one morning when two bitches whelped at the same time. One litter was born in the studio, the other in the laundry. Dark Impression had four pups in each corner, including two on a slate ledge, leaving them where they had been born; eight pups survived, mainly because we arrived before it was too late. I then went to see Heatherglen Cliquot and was greeted by an ecstatic mum who carried a pup from behind a table, dumping it at my feet in triumph. She then proceeded to have another dozen.

Our drill is to record the time and examine and weigh the new pup, putting a piece of coloured wool around its neck; this is changed, two days later, for the same colour bias binding. Sometimes we may have to wait until a number two is born before examining number one. We open a whelping diary two days before the expected birth. All pertinent facts are recorded and a pattern of individual behaviour emerges after two or three litters. The person arriving on duty in the middle of the night may thus read the diary to acquaint himself of the current position. When the pup is born, time, sex, weight, whether the afterbirth was present, and similar details are written down. Bitches should be allowed to eat some of the afterbirths, as they provide protein and minerals. Soiled paper is removed from time to time; sometimes a few sheets of fresh paper are placed under her rump. After a couple of hours the bitch may be given a cup of cold milk and water, and also a spoonful of glucose. Warm milk is given only when whelping is over and the bitch has been allowed to sleep. If there is a long interval between whelps, the bitch may like a short walk.

Whelps can slide out so easily that they can be missed even if one is sitting a foot away. On one occasion I took a bitch for a walk on a lead, thinking that whelping was over. It was dark and she stopped to spend a penny, or so I thought; the next morning I found a dead pup near the spot!

Sometimes a bitch may go the full term without showing signs of imminent whelping, but it is a mistake to take action too early. On three occasions, bitches that were mated to our stud dogs failed to whelp by the sixty-third day. In each case a caesarian section was performed, and in each case the litter was lost. Some breeds are prone to whelping difficulties – larger, or dead, pups blocking the passage, uterine inertia or such – but the Rottweiler whelps with the greatest of ease. On rare occasions, assistance may be necessary to ease a pup out of the mother. This sometimes occurs with a breach birth: using the square of rough towelling, grasp the whelp gently and draw it down and under as the bitch pushes. This is done to save the pup drowning in fluid if it is separated from the sack.

A nursing bitch requires plenty of fluid in order to produce milk. Milk should, however, make up only part of this fluid intake; it does provide some natural calcium, but too rich a diet can produce diarrhoea. Our bitches are partial to a boiled egg which is consumed together with the shell. She should have a little meat, white for preference, on the second day, followed by increasing quantities of semi-cooked red meat. She will not eat dry food for five to six days, but she should be encouraged to do so as soon as possible, to enable her bowels to return to normal. Food intake should be gradually increased, depending on the size of the litter. Most bitches will come into milk when the pups are born and pups will suckle minutes after birth. Puppies should be left with their mother, as new-born pups cannot generate their own heat, and warmth is vital in the first four days.

Some pups inhale a small quantity of fluid during the process of birth. This can be heard as a gurgle and the pup will splutter in an effort to rid itself of it. The pup can be held upside down for a few minutes until it cries. The mother will lick and massage the pup for several minutes, sometimes doing this until the next pup arrives. An apparently dead pup can be revived by artificial respiration, mouth to mouth resuscitation, or by massage. If the mother refuses to notice it, however, the pup is not worth saving and the best time for a weak pup to die is shortly after birth.

We have not experienced complications, but should a bitch indicate that she is in difficulties, the veterinary surgeon should be alerted. Panic is generally associated only with the first litter.

We do not give our bitches a post-whelping injection or any antibiotics. Some years ago Ch Auslese Heidsieck was given three injections after a litter. On the third day she refused food and ran a temperature of 40°C (104°F). She was taken to the surgery immediately. An X-ray revealed nothing, but I insisted on another. While the picture was being developed, I formed the opinion that something had been retained. The second X-ray also showed nothing, but on examination the surgeon removed part of a pup. She was operated on immediately and recovered to lead a healthy life, although she did not have another litter.

I have heard of one bitch dying of eclampsia, and we experienced one case in 1969. Dark Impression started to shiver, refused to eat or stay with her pups and her temperature dropped to 37°C (98°F). She was on the point of collapse when the veterinary surgeon injected a calcium solution into a vein. This was fifteen days after the litter was born. We always keep a syringe and calcium in case of necessity, but have had no other occasion to use them. We do not give the bitch any calcium until after the birth. The calcium drain on the bitch is greatest when the pups are about two to three weeks, that is just before weaning.

After some years of experience, my wife is able to tell by feeling a pup whether it is losing or gaining weight. Daily weighing is necessary; we weigh problem pups more often. Puppies will lose some weight due to the trauma of birth, but they should then gain steadily except, perhaps, for a check when tails and dew claws are removed. A normal pup that does not gain indicates that the bitch has no milk. The Germans frown on any assistance in feeding and many of my European friends, who have had more experience than I, report poor results with supplementary feeding. Our experience has been entirely the opposite. We bottle-feed as soon as the litter requires feeding, using an ordinary baby's bottle with an ordinary teat. Some breeders use a tube but we are firmly of the opinion that a pup should enjoy his suckling. This is obvious when he sucks, and he exercises his jaws, muscles and the whole body. The formula we use is a cup of cow's milk – unpasteurised if possible – an egg yolk, eight drops of infant Pentavite and a teaspoon of glucose – the whole well beaten. When they are older a spoonful of full-cream powdered milk is added. All bottle feeds should be strained to prevent the teat hole blocking. If the litter is large, say more than eight, the pups should be placed on the mother in relays. Larger pups should be placed in a basket for an hour or so and then changed over. We feed at three-hourly intervals, with a gap between 11 pm and 4 am. We put the large pups in the basket around 10 pm and feed them all at 11 pm. The bitch must not be left without her puppies even if she apparently has no milk. Sucking will stimulate milk flow. The bitch must be suckled from all teats, otherwise one or two will block; pups will not drink the stale milk and the situation will be aggravated. If the gland swells into a hard lump, mastitis or an abscess can result. Hot fomentations, stripping with the fingers and the attention of the strongest and hungriest pup will help.

After whelping, the bitch will be reluctant to leave the nest for twenty-four hours, but she must be placed on a lead and given a short walk. Her bowels will move the next day and motions will be very loose and black, gradually returning to normal over a week. Two people in attendance are useful; one takes the bitch while the other cleans the box. We sponge the bitch's rear with warm water each time she returns, giving her a brush to freshen her up. It is useful to trim the flanks some days before, as this will prevent mats forming in the hair. Puppies must not be allowed to get cold and the bitch must be kept quiet. Puppies that cry are hungry, cold, hot or ill. If they are cold they cluster together, if over-hot they will separate. Healthy pups should sleep most of the time. During sleep they are never still. Muscles, particularly around the head and feet, will twitch. This is quite natural and will gradually diminish about the time the puppies are able to stand. Eyes begin to open on the fourteenth day and a sliver of a gleam of light may be seen.

Tails and dew claws should be removed about the third or fourth day. The Germans leave the front dew claws and we do the same. Some pups may have no dew claws, especially in the rear feet.

Pups have very sharp claws and these can hurt the mother. They must

A labrador bitch, owned by the Royal Guide Dogs for the Blind, reared her own litter, did the same for another guide dog litter and then reared these orphaned Rottweiler puppies

be cut regularly after the fifth day. Using a pair of nail scissors, the 'hook' of the claw is snipped and the best time to do this is when the pup has been fed and is content. They object more to this being done with rear claws.

Pups are devoid of all senses, except that of awareness of warmth and taste, until the eyes are open; this is followed by the hearing sense. Around the end of the third week pups begin to notice people. We handle them very gently and they enjoy and expect a cuddle after the fifteenth or sixteenth day. They will accept this from anyone until the fifth week when they begin to differentiate between 'their' people and 'foreigners'. The whelping room should be private, without any outside traffic. Strangers, including dogs, will worry the bitch and she may react violently. Cliquot, on one occasion, stood on two pups when a stranger accidently walked into the whelping room.

Weaning

We start to wean pups about the eighteenth to the twenty-first day. Milk formula, plus a little high protein cereal – Heinz 35 per cent high protein or Farex – is placed in a saucer which is held up at a slight angle. The pup's face is pushed gently into the milk. Some will lap almost straightaway, but others will take two to three days to learn. Three or four days later, meat, minced very finely and made into balls of walnut size, is fed by hand. It may be placed in a saucer soon after, because by then the pups recognise meat and will get quite excited by the smell. When they are a month old, two meals of meat, including soaked puppy chow, may be given, plus three milk feeds a day. The mother will lose interest after five to six weeks, and the number of meals can then be increased to five per day. When the pups have been weaned, and before they depart, at eight weeks, for their new homes, the feeding routine is as follows; 6 am milk brew plus cereal; 9 am finely chopped meat mixed with chow soaked in hot soup, the soup made from bones, vegetables, perhaps rice or sago. Calcium is added to this meal. 1 pm a drink of milk; 4 pm the same meal as at 9 am without the calcium; 9 pm milk brew. Puppies should not be allowed to over-eat and their meals should fit the stomach which must not bulge.

During this early phase we find that the most economical meat is the most expensive. We use topside, minced under supervision; there is no waste. Each pup has its own feeding bowl. We know, then, that the greedy ones are not eating more than their share.

We find that worming is not successful until the fourteenth day. This is carried out three or four times at ten-day intervals until the pups leave for their permanent homes.

Selection: Matching Pups to People

One of the responsibilities of which genuine Rottweiler breeders are most conscious, is the placement of puppies. A Rottweiler is not every-one's dog and care must be exercised in selecting suitable homes and owners. Care must also be taken to ensure that owner and pup suit each other. This means that the breeder must know his puppies well and he must be reasonably familiar with the background and environment to which his pup is committed. It is quite impossible to exercise this responsibility at the time the puppies are ready to leave the kennel. When we first have an enquiry about the breed, we discuss several points with the person concerned, either by telephone or letter. If they appear suitable, we invite them to visit us; this gives us an opportunity to 'test' them and they are able to see parents, grandparents, other puppies and the environment from which their pup will come. An enquiry for a pup to be picked up at the weekend, or as a present for Father's Day, meets with advice to try another breed as the Rottweiler is unsuitable. Economics play very little part in selecting new owners. A Rottweiler requires affection, discipline and companionship and he has a desire to share his life with his owner. These may be provided by an itinerant who has very little but is prepared to share his meal with his dog and only sleeps when his dog has shelter; it may be absent in the case of a millionaire who keeps his dog in an air-conditioned suite and sees it one day a week!

If we think that a person is suitable, he or she is placed on a waiting list; the wait could be a long one. A German who wanted a pup from a particular breeding waited two years. During this period he visited us regularly; sometimes he would just sit in his car and watch the dogs without speaking. We do not take a deposit. If people change their minds, we prefer them to go elsewhere. We disregard circular letters, which generally come from agents, and enquiries for whole litters. We never sell a pup intended as a present unless we meet both people concerned. If a person has waited a year or more, the indication given is that he really wants a pup from our kennel.

There are two categories of prospective owners. The first category is that of the experienced Rottweiler owner; he generally wants a pup from a particular line or sire. The second is that of the uninitiated purchasing a pup which may be his first dog; special care must be taken with this type. We do not sell a dog to a couple who work; if they do it means that a young pup will be left on his own for the better part of the day. A pup left on his own grows up to be too wary and suspicious, or too fearful.

We inspect a litter from the moment it is born. Some idea of conformation may be gained at birth. There is no guarantee, however, that a pup will measure up to conformation expectations. Character and

A Rottweiler pup about to get its first lesson in the law of gravity! (Photo: courtesy Mrs Hyden)

emotional and sensory reactions can be gauged more accurately, but these only start to appear after two weeks. Notes are made as various characteristics become apparent and an attempt is made to gauge each pup's suitability for the various people on the waiting list. The responsible breeder will place his pups so that the pups themselves, the new owner and the breeder are happy. There are a number of factors to consider. We do not sell show-quality pups *per se*, but a purchaser whose main interest is in showing must have a pup with this potential. A working owner must have a pup with qualities that he can develop. A dominant pup may prove too much of a handful for a novice. Puppies reveal certain aspects in their make-up after the second week, and this continues as the senses develop.

Puppy Development

Puppies are born with two fairly well-developed senses, taste and awareness of temperature: they have body sensitivity, ie they can feel pain, cold and heat.

They can taste the difference between mother's milk and the simulated variety. It is amusing to see how they sometimes reject bottle and teat, literally spitting the milk out. This is the neonatal stage, when the pups are entirely dependent on their mother. She feeds them, regulates their heating mechanism and controls elimination. She induces evacuation by licking them and then cleans up. This instinctive action goes back to the days when dogs hunted their food. If pups evacuated when the mother was away, the nest would be fouled. She allows this only when she can clean up. When pups are able to walk, they leave the immediate area of the nest to do their business. During this stage – when pups are handled to weigh them, cut nails and clean the whelping box – the breeder begins to form an impression about which pups are dominant, vigorous or placid, those that cry, and pups with high or low body sensitivity.

After some fifteen days, the neonatal stage gives way to the transitional stage which lasts for about a week. The change in the pup during this week is dramatic. In a matter of days it changes from a baby that was entirely dependent on its mother, to a personality that resembles a Rottweiler, with an identity all of its own. The first sign is the slit of light that shows in the eyes. They will be open in two days, but will not focus for three or four. This will be followed by the sense of hearing; noises will startle the pup. Its motor and sensory capacities develop quickly and it is conscious of its litter mates. It even leaves the nest to exercise its bodily functions. The puppy becomes an individual and is no longer insulated in a world of its own. At the end of this week, the teeth may be felt; they feel like the serrated edge of a blunt saw but soon develop a needle-like sharpness. During the neonatal stage pups sleep for 90 per cent of the time. At the end of the transitional stage, they sleep less, and can move on all four legs, although shakily. The action of the jaws changes. Instead of merely sucking, pups will mouth each other in more adult fashion. The timing of these changes varies from pup to pup, but they can be predicted to a period of two to three days. The transitional stage – the third week – is a prelude to the most important stage in its life, the socialisation stage which lasts in the kennel until the puppy goes to its new home at the age of eight weeks.

During the neonatal stage, the pup is insulated against the world; it has had no influence on its environment and this has very little influence on it. During the transitional stage, the puppy begins to learn that there are other elements in its environment. This stage prepares it for the socialisation stage when it learns that it is part of a community with which it must live in harmony. In the wild, it would be taught by both parents and later by senior members of the pack. It would learn to accept the discipline of the pack, find its place in it and, in time, make its contribution. In a kennel situation, the father plays no part, but it is vital that the mother and the litter be kept together for at least six weeks; she must then still have contact, even if only occasionally, until the pups leave for their new homes.

It is the reaction of the pup to its environment, at this stage, that makes a large contribution to its personality. The expression, sound temperament, is the uniform manner in which a dog reacts to stimuli encountered. Dogs will be exposed to a great variety of stimuli and reactions, therefore, will be very different. If the required reaction can be predicted, then temperament is sound. Irrespective of the role to which they will be assigned – guarding, companion, herding, working or pet – all pups should have the same basic socialising during the second month of life. It is during this stage that the breeder assesses the pup's suitability for the people on the waiting list.

Puppy-Testing

Puppy-testing today seems to be very fashionable. People arm themselves with pencil and score sheet, they subject puppies to tests, with scores of 0–+5, or −2–+2 being carefully recorded. It is not difficult to test pups and explanatory notes about each test are clear and simple. To interpret them, however, and make value judgements on such characteristics as courage, protective and fighting instinct, hardness, intelligence, loyalty, affection and a dozen others is another matter. There are very few useful tests that can be made on a seven-week old pup. Another

A two-year-old bitch trained at the Austrian Military Dog School (courtesy Adolf Ringer)

Dogs trained at the Austrian Military Dog School must wear a muzzle in public (courtesy Adolf Ringer)

Ch Auslese Bacchus

'Do I see a missing molar?' Kanausens Bamse (owned by Harald Brastad) with inquisitive puppy (courtesy Ove Enger)

criticism of puppy-testing, as carried out by enthusiasts with little experience, is that the object is lost sight of and the drill of testing becomes an end in itself. Observation is more purposeful than ritual testing, and although uniform tests and comparative scores are necessary when testing dogs for institutions, continuous observation of a Rottweiler litter, to enable selection of pups for a wide variety of owners, is more useful.

During the kennel socialisation stage, we take our puppies for a walk three or four times a day. They cover broken ground, go through brush and bracken and run over rocks and logs. They are exposed spontaneously to a wide variety of situations. If an area or obstacle presents a problem, the solving of which teaches us something about the pups, we go back deliberately the next time. Pups go out in a group, in pairs and singly. We observe their general behaviour without a particular object in mind and assessments are made as situations arise: how pups respond emotionally to being on their own; the venturesome pup versus the inhibited; how they respond to the noise of cows, birds, tractors and strange objects; the agile ones that negotiate gullies and obstacles; the independent pup; the dominant one; the curious one (curiosity being very close to intelligence); the shy one; who leads; who is bold enough to come down the steep bank first; the reaction to sticks and stones that are thrown; who finds the way back first. A pattern gradually begins to form. Observation is related to the open range in an atmosphere of spontaneity, and it is made over a period of three or four weeks. I have seen a prospective owner make his selection because of one action, although this pup had behaved quite differently at other times. Generally speaking, pups are not affected by individual moods; but the time of day, before and after meals, or sleep, or after a lot of exercise does influence behaviour. Notes are kept in an effort to match puppy and owner and such observations may be recorded as follows:

> Red dog will *not* suit Mrs X; she hasn't the experience to control a dominant dog. Pink bitch will suit Mrs X as she is submissive and will fit in with her other dogs. Blue dog will suit Mrs B; she wants an obedience dog and blue is very responsive.

There are two tests that are more deliberate. One of these was devised when I discovered an ancillary quality in a lady's hair dryer! A pup had fallen in the water and had to be dried off quickly. During the process of drying, the pup revealed some interesting characteristics. I now use a dryer on all pups, partly to dry them, but primarily to test body sensitivity and dominance, as well as to teach them to trust and have confidence in me. We also used to carry out simple tests on gun shyness by using crackers, but the manufacture of crackers is now outlawed. We now use a variety of objects, including a cow bell which my wife picked up in Oberammergau.

Some testers are apt to conclude that a pup has poor nerves purely on its reflex actions. A pup with acute hearing will jump at a sudden bang; it is the deliberate action that follows that is important. The object of testing, at this early age, should be clear. Firstly, what is revealed by the pup is a predisposition rather than an accurate measurement of capacity. Secondly, this predisposition can be shaped or mis-shaped in the process of testing.

We try to learn as much as we can about a litter so that we can advise buyers without giving them the impression of trying to force a course of action.

After Sales Service

We find that people purchasing pups ask many questions. These concern the breed in general, feeding, exercise, ailments, immunisation, the standard, showing, obedience, Rottweiler organisations and so on. My wife has now produced a twenty-two page booklet which is given to every new owner. The day after the pup leaves we ring to see how it has settled into its new home. We have regular calls, and we encourage people to tell us of new developments and the pup's exploits and to ask particular advice. These people join our Rottweiler family and we have found over the years that we have made many friends. This has given us a great deal of pleasure and assisted greatly in our resolve to breed better Rottweilers.

Puppy Socialisation

The pup, having gone to its new home at eight weeks, is still very much at the socialisation stage. It will continue to develop, using the foundation that has already been established. The sort of dog that it will grow into will be an amalgam of inherited traits and how these have been modified by reaction to its environment. There is no doubt about the time its learning capability starts, but there is a difference of opinion about the genetic influence on this capability. According to Konrad Lorenz, an organism is programmed to react in a genetically prescribed manner and 'imprinting' cannot be equated with learning. His early work was with geese; these precocious birds come into the world with a sensory and motor capacity that the pup only *starts* to acquire after two weeks of neonatal existence. The period when the pup begins to react with the environment begins later and is gradual, and imprinting, therefore, is not precise or dramatic. Lorenz also states that imprinting is an irreversible process; certainly it is much easier to teach a pup at this stage. If the joyous exuberance of puppyhood is contained and the pup induced to concentrate, memory is sharpened. Learning should be on a permanent foundation and development should be step by step. Bad habits are easier to acquire than break, and what the pup learns during this stage will determine the kind of dog that it will be.

The late Mr Pfaffenberger, whose work in training guide dogs at Hamilton Station provided a new insight into puppy development, proved by exhaustive tests that good socialisation during this period was imperative to the successful training of guide dogs. Another aspect of development, which he discovered by accident, was the importance of encouraging instinctive behaviour rather than frustrating it. Lanny, a black labrador pup, having passed his initial tests, was given to a puppy walker for the usual period of nine months. Strict instructions were given that Lanny must be restrained from hunting. When Lanny returned for his final testing, he not only failed, but was savage into the bargain; he was returned to the puppy walker. Being a reject, and no longer under the school influence, Lanny was allowed to run free; his hunting instincts were given free rein. A year later Mr Pfaffenberger returned to the same puppy walker to collect another guide dog. He was amazed to see the change in Lanny who was very friendly. Mr Pfaffenberger took the unprecedented step of taking Lanny back to the school. His tests recorded below, are self-explanatory.

The best of pals. Rintelna the Bombardier CDex, UDex seen in an 'off duty' tug of war with the Dobermann, Bowesmoor Hans (Photo: courtesy Mary Macphail)

	Scores when tested prior to leaving school.	Scores when tested at one year. (During this period he was restrained.)	Scores when tested at two years. (During this period he was allowed to hunt.)
Come	4	2	3
Sit	5	2	4
Fetch	4	1	4
Eye test	3	1	2
Intelligence	4	0	2
Willingness	4	0	4

The New Knowledge of Dog Behaviour, Clarence Pfaffenberger.

Trust and confidence are essentials that must be established during this stage. The first lesson to be learnt is to come immediately when called. A pup will always do this if it gets pleasure from the action. We find that picking a pup up when it comes, and cuddling it goes a long way in establishing rapport. When a pup is first exposed to a situation that will elicit a fear response it should be in a position of security. It should be cuddled (softness is comforting), stroked gently (hands impart confidence), and reassured softly (the voice has a soothing quality); this will cushion its response to fear. If it is by itself, fear response will be greater. Trauma and stress must be avoided. One can teach a child to swim without throwing it in at the deep end. A pup should be exposed, at this stage, to a wide variety of situations and encouraged to explore the horizon, but it should not be frightened. Fear response will always be greater when it is in a strange situation or in the company of strangers.

House training is another important aspect during this stage. Rottweilers are clean in their habits and this is noticeable while the pups are still in the whelping box. If this instinct is not developed, however, the grown dog, particularly males, will be a source of embarrassment. A baby pup will always urinate when roused from sleep, after a meal or drink, or at the start of an active period. It should be picked up and placed where it can relieve itself; it should be praised lavishly when it does. The barbaric practice of rubbing a pup's nose in its dirt only humiliates and confuses the puppy, giving the impression that it must not do this in the owner's presence. A pup will be encouraged to use the same place because of the smell. If an accident does happen elsewhere, then the smell must be removed.

The Rottweiler, particularly some males, has a dominant characteristic that emerges at about the time of sexual maturity. The owner must now exert his authority as the pack leader. This cannot be left for a later stage. This characteristic was prominent in one of our early dogs. I gave Lirac a bone when he was seven weeks of age and my wife tried to take it from him. The aggressive response was quite surprising, though not unexpected. I ordered him to 'leave' picking him up by the scruff and shaking him. (Dogs will not bite or continue to hold when lifted off the floor; naturally this is easier with a puppy.) Lirac dropped his bone, it was then given back to him. The exercise was repeated on five mornings, with each lesson producing a less aggressive response. On the fifth morning he left the bone immediately and the problem was resolved.

Car sickness is another problem that faces some Rottweilers. There are drugs that can alleviate the problem, but it is far better to condition a dog without recourse to them. The pup should be encouraged to stay in a stationary car; a toy or a bone will keep it occupied. It should then be taken for a short ride. The object should be to give it pleasure rather than serving a specific object like taking it to the vet for a distemper vaccination. Pups should not be fed before this exercise. When it associates the car with a pleasant outing nothing will keep it away and it will not be sick. Our problem is to keep our dogs out of cars.

All dogs have to be handled by a vet at some stage in their lives. Regular examination of feet, ears and mouth will condition it to accept handling of this kind. If this is not done the dog could present a vet with a problem, by refusing to be handled in later life.

Pfaffenberger demonstrated the vital role that socialisation played in the successful training of guide dogs; isolation also has a large bearing in the reverse direction. Some years ago we visited a friend with a litter of four-week old pups. They had not left the cellar in which they were born and were in excellent condition and most friendly. We advised the owner to give them some access to sunlight. A month later we visited them again and were proudly told that the litter was being brought up 'naturally'. We were taken to see the run which resembled a modern zoo. A kennel, open space, bushes and a place where food was left, was enclosed by a fence. The pups who were healthy, physical specimens, behaved like a litter of fox cubs. They took cover immediately we approached They could not be handled and would yelp and bite when picked up. On the other hand, pups that are exposed only to human beings grow up to regard other dogs as pieces of furniture. Both forms of upbringing are equally wrong. Development includes, in order of importance, the influence of the mother and the siblings, owner, other dogs, other people and a whole range of interesting stimuli. A pup must grow up with this whole influence if it is to become an acceptable member of modern society. The most important time when this conditioning must be experienced is during this period of socialisation. It is one of the most interesting phases of a dog's life and it gives unlimited pleasure to witness a puppy's development, to learn from it and, in some small way, to influence it through our own contribution.

Practical Breeding and Genetics

The first consideration, when breeding a dog, should be the existing gene pool and the influence on the breed as a whole that would be exercised by the dog being bred. The next consideration should be the dog himself, to ensure that his qualities would be an asset and that maximum benefit would be derived from his genes. These considerations, naturally, apply only to countries where the breed is already established. I discussed these implications with the late Captain Roy-Smith who was responsible for regenerating interest in the breed in Britain after the last war. It was clear that people importing dogs were not conscious of these considerations and I doubt whether much attention is paid to them even today. The chief considerations of people contemplating imports, unfortunately, appear to be phenotype, and the impact the dog will have in their show ring.

Imports are very costly, and, in countries protected by quarantine regulations, much time elapses between initial purchase and the actual time of arrival in the new owner's kennel. Much can go wrong and the risk is considerable. Consequently, thought should be given to the maximum benefit that any import would bring through his influence on the gene pool. A conscientious breeder has a responsibility for the development of the breed in his or her country.

It would appear, from an analysis of the exports from Germany, that Scandinavia, and particularly Sweden, has benefited most when one equates quality, the number of imports and their influence on the gene pool to the money outlayed. Whether this is purely fortuitous, or whether it was inspired by a knowledge of German dogs is a matter for conjecture. Knowing Gerd and Sven Hyden, who have guided the destiny of Swedish Rottweilers for fifty years, and Olavi Pasanen, the Finnish Rottweiler Chairman for the last thirty years, I would say that the quality obtaining in Scandinavia today was determined very largely by their appreciation and intimate knowledge of German Rottweilers.

Genetic Principles and the Breeder

One of the factors influencing a selection of breeding partners is a study of the pedigrees involved. The form itself, although it contains names, numbers and, where applicable, titles and working degrees, gives very little information of real value.

Value lies in the amount of genetic information supplied, and, unless the breeder is familiar with the animals named, very little useful knowledge is gained from a pedigree. German pedigrees show much more detail and critiques of parents and grandparents give a good idea of phenotype. No genetic information is supplied, however, and to get this one must have an in-depth knowledge of parents, grandparents and siblings, particularly half-brothers and sisters. Results of matings of parents to other partners is probably the most vital factor in assessing the genotype of breeding animals.

What is the breeder's object when two animals are mated and what result does he expect to get? He must have a goal of several factors in mind, and must allocate priorities. The following four traits, related to the appreciation of a breeding programme, are set out for discussion. Most breeders would accept them, although individuals will have a different order of priority. Much argument would attend the separation of the first three. Breeders would opt unhesitatingly for all three, but most would find that sacrifices have to be made and one is fortunate if the material available reduces these to a minimum.

1 Type
2 Character/temperament
3 Soundness
4 Beauty

I have placed type first because the prime consideration in breeding purebred dogs is to breed a typical animal as near the standard as possible. A breeding programme must be realistic; one can be too ambitious regarding quality and the time span in which this can be accomplished. A programme must be based on material already available in the country and a programme for one country may not be suitable for another. A programme devised for Germany would not suit conditions that prevail in Australia. The depth of quality in brood bitches and sires simply does not exist in the latter country. One could develop a line in Germany to produce stock of the highest quality within three to five years. The records will show that this has been done. Eugene Schertel adopted the kennel name Kohwald in 1946 and bred five consecutive *Bundessiegers*, starting in 1951. Gunter Czeckowski, Vom Mägdeburg, bred his first litter in 1977: Babette v Mägdeburg, a bitch from his second litter, was the Hans Korn memorial prizewinner for the best Rottweiler at the 1980 annual show, and his stock figured prominently the following year. The 1982 *Klubsieger* was Bronco v Rauberfeld, whose breeder Gottfried Fahbender had entered the Rottweiler fray only three years earlier.

Kennel names such as Hause Neubrand, Haugenfeld, Rauchfang and others all produced quality dogs within three years of the start of their breeding careers. Depth of quality is available for a sensible breeder in Germany to produce a top-quality line in a short space of time. We in Australia are forced to use dogs with faults that have to be bred out.

With regard to character, the differences associated with assessing hereditary influence would appear anomalous when one remembers that character requirements have remained unaltered since the first standard was produced. The thrust has always been to breed a good-natured, incorruptible, courageous dog of the purest integrity. Conformation requirements, on the other hand, have altered with the writing of each standard revision. This is due to two factors. Firstly because of the differing interpretations and different values that are placed on such words as aggressive, protective, fighting and hardness. Secondly, because of the confusion that exists about the influence of environment in this context. It is simple to deal with matters of fact and quantitative values that can be measured; character/temperament is a matter of opinion.

Some people may place soundness above character in our list of priorities. Others may say, with good reason, that soundness includes the properties of both body and mind. One could argue that an unsound, though typical, Rottweiler is of little value either in the work place or the show ring. Both features are essential, but is it easier to introduce type or is it easier to eliminate weaknesses? In my opinion, type is something peculiar to the breed, and it is difficult to separate it from soundness. There is no denying that one can make a good case for both. 'What about movement?' comes an irate cry. I feel that a sound, good-type Rottweiler will always satisfy the purist in this respect and any weakness of gait, due to lack of proper exercise, can be easily remedied.

With regard to the last trait, beauty, there is no denying that a striking black dog with rich mahogany markings, dark brown eyes and small well-carried ears, both working in harmony to give expression, creates an immediate impression when he enters the ring. Beauty faults do not lower the working value of a dog but too many such faults, or faults that are too striking, do affect type. Large ears, for example, are a minor fault that does not lower working value, but large, heavy ears, set too low and too far back, alter the shape of the head and therefore affect type. Light brown eyes are not as desirable as dark brown, but they do not reduce a dog's rating to any extent. Yellow eyes, or eyes that are dissimilar in shape or colour, make for a head that is unacceptable. Markings that are a pale yellow, or brown markings that cover the entire forechest, or legs that are too black in colour, do not disqualify a dog, but markings are a distinct characteristic of the Rottweiler and too great a departure is unacceptable. It would appear, therefore, that severe beauty faults can affect type without reducing working capacity. This tendency should be noted when choosing breeding partners, so that the degree of a beauty fault does not degenerate into a fault of type.

Breeding: Art or Science?

Most of the great breeders of the past, one suspects, relied entirely on their 'eye' when choosing breeding partners. This worked extremely well in practice as results show. Phenotype – what we see in the ring – however, can sometimes be at variance with genotype – the inherent characteristics that a dog is most likely to pass on to its progeny. Most breeders with whom I have spoken rely on a selection of phenotypes and trust that breeding partners will 'click'. The difficulty of the scientific method is that one cannot 'see' genes or identify the characteristics that are most likely to be passed on. Theory, although complicated, can be explained, but to implement what one understands is time-consuming, costly and often impractical. In the back of every breeder's mind there is, in varying degree of clarity, an idea of the mechanism that transmits traits from one generation to the next. We know that the influence of parents and immediate antecedents works through the genes, but the laws based on Mendel's experiments have little conscious application in the practical sense. Genetics is a most complicated subject and we are often forced to accept conclusions that are difficult to understand fully.

The unit of the transmission system is the reproduction cell. Each cell has a nucleus and the blue print for reproducing itself lies in the cell nucleus and it is called a chromosome. Chromosomes are a thread-like substance which can be seen under a microscope. Genes are located on specific parts of the chromosome and each expresses specific traits. These traits are controlled by chemical changes that occur at a particular point on the chromosome; this point is known as a locus. Chromosomes are passed from parents to progeny, the dog having seventy-eight, or more correctly, thirty-nine pairs. When the egg is fertilised, each parent provides a single chromosome from each of its thirty-nine pairs. Each chromosome has something like 100,000 genes, each one expressing a specific trait. On the surface, it appears that both parents contribute half of the characteristics that are expressed in the progeny. In order to understand how the system works it is necessary to clarify certain terms.

Genetic Terms

Each pair of genes is made up from the contribution of the parents. When both genes in a pair express the same trait the pair is homozygous. When they express different traits the pair is heterozygous; the trait that is visibly expressed is governed by the dominant gene. The gene that is masked or hidden is the recessive. The influence of a dominant gene is expressed when present in a single dose, ie the trait comes from one parent only. The influence of a recessive is expressed only when present in a double dose, ie the trait is passed on by both parents. Dominance therefore may not be complete because recessive genes will express traits that have been hidden for two or three generations, when paired with a similar recessive. Genes do not blend and they retain their particular ability to express specific characteristics.

Their behaviour may be likened to a double brick wall, built with pairs of black and white bricks. The bricks cannot be blended to produce a pastel grey. One can build a wall of the same colour by using bricks of only one colour on the outside. If the wall is demolished, the bricks will still be either black or white and may be rearranged in a different pattern. The colour of a cup of white coffee, on the other hand, poured from a pot of coffee and a jug of milk, can be varied to provide the desired shade by pouring more milk or more coffee. Once poured, the mixture cannot be restored to its original constituents. Genes cannot be varied in this fashion.

In genetic parlance, each member of a gene pair expresses a characteristic and when the pair is homozygous, the characteristic expressed is denoted by capital letters HH; the absence of the characteristics (or more correctly its alternative) is denoted by small letters hh. In a heterozygous pair dominated by the characteristic the letters would be Hh. H represents the characteristic and h represents the alternative gene or characteristic. A characteristic in a pup could therefore be HH or Hh or hh.

When Mendel crossed a red flowering pea with a white, the result was red because of the dominant gene. The phenotypes of the red peas were similar, but the genotypes were not, because the red pea was not pure and would not breed truly. When he crossed the hybrids, the result was three reds to one white. The flowering peas had two phenotypes, red or white, but three genotypes. The white was double recessive, but, to identify the pure red, a further breeding was necessary. Again, the average ratio of 1:2:1 would apply to a large sampling, and, in a kennel situation, a series of matings over many years would be required to ensure that a trait would breed true. There have been many well-documented cases where carriers of a serious fault have been identified by a series of test-matings. A good example of this is how the Progressive Retinal Atrophy Syndrome was arrested in Irish setters. The breed was in danger because the disease was being spread by dogs who carried a recessive gene, but who appeared normal. Test-matings were carried out, using dogs that were already blind. The only certain method of identifying carriers was by test-mating dogs to known carriers, thus bringing a pair of recessives together.

There is another source from which disease is introduced, and that is when genes are altered so that a different trait is expressed. This occurrence is called a mutation. This can be extremely dangerous, but fortunately it is rare. Mutations can, however, appear in one generation without warning and with devastating effect. The nuclear age has made us more conscious of the effects of radiation causing mutations and the effects of many herbicides are also now emerging. Genes have been altered over the years by natural radiation, but the process has been gradual. Man himself has added his contribution to the modifying effect of genes, by selective breeding, but results have not been dramatic. Alterations deliberately undertaken by genetic engineering are spectacular, and one wonders whether all side effects have been considered. Variations are a necessary component for progress and we are all familiar with Darwin's theory of evolution. There are many examples of how nature selects for survival those individuals and species that are best adapted to their environment. The weak perish and the strong survive. Rabbits that survived the myxomatosis era, and bacteria that have proved resistant to antibiotics, have recolonised their environment. What can we learn from these examples when we breed dogs? We should be conscious of the long term, and resist promises of dramatic and immediate improvement.

We have had a brief look at the action of single genes expressing a trait because of their dominance, single or double recessives and the problems caused when phenotypes express traits that are not reproduced. There is another way that a gene can have a significant bearing on the breeding of dogs. This gene, although exerting little influence by itself, acts in concert with similar genes. This type can help to express a useful trait, like a high milk yield, or it can be a contributing factor in producing a disease. The contribution of a single pair is not significant, but the cumulative effect is considerable. One may say that the gene predisposes an animal, rather than causes the trait to be expressed. It is now accepted that hip dysplasia is not caused by a dominant or recessive gene, but that inheritance is polygenic. Polygenic diseases are susceptible to modification by the environment and a wide variation in the severity of the disease, due to this factor, is possible. With regard to HD, the effect of environmental factors, such as overfeeding, resulting in weight increases out of proportion to muscle growth, stress placed on the coxofemoral joint before ossification is complete, exercise on steep or slippery surfaces – which not only places stress on soft joints, but alters the angle of thrust, causing remodelling of the acetabulum – should be borne in mind.

A striking example of the environmental effect on HD is the modern-day usage of the diaper, or nappy, for human babies. Diapers help to hold the femoral head firmly into the acetabulum during the early years of a baby's life. This practice makes a significant contribution to the status of the hip joint later in life. The incidence of HD in Red Indian tribes, where mothers carried their babies on their backs – providing much the same support – is low; whereas incidence of HD was high in tribes that transported babies in a cradle.

In an earlier chapter we saw how the reaction of hereditary traits to the environmental factor of socialisation affected behaviour. Genetic traits are also modified by environmental factors. Climate, especially on coat, nutrition, especially during gestation, and the natural balance of calcium/phosphorus/vitamin D are all factors that cannot be disregarded. We have always been conscious, for example, of large, even teeth in the Rottweilers we breed. We noticed many years ago that when a bitch was deprived of proper nutrition during pregnancy, the resulting litter had poor dentition and no amount of feeding would change the quality of teeth in the progeny.

The science of genetics has been of great benefit to producers of livestock, but this has been confined almost entirely to animals where only one or two traits are important. These traits have been influenced by a number of genes acting together to produce a cumulative effect. The traits desirable in dairy cattle, for example, are a high milk yield and butter fat content, rapid growth and early maturity. In sheep, the farmer looks for increases in meat and wool. In poultry, the accent is on meat and eggs laid per annum. These are quantitative traits that are easy to measure. Their improvement depends on the influence of many loci acting in concert to express only a few traits. In the short term, the gene pool can be compressed to advantage by close breeding with animals that express these traits. The disadvantage, in the longer term, is the emergence of characteristics like infertility, lack of resistance to disease, and so on. Out-crossing is then necessary, to introduce new genes that bring fresh vigour and give further impetus to the expression of the desired characteristics.

The sex of pups is influenced entirely by the male partner. We know that dogs have thirty-nine pairs of chromosomes. Of these, thirty-eight are similar. The thirty-ninth pair, in addition to passing on its characteristics, serves the special function of determining the sex of the progeny. The female pair of sex chromosomes is similar and are labelled XX. The male pair is dissimilar and is labelled XY. The bitch can only pass one of her X chromosomes. The dog may pass either. If it is an X it pairs with the female X to produce a female puppy XX. If it is a Y, the result is a dog, XY.

The Essence of Genetics

The most important consideration of all the proven facts and theories concerning reproduction is, 'What have we gathered from this mass of evidence and what can be applied in practice?' The following details have emerged.

The dog has thirty-nine pairs of chromosomes. Each parent contributes one from each of its pairs. Each chromosome has approximately 100,000 genes located on its thread-like substance and these genes are concerned with the transmission of hereditary traits. Specific traits depend on the position that genes occupy on the chromosome. The factors that express these traits must have a degree of commonality. Thirty-nine (pairs) $\times$ 2 $\times$ 100,000 (genes) = 7,800,000. How many individual traits are there in the make-up of the total dog – 100 . . . 200 . . . 500? Whatever this number may be, it can only be a small fraction of the total number of genes. Therefore many genes must express the same trait, providing a cumulative effect. Chromosomes are visible under a microscope, but we can only postulate the influence of genes by the phenotypical characteristics expressed by progeny.

Imagine a pack of seventy-eight cards, each card having 100,000 characters. One character only, selected at random in a mating, plays a part in transmitting hereditary traits. The element of luck is brought into even sharper focus when we realise that a dog produces something like 500 million sperm at a single service and that only one of these can fuse with the egg to produce a puppy.

Thus, seventy-eight cards are selected, and each has only one character, selected at random out of a possible 100,000. The selection of characters can be influenced by narrowing the field. This can be done immediately, by recognising the influence of recessive genes that show up by accident. When a fault shows up, the mating pair should both be mated with other partners. In a kennel situation test-matings are not always practical, but much can be done by observation. The first step is to breed the desired phenotype. If the fault is serious, then further steps can be taken to weed out carriers. More positive steps can be taken with dominant genes by recognising sires prepotent for desirable character- istics. This can be done by a series of normal matings. The next step is to promote a homologous gene pool by selective line-breeding. One must remember that 'a good thing' is never permanent and the vigour of the pool must be kept in repair by the occasional introduction of fresh genes.

When choosing breeding partners, particularly the stud dog, most breeders concern themselves with phenotype. A question that is sometimes asked is, 'Should I use dog X in spite of a fault?' No single characteristic can be judged in isolation, because transmission depends not on the individual animal, but on its immediate antecedents, as well as the breeding partner. A useful tool, to evaluate breed worthiness in the animals available in a breeding colony, is to analyse the results of matings of *all* progeny. Weak partners can be eliminated, and half-siblings mated to establish a homologous gene pool. Few breeders have the capacity to undertake this and breed societies are concerned with organising breed shows, social activities and the generating of funds. The aim could be achieved, however, if breeders would co-operate to pool their knowledge.

Many years ago my wife and I attempted to form a breeders' association with the express purpose of analysing the breedworthiness of the animals available to us. Most people were not in sympathy with our aim. A few thought that this should be left to the club. Others felt that a breed warden system was the answer. The breed warden system works excellently in Germany where the ADRK exercises sole authority over a single breed. It would not work in Australia because we do not have the basic knowledge, skills and experience possessed by the individuals who are responsible for the efficiency of the German system. Authority, in Australia, is vested in a council that is responsible for over one hundred breeds and caters for the needs of a dog-showing community that is harnessed to the all-breeds syndrome.

No country can abstract a system that has taken years to evolve and superimpose it on conditions existing in a different environment. Each country must accept and adapt prevailing conditions, tailoring its canine philosophy accordingly. Breeding regulations, rules of conduct and the establishment of goals must be compatible; if they are not, more harm than good will result.

The effect of mutations and lethal genes is extremely rare with our breed. If, however, one is unfortunate enough to encounter these circumstances, immediate action should be taken to identify the culprit. We are particularly watchful of the bitch in whelp, especially in the first six weeks of pregnancy. No drugs or vaccines should be administered, and, although the nature of any faults that then occur would be congenital rather than genetic, unnecessary risks should not be taken.

Man has used selective breeding as a tool for improving his livestock long before Gregor Mendel started the experiments on which the laws of genetics are based. Man's attitude to breeding was governed by dominant genes and prepotent sires. It did not extend to a programme and, if it did, it was probably confined to a single generation. It was only in the latter part of the last century that breeders started to become conscious of a breeding programme. The approach was intuitive and empirical, rather than curricular, and I doubt even today if the tenets of such laws as independent assortment or segregation play any part in the selection of breeding partners. Our own humble approach is based on what I call 'pillars' and 'links'. Pillars in a pedigree are the names of the great dogs. Links are the names of those dogs in between. Desirable traits are more likely to be expressed when there are a good number of pillars.

A brief look at some of the early pedigrees will illustrate what is meant by pillars in a pedigree.

Each dog is a link between generations but only dogs of outstanding quality can be described as pillars. A study of chart 2 (page 27) will show the dogs that possessed this quality. Alfon, and his sons Hackel and Ido, and Arno and his sons Odo, Oleo and Vogt not only possessed notable Rottweiler phenotype but they exuded that indefinable capacity to pass greatness on to their children and to the generations that immediately followed. Chart 3 (page 29) shows the influence of Hackel through to Igor v Kohlwald in the seventh filial generation. This was the era into which Harras was born. Could it have had a bearing on his own contribution reflected in his sons like Erno, Farro, Falco, Kluge and Kurt and grandsons like Kato and Barras shown in pedigree 23? This era stands out in the history of American Rottweilers. The quality is obvious. The challenge to the dedicated Rottweiler disciple concerns the preservation of this essence in an ocean of twenty thousand registrations per annum!

The pillars stand out in the chart and they are linked to a succession of other pillars: Fels, Alfon, Hackel, Ido. Hackel (82 litters, 375 pups, over 100 rated SG and many rated V) was probably the greatest. His sire, Alfon (26 litters, 130 pups) was another pillar. Fels, another noted stud dog, passed his quality to few dogs, but they ranked with the best. The links in this line are excellent, without a single poor specimen. Igor was not only a *Sieger* but he put his stamp on many modern champions especially those coming from Harras.

It is interesting to follow the breeding Fels – Arno v Zenthoff – Odo v Gaisburg – Grief v Bexbach – Arno v Gunthershof. It is an excellent line of dogs. Arno was the great grandsire of Rudi Eulenspiegel who was imported into England. Rudi was one of the best Rottweilers imported from Germany, but he did not continue his own excellence. He was probably not good enough to be classed as a pillar, but he was a good link.

Probably the greatest dog and the most influential sire to go to the United States was Triple *Bundessieger* Harras v Sofienbusch. Although used on only ten occasions in the States, he left a lasting impression. If you follow his pedigree and note the pillars and links, the reason is obvious.

Pedigree 23

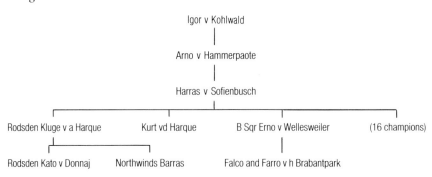

Igor v Kohlwald

Arno v Hammerpaote

Harras v Sofienbusch

| Rodsden Kluge v a Harque | Kurt vd Harque | B Sqr Erno v Wellesweiler | (16 champions) |

| Rodsden Kato v Donnaj | Northwinds Barras | Falco and Farro v h Brabantpark |

Harras had a tremendous influence in the States and it is difficult to find the pedigree of a top American Rottweiler without his name in it. Erno won the *Sieger* title before being exported. He was responsible for many excellent dogs, some sired in Europe. Kluge sired thirty-four champions and twenty-three obedience winners. Kurt was the first dog to win in group consistently. His grand-daughters, Quelle and Wilma vd Harque, were top obedience bitches. The pillars and links are obvious. On the other hand, a number of dogs have distinguished themselves in the ring, but have not produced any progeny of the same quality. An examination of their pedigrees will show that their immediate forebears were animals of little distinction. An excellent phenotype is not a good breeding proposition when his links go back to genotype mediocrity.

13 Understanding Your Dog

Animal behaviour has always interested me, but until my association with Rottweilers this interest was uninformed and my knowledge indifferent and cursory. In my study of Rottweilers I have arrived at conclusions – which are still the subject of analysis – by a process of retrospection. Memories have been stimulated by observation and interest sharpened by what has been written by those disposed by nature and trained by science to observe what I have also perceived in a more untutored fashion.

The dog reacts to a range of stimuli that, in large measure, are common to those experienced by his master. Authorities differ on such questions as a dog's intelligence and its capacity to learn and to apply this learning. Man is acknowledged to be more intelligent! His brain is larger than the dog's and part of it – known as the association area which reacts to symbols – deals with processes that are simply beyond a dog's capacity.

A dog senses, but does not perceive. When an animal senses, a nerve cell in its brain is stimulated and produces a response. If it is cold or hungry, it looks for warmth and food. When a man perceives, his brain is stimulated, sense being reinforced by memory of what he has previously seen or been told. Response is stimulated by a symbolic process. The dog is stimulated by his senses and he merely reacts to smell, sound and the like. The more one sees of Rottweilers, however, the more one questions this difference. Undoubtedly man has many advantages. He can analyse his past experiences, he can learn by language transfer and he can learn from the experience of others. The difference, however, is one of degree rather than of principle. Man has the capacity to generate a chain reaction of symbols, and individuals have a great range for interpretation. Symbolic response, I feel, may be within the scope of a Rottweiler, although it stands much lower in the evolutionary scale and it cannot exercise man's faculty for reason. A close association with Rottweilers has clearly demonstrated that they possess cognitive ability that I had previously thought to be outside the realm of the animal kingdom.

These three examples will illustrate a Rottweiler's ability in this context. I returned home one evening to find my wife's shoes in the laundry; her Wellingtons were missing. I said to Chab 'Where's Pop, go and find her'. He sniffed around for a few seconds and then set off on the trail. My wife had walked over a mile inspecting fences; Chab tracked her within minutes. He did the same with the cat. She could not be located for the evening meal so Chab was ordered to find her. He circled the house, picked up the scent and found her three hundred yards away in a pine tree. On another occasion I wanted my Head Curator in a hurry. When last seen he was on the second green. I drove to the green, let Chab out with the command 'Find Jim'. Jim was several fairways away but Chab tracked him down following his trail.

Man and dog are each born with a certain potential. How close each comes to reaching this depends on the environment and the opportunities afforded. We are fortunate, in the western world, that almost every child is given the opportunity to develop this potential. Can we say the same for a dog? We assume that it is capable of simple responses that do not involve reasoning and so fashion its curriculum accordingly.

According to some psychologists, a dog recalls no past experience when meeting someone it has known well; it merely senses that it has met up with something pleasant. A few weeks before my Chab died, a friend whom he had not seen for three years, visited us; he was Chab's friend too. I went to Chab's day kennel and explained that Paul was visiting. He understood in a flash, went through three gates and a door and flung himself on Paul in joyous welcome.

Rottweilers make very accommodating friends – here Emil from Blackforest CDex transports a Pekingese around (Photo: courtesy Mary Macphail)

Do Rottweilers think? What do they think about? How does thinking affect behaviour? What can we do to make our Rottweiler a good citizen? These are the questions to which we Rottweiler owners should address ourselves, yet we are not encouraged to think along these lines. New owners are presented with vaguely understood formulae which are applied without modification and without regard for individual differences. No two Rottweilers are alike. Each has many thousands of paired genes inherited in a genetic lottery, the permutation of which creates a range of individual variants. The individual owner is responsible for his dog's upbringing. He should not do this by following a general formula. An analytical presentation would allow him to make his own appreciation and fashion the syllabus that will be of service to him and benefit to his dog.

Our attitude to animal psychology has undergone many changes and this pattern will continue as we learn more about animals. Julian Huxley echoed the sentiments of the late nineteenth century when he wrote that animals were little human beings with the same thoughts and emotions, but without the ability to express them. There was the usual sharp reaction. The psychologists were diametrically opposed, holding the view that animals had no conscious thought, behaviour being determined by responses that are innate and involuntary. Balance was restored by the information which resulted from experiments carried out between the wars. This is summed up by D. O. Hebb, *Emotions in Man and Animal* – 'The true objection to anthropomorphism is not to discovering a similarity of mechanism in human and animal behaviour but to inventing similarities that do not exist.'

The extreme was reached in a book published by Charles P. Eisenmann entitled *Stop! Sit! Think!* It is described as a documented account of an intellectual breakthrough between man and dog. 'Chuck' Eisenmann is known for his remarkable dogs trained for the film industry, the most famous, perhaps, being a TV series called *The Littlest Hobo*. Some may smile in disbelief at the capabilities of London, the German shepherd dog, and his friends. For example, during a media interview, one dog was told 'This man's shoes are dirty. Fetch something to clean them with.' The dog left the room, returning again with a shoe brush.

How far have we probed the dog's mind? What is *meant* by 'mind'? How does the human brain compare? Terms can be confusing and we must be clear about entities and functions. The human brain is similar to that of a dog, except for two main differences. It is larger and biologically older, and it has an area that is peculiar to it, which has been referred to as the association area. The sensory, motor and emotional areas work in the same way, the only difference being in their relative size.

Mrs Blackmore's Gamegards Basula v Sachenhertz (left) and Emil from Blackforest are both safe and gentle with this tiny kitten (Photo: courtesy Mary Macphail)

Much of our knowledge of animal behaviour is based on experiments conducted in laboratories. Pavlov devised a method of measuring the amount of saliva produced by dogs in response to certain stimuli. His work on conditioning responses was unique, but it is difficult to disregard the cloak of artificiality. Results of experiments are open to a wide range of interpretation. It is acknowledged that human subjects undergoing tests respond differently when conscious of being studied. It has been proved that domesticated wild animals are more efficient in problem-solving than their wild brothers. On the other hand the late Mrs Joy Adamson demonstrated clearly that wild lions are capable of looking after themselves far better than pets released from captivity for rehabilitation in the wild.

Let us not downgrade a Rottweiler's intelligence because we look down from a pinnacle occupied by the higher-rated primates. It may not think exactly like its master, but it responds to much the same stimuli and in much the same fashion. It wants much the same from life – recognition, preservation of dignity, praise when it thinks that performance warrants it, and acceptance as a member of the team. It comes into the world with many of the same primary drives. As it develops, some characteristics appear more brutish or bestial by comparison, not because it is baser, but because man is more practised, and therefore more proficient, in the act of sublimation.

Many years ago a young friend of mine, aged four, struck a female acquaintance of the same age. Replying to his father's admonition he said 'I only hit her second.' Twenty years later his action would have been different. He would have been inhibited by his upbringing in a society that requires young men to behave like gentlemen.

An owner should have a basic knowledge of Rottweiler instincts and a clear understanding of what it can be taught and how it can be taught and how it should be corrected. The dog can then, by education and understanding, be encouraged to fulfil a useful role in society. The owner must be on guard, however, because instincts can be easily aroused, particularly when two or more dogs act in unison. Instinct is a term that is freely used; it may be interpreted in many ways. It has much to do with the education of Rottweilers, so let us examine it more fully.

Instinct

Eugene Marais, the South African naturalist, brought a refreshingly new understanding to the words 'instinct' and 'learning' by inventing two simple phrases, phyletic memory and causal memory.

Phyletic memory is the unconscious part of the psyche; causal memory is the conscious part, being the result of what has been learned. If phyletic memory is strong, response will be immediate; the inhibiting influence is provided by the discipline that has been acquired by causal memory. I saw this work with my dogs. One evening a fox crossed immediately in front of us while we were walking on the farm. The dogs set off in instant pursuit. I called loudly for them to drop, but only Chab obeyed. He returned and was praised lavishly. The miscreants returned at intervals, and I feared that my admonition had had little effect. A few days later the same thing happened with a rabbit. The other dogs gave chase, but not Chab. He started, but then had second thoughts, looked at me and returned. I did not take any overt action to stop him.

This bears out the statement that dogs are stimulated by innate impulses. Whether they respond or refrain depends partly on the strength of the impulse and partly on the discipline that has been learned. In the education of a Rottweiler, owners must remember that phyletic memory is never completely submerged. How far it is allowed to control behaviour depends entirely on the discipline taught to the dog. The strength of the influence of phyletic memory depends on the individual circumstances, and this influence will always be greater when there are two or more dogs to get out of hand.

People have complained about three-month old puppies chasing a

Mrs Margareta McIntyre (USA) and Mr Setterfield seen after the 1981 Victorian Speciality with Aus Ch Auselese Bold Lorenzo pulling a cart (Photo: Robinson)

kitten or chicken; I would be worried if they refrained. A healthy child goes through various stages of development. If they behaved like angels at all times, something could be amiss. When a boy of four is smacked by a girl of the same age, a healthy reaction is to give the girl a thump in return. The same applies to a pup. If a hen runs through its yard, a healthy reaction is to give chase. It can be taught more genteel manners as it grows older. Some owners feel that bad behaviour should be knocked out of a pup in the early stages, and thus a pup relieving itself on the Persian rug may have its nose rubbed in the offending puddle. The action is quite unfair and only harm will result. Energy produced by phyletic memory is not only natural but necessary. It should never be suppressed by punitive measures. When a pup chases a hen for the first time, it should not be punished. Punishment – something it cannot understand – will destroy its exuberance and confuse it. Energy should be directed into more useful channels. It should be stopped from chasing the hen and encouraged to retrieve instead. It could be exposed to the temptation again, but discouraged from the chase. This may be done when it is small by holding it back. When it is older, a sharp tug on the choke chain will convey the message; a ball may then be substituted.

Genetic inheritance – disregarding the influence of dominant genes – is exactly 50 per cent from each parent, but there is a belief that a pup inherits more characteristics of temperament from the dam, some of which have no genetic base whatsoever. The dam does indeed have a greater influence on the litter; the sire, apart from his contribution of genes, has little if any. Nervousness may be hereditary, but it can also be acquired through association, generally between the fourth and eighth week.

Behavioural traits, of course, may have a genetic base. An interesting experiment was carried out by Drs Scott and Fuller to establish the genetic influence of barking. They took a known barker and a poor barker, in the shape of a cocker spaniel and a basenji and exposed them to similar stimuli. The spaniel barked on 68 per cent of the occasions, the basenji on 20 per cent. The same experiment was carried out on the F1 generation which was a cross between the two. Barking was reduced to 60 per cent which showed that the basenji genes had an inhibiting influence. The crosses were then mated back to cockers and these pups barked on 65 per cent of the occasions when exposed to the stimuli; the back-cross to the basenjis only barked on 50 per cent of the occasions. There is a possibility, however, that cocker mothers may have induced more barking although the genetic component was the same.

A bitch, acquiring a pattern of behaviour, will teach it to her offspring. This appears on the surface to have a genetic base, but the characteristic may also be acquired by a foster child brought up in the litter.

An understanding of phyletic and causal memory will influence the attitude to corrective measures. Undesirable behaviour, triggered by phyletic memory, should not be checked with the same force as behaviour emanating from causal memory. I have found that a dog is more conscious of guilt when misbehaviour stems from causal memory. Checking misbehaviour stemming from phyletic memory, especially when it is done forcefully, confuses a dog.

Instincts or innate drives do serve a biological purpose. The energy produced from these sources has helped to preserve the species, and an understanding of particular instincts will help in the education of a Rottweiler.

Hunting Instinct
According to some of my German friends, the Rottweiler has a poorly developed hunting instinct. Working with Rottweilers over the last twenty years, I have formed the opposite opinion. Hunting has, in the past, been one of man's chief activities and dogs have always played a key role in it. Man first hunted to provide himself with food and clothing and to defend himself against predators. As more food was produced

from farming, and predators were reduced in numbers, hunting assumed a more sporting flavour. When man hunted in order to survive, dogs were used to drive game into nets or pits, or towards a line of men armed with spears or bows and arrows. Egyptian noblemen hunted as a form of relaxation some 3,000 years ago. The first dogs used were sight hounds which suited the deserts of North Africa admirably. Man adapted the dog's hunting ability to suit the terrain and the weapons available. In woody or marshy country, the spaniel became popular and a sense of smell replaced fleetness of foot as the main hunting attribute. The plains of Scotland and Ireland produced the deerhound and wolfhound; the frozen wastes of Russia produced their counterpart in the borzoi. The pointer, the perfect foil for the muzzle-loading flintlock, was replaced by the setter and retriever when the percussion breech-loading shotgun was invented.

The role of the Rottweiler in this activity has not been recorded, but we can draw a conclusion from two well-established premises. Boar, bear and deer were hunted in northern Europe throughout the Middle Ages, and the Rottweiler, with its powerful physique, excellent nose and great stamina was an ideal partner. Its inclusion in the hunt, particularly in a country like Germany where sport was so important and where the skills involved were a source of national pride, is a foregone conclusion. I have found that a Rottweiler's hunting instinct is easily stimulated, with the strength of response varying from dog to dog.

Our first dog, Chab, retrieved from land and water and he did this instinctively. He was eight months old when I first took him on the golf course. A rabbit ran across the track and I fired at it with a shotgun, turning to see Chab's reaction. He was most excited and, when I opened the door of the wagon, he was out like a flash. After some minutes he returned with the rabbit and jumped into the wagon with it as if he had done this all his life. I shot a few more and each time he retrieved without me ever leaving the car.

The golf course was overrun with rabbits and Chab and I made a concerted attempt to contain the population. One night I was driving a friend who was seated on the roof of the wagon. He took a long shot at a rabbit which moved off into the bush, apparently unhurt. Chab, as usual, went after it. He returned some twenty minutes later with the rabbit; I examined that rabbit and found only one pellet in its body. When the rabbits reached plague proportions, I invited the local gun club to ride shot gun for me. We set off, with two men armed with Browning automatics and one man with a spot light. I drove the wagon, with Chab occupying his usual position in the back. We collected ninety-two rabbits, with only Chab leaving the car.

Chab retrieved duck equally well, having had early practice with sticks. I dropped a duck some forty yards out in a pond. Chab looked quizzically at me and, on the command 'fetch', he did just that. If I shot two ducks, he would collect one and then swim to the other, always retrieving the pair.

All our dogs respond to the thrill of the chase and their scenting ability is extremely high. The scent of a koala bear in a tree a hundred yards off does not escape them. Elizabeth Harrap, the secretary of The Rottweiler Club who was staying with us, wanted to see a koala. I sent the dogs off into the bush, something they did regularly, always beginning to bark when they located a bear. To Elizabeth's joy they found two and barked until we arrived.

On one occasion, I saw a bitch point. Auslese Bordeaux Begum put up a quail on our morning walk. The quail pitched some two hundred yards off and I followed the dog to see what she would do. She located the quail, approached to five yards and held a perfect point. I flushed the quail and the same thing happened again. I have seen dogs flush quail many times, but I never saw one point before or since.

I have no doubt that my Rottweilers could be trained to tree a puma, or cougar as he is called in some parts of America. Some of my dogs would make excellent companions in rough shooting and could be of much use, both in walking game up or in retrieving it. The instinct to hunt in a pack by sight and smell is very strong. Mr Mummery informed me that the best pig dog he owned – he has been shooting for thirty years – was a Rottweiler/mastiff bitch. Caliban of Mallion, owned by Mr Roberts, attended shoots and collected the birds that the retrievers failed to locate; this was reported in the English club's April Newsletter, 1963.

Following a wounded tiger is a hazardous and nerve-wracking business as the animal may be either ten yards or ten miles away. A good dog would be of enormous assistance, but the dogs that I have had were always terrified of the scent of carnivores. I am quite sure, however, that Chab would have understood what was required, following the trail and warning me when the quarry was approached. Steadiness is essential in this operation and a nervous, highly strung dog would be quite useless. I understand that huskies are trained to track tigers in Siberia and I am quite sure that a Rottweiler's hunting ability could be put to good use in this field.

Herding Instinct
A number of people who have purchased puppies from us and who live on farms, or in the country, have reported incidents where their Rottweiler has exhibited spontaneous instincts for herding. We experienced this very early in our Rottweiler association and have harnessed

the quality to good effect. This ability is not surprising, as Rottweilers have been associated with farm animals for over a thousand years. The working instinct may remain dormant for several generations, but slumbering phyletic memory can be awakened by the proper stimulus and the consequent response can be quite striking.

Our introduction to sheep herding was accidental. A gate had been left open and a small flock of sheep had wandered off. My wife said, 'Chab, go and bring them back,' pointing to the errant flock; he did just that and it was the start of a long association with herding.

The herding technique of the Rottweiler is not suited to working sheep. Unlike cattle, sheep do not run in a straight line but tend to break right and left and disperse. The sheepdog's instinct is to keep the flock together by working on the perimeter, while the Rottweiler maintains direction, thus dividing the flock. We invented an unconventional tactic to counter this. When the flock approached a gate Chab would sit behind them in the centre, my wife and I moving to either side. We would then all move slowly forward until the lead sheep went through the gate.

Chab's forte was to catch a particular sheep in the paddock; this was a great saving in time when only one or two sheep needed treatment for fly strike. Blow-fly strike is prevalent in the Australian summer and normally the whole flock is yarded so that the affected sheep can be caught and treated. I would point to a sheep in the paddock, Chab would

Mr and Mrs Axten's Auslese Cora seen at six months old bringing in a goat. The herding instinct is very strong in Rottweilers (Photo: courtesy Mrs Axten)

catch it without ever causing it harm, and I would treat it on the spot. We made a film of this in 1968 for Charles Tuttle of the Colonial Rottweiler Club.

My best sheepdog was Jimbo – Auslese Pedro Ximenes – who was obedience-trained. He worked slowly and methodically, whereas Chab always injected a measure of urgency into the operation. Jimbo's great contribution was to put sheep through a race so that I could separate them. He would bring a dozen or more sheep from the holding paddock, pushing them towards me through the race. If a sheep turned about, causing a jam, he would walk across the backs of the others to clear it. He was also adept at bringing back a steer when it escaped from the yard. The steer would gallop away with Jimbo following sedately. He always brought the miscreant back slowly, the operation sometimes taking half an hour.

The history of the Rottweiler has clearly shown that the herding instinct, together with that of protection, is the foundation on which its service to man was built. The opportunity to express it, unfortunately, is rare in the environment in which it now lives. When this opportunity does occur, the instinct, which may have remained dormant for several generations, is roused instantly. The immediate uncompromising response measures the integrity and strength of this cardinal impulse.

Guarding
The guarding instinct in dogs has been recognised for at least 4,000 years, and has been adapted to suit particular requirements and regions. Early guarding dogs may be divided into two broad groups.

The first probably originated in the mountainous regions of Tibet, northern India and southern China. These dogs guarded property, the guarding propensity being extended to animals that required little or no herding. Accounts of life in Tibet describe these dogs as being chained outside houses where they presented a formidable obstacle to anyone trying to enter.

The second group were dogs of the spitz breed, used in the far north to work herds; the emphasis here was on rounding up and herding rather than on guarding.

The development of animal husbandry on the Hungarian plains and in the Caucasian mountains demanded yet another type that would herd and guard equally well. This was provided by a fusion of the dogs from both north and south: the Hungarian komondor and kuvasz probably originated from this merger.

The role of the Rottweiler, which emerged in the early Middle Ages with the development of the Rottweil cattle market, followed this herding/guarding pattern. These dogs, however, were more mobile, because the distances covered were much greater. The nomadic nature of the operation placed the emphasis on the transport of herds rather than on grazing. It was over this period that the Rottweiler's unique relationship with his master was formed. Korn refers to the constant companionship of man and dog, and it is not difficult to imagine how this came about. The team of man and dog would negotiate the difficult and dangerous country, keeping the herd together, fending off wolves, urging the laggards and subduing unruly bulls. Both were on duty for the whole journey, snatching sleep and food when they could, but always conscious of the bond between them and of their duty. The dog's purpose was to defend his charge and not rush off in pursuit of those that would prey on it. The dog was not on the offensive.

Demonstrations of the guarding instinct in wild animals and domestic dogs reveal a pattern of simulated attack. The object is to protect food, young, or territory; it is not logical to press the attack home unless this course becomes imperative.

Many years ago, a friend and I rented a shooting block in Central India. He left camp one evening to shoot a fowl for dinner, armed only with a shotgun and a handful of No 4 shot. A tiger suddenly appeared from some fifty yards away, closing the gap with three or four gigantic bounds, each bound accompanied by an earth-shattering roar. It braked hard some twenty yards off, ripped a bush out of the ground with a blow from its forepaw, emitted another roar and then bounded off into the jungle: the whole episode lasted less than ten seconds. My friend, for reasons that he considered sound, turned about and returned to camp!

In the course of discussion he remarked that the tiger had not meant to attack. He used the word 'demonstration', something that I have since seen many times and which describes exactly the display of guarding or protective instinct in the pure state.

A Rottweiler, brought up to regard all strangers with suspicion, will menace an intruder who ventures on its territory. The attack is not pressed home unless the intruder makes an aggressive move or attempts to run away. The Rottweiler brought up in a friendly atmosphere will close with an intruder, smelling him in a manner that suggests curiosity rather than aggression. Should the intruder pick up something belonging to the owner of the dog, then it will demonstrate.

Generally speaking, if the dog can approach the intruder and smell him, behaviour will be low key. If the dog is confined or separated by a fence, the demonstration will be made with greater force. The ability to identify felonius intention is highly developed in a Rottweiler. It is suspicious of behaviour that is tentative and will test such suspicion by investigating.

I am often asked how the protective instinct can be aroused and a young dog made more aggressive. An attempt to provoke this in some direct fashion could create an undesirable situation. Moreover, it is quite unnecessary in the family/companion role. A pup must be taught to recognise its family, and the property and possessions of the family. When it identifies them, it will take the necessary action when they are placed in jeopardy. It does not need to be taught how to protect. If the dog is regarded as a member of the family, it will come to the assistance of its fellow members whenever danger threatens.

A dog can, of course, make an error of judgement and attack when this is not warranted. But then we are all prone to error! If a dog is *trained* to attack, these occasions are more likely to arise if it does misread a signal!

Each dog reacts to a situation in an individual way. This depends partly on its innate ability, but more particularly on how and what it has been taught. I have found Rottweiler behaviour follows the same pattern as that of its master. If the master is excitable, nervous or aggressive, the dog is more likely to attack. If the master is a friendly person with a placid disposition, the dog is less likely to demonstrate. Again, a Rottweiler is particularly sensitive to its master's likes and dislikes; it will sense immediately whether its master is hostile or cordial towards a person.

As a general rule, one may say that if a man is looking for trouble, his Rottweiler will always be there to lend him a hand.

Aggression

Is there such a thing as an instinct for fighting? Some psychologists hold the opinion that aggression is not the expression of an innate drive but something that is learned and expressed when stimulated from outside.

I have some doubt about the evaluation of fighting instinct and have found that there is considerable variation in both its arousal and strength. One dog, with a fairly high threshold, will fight savagely when eventually aroused, but it will not go about with the sole intention of fighting every other dog. Another will try to attack every dog in sight. This type has a deranged mentality. It is a liability, bringing little joy to itself or its owner. A dog appearing for his ZTP or *Körung* in Germany, must possess a very high degree of courage, and fighting and protective instinct. Considerable expertise is required to analyse the connotation and parameters of fighting instinct and place them in perspective.

There are many ways in which aggression can be stimulated. The training sleeve, or even a hessian bag, will elicit the required response. An eight week old pup can be given his first lesson in aggression by using a stocking. A pup we sold developed a most aggressive attitude to children. After some investigation, it was discovered that it was tormented by boys riding bicycles outside the fence. The pup was encouraged to chase them and then beaten with sticks. Frustration provokes aggression. Think of a frustrated dog that has been chained or confined within a small yard. A dog subjected to this treatment will harbour resentment, with a tendency to vent its spleen on whatever comes within range.

Aggression can be provoked in other ways. Mental activity creates a certain energy which must be expended in useful ways. If development is to continue smoothly, this energy must find an outlet. If suitable opportunity is not provided, the more intelligent the dog the greater will be the problem. The attitude of some well-meaning owners often produces a result that is not intended. There is a tendency in some too-careful owners to protect their dogs. The dog is never allowed to go near another in case of a fight. Dogs have a natural curiosity and a wish to explore. If this is continually frustrated, the dog may become aggressive.

Experiments have shown that aggression can be stimulated artificially by mild electrical currents, although any outside stimuli to induce it is not present. Problems are easier to avoid than to solve and knowledge of this danger may help new Rottweiler owners because Rottweilers have an enormous potential for destruction when acquired by the wrong people.

The terms used to describe character can be confusing, and the distinction between innate and acquired characteristics is not always clear. For example, if a dog has a timid disposition – phyletic memory – which is directed towards a particular object, this can become a fear of somebody or something – causal memory. This fear can be expressed in different ways, such as biting or running away. If the dog wastes no time in biting, because of its fear, it is sharp. If another dog, with a fearless disposition, takes a dislike to some person, and it wastes no time in biting, it also is sharp. One is sharp because it is frightened, the other because it is not. A true assessment of character should be based on a dog's innate disposition. Is it born with character or is this acquired through its environment?

Scientists have discovered a great deal about this in the last century, and, while the hereditary influence has always been acknowledged, the vital role played by other factors – political, social, cultural, family – has now been placed in better perspective. Recent research has revealed that the contribution of maternal love and affection in the very early stages of infant development, and, later, the close relationships formed within the immediate family, are the cornerstones in the arch of development and character forming. We should not lose sight of this in the Rottweiler context.

Courage

Webster's dictionary lists fearlessness as a synonym of courage. Fearless means the absence of fear. In my view, the scope of courage includes the recognition and conquest of fear. To have courage, one must also know fear. The word fearlessness should not be included in the anatomy of courage.

All living things have an innate urge to preserve their life, to want comfort and to avoid pain. A decision to take action that places this urge in jeopardy requires energy which can be drawn from many sources. When the factors are considered in cold blood and a decision made which may involve the subject in pain or worse, the energy to carry out the action comes only from an intellectual source; something that a dog does not possess.

The media often refers to the courage of a race horse. Korn listed courage as an ingredient of Rottweiler character and one does not enter into dispute with Korn lightly. I do not believe that courage has any part in the make-up of a dog and I prefer the phrase, 'breeding integrity'. Courage is part of the human psyche. A race horse with breeding integrity has the will to be in front and will gallop his heart out to do so. A Rottweiler with this quality is a loyal and devoted companion, guaranteed to act in a stable and confident manner. To say that it does not possess the intellectual equipment to exercise courage is in no way an imputation of its character.

Temperament

What is meant by temperament and what is expected from good temperament? If the dog's response is consistent and reliable, its temperament must be considered good. Temperament is the dog's response to society. It interprets a situation by what it has learned and its response depends on inborn qualities. In some countries this response is aggressive and unfriendly; in others it is the opposite. Provided the dog's response is predictable, one must agree that temperament is good and that it is an 'honest' dog.

Many years ago we sold a dog and a bitch from the same litter to two different people in New Guinea. Following our custom, I rang the lady who owned the bitch to enquire how she was progressing. She was enthusiastic. I asked about the dog who lived a few miles away. Oh! he was very different and his temperament was poor. I rang the owner of the dog with some concern. He reassured me about the dog, saying that the temperament was excellent. I then asked him about the bitch and was told that her temperament was shocking! Pressed for details, he said that the bitch would attack on sight, unlike his dog who could be trusted with anybody. Both owners seemed satisfied.

If a dog is brought up to treat all visitors as dangerous, it will corner people, or even attack. If it is taught to treat people as friends, particularly when ordered by its master to do so, its response will be friendly. However, should the occasion warrant, the friendliest of Rottweilers can still produce the steel that is not very far below the surface.

In Germany it appears that dogs are more aggressive when in the presence of their owners. The inference drawn is that the dogs behave in a manner that they think will please their owners. Outside Germany, we saw dogs of German breeding, or sired by German studs, behave in quite a friendly fashion. It seems likely, therefore, that the customs and behaviour patterns of a country can influence a young dog. I am of the opinion that a dog begins to acquire an 'attitude' at about the age of two months. The wise owner should recognise this and shape the dog accordingly. It is easy to excuse something in a puppy of six weeks, but in doing so the owner may be encouraging an attitude that will most certainly cause problems a few months later.

A baby Rottweiler, like its human counterpart, needs something more than attention to its physical needs if it is to grow up into a wholesome dog. It must have affection – and the outward manifestation of affection – and a feeling of security in order to establish a relationship with its mother and other members of the litter. This relationship of trust is later extended to include its breeder and the immediate human family. A pup brought up in this atmosphere develops confidence, not only in itself, but also in its environment. The success of its future role – and this may be in the show or obedience ring, as a police dog, a working dog, or as a companion and friend – will rest on this foundation.

It is appropriate, at this juncture, to refer to the confusion that exists about aggression and the need for its suppression. The aggressive impulse, and the energy generated, is a vital part of Rottweiler make-up and it is a pity that our understanding of the term is so restricted. Aggression is not confined to vicious and savage behaviour. Indeed Gibbon, in his famous *Decline and Fall of the Roman Empire*, speaking of the love of action – his term for the instinct of aggression – states that when properly guided it becomes the parent of every virtue. We have already discussed courage in the context of Rottweilers, but the importance of using the energy that springs from aggression should not be lost on us.

Man has survived, elevating himself above all other species, partly because of his ability to adjust to the various pressures of environment, and particularly because of his aggressive drive which enables him to compete, to achieve and to master the difficulties that assail him. Aggressive energy, which has been responsible for so much hatred and

Heatherglen Chablis Khan (whelped 1965), the author's first working dog

Ch Auslese Bold Banner CD, giving her son a ride (courtesy Mrs Read)

Graf v Grüntenblick w 30.12.84 Jugendbester Rüde 1986. Imported by the author. The most important dog to go to the UK and then on to Australia

Ch Auslese Droll, the only Sch H2 Rottweiler in Australia, trained by Mr Axten (courtesy Mr Axten)

brutality, has also produced great feats of achievement.

It is a pity that the attitude to aggressive behaviour is so polarised. Some German dogs, and the best come from that country, would not be permitted in our rings, while the casual German spectator would regard our dogs as lacking in protective and fighting instinct. No judge should feel apprehensive about entering a Rottweiler ring, and no entrant or exhibitor should be disconcerted by the uncontrolled behaviour of another dog. It would be a pity, however, to eliminate the spectacle of a male Rottweiler bounding imperiously into the ring, surveying the arena with a confidence amounting almost to arrogance and, implicit in his bearing, the unspoken comment, 'Well, who is going to run second today!'

A reasonable balance is struck in the last sentence of the opening paragraph of the current standard: 'His bearing displays boldness and courage; his tranquil gaze manifests good nature and devotion.'

14 Communication – The Basis of Training

We are becoming increasingly aware that communication is a vital element, not only in the conduct of everyday affairs, but in the life of every living thing. The thrust of our concern is directed to the explicit and formulated methods of communication. Attention is confined to the material side; to the improving of discipline and clarity in the reasoning process, and exactness and accuracy in expressing the conclusions reached.

People communicate without the use of words. We use this form of communication a great deal without being conscious of our dependence on it and without understanding its importance. It is infinitely quicker and more natural. We communicate moods, feelings, attitudes, intentions, trust, affection, confidence and a host of things that defy accurate description.

The life of a gazelle depends entirely on communication within the herd. While the herd grazes, a sentinal keeps watch. Safety depends not only on the vigilance of the sentinal, but on its ability to communicate. The herd rests or grazes, or is galvanised into action, depending on intelligence communicated. Direct assimilation of mood plays an important part in immediate behaviour. People can become overly concerned with the mechanics of communication, looking more at the shell and ignoring the soul.

I have found that this attitude prevails in the dog world, particularly in the field of obedience training. The immediate post-war attitude to training has changed, but the emphasis, in some quarters, still remains on the compulsive methods of primary and secondary inducement, reinforcement and the mechanics of training applied to the physical side of the dog. Little is done to help the newcomer understand the mind of the dog; no distinction is made between individual dogs, and no attention paid to the necessity of establishing a rapport before training is undertaken. The emphasis is on the drill which, when executed with precision, produces a qualifying score of 170 points. Repetitive drill reduces the dog to boredom, and it becomes a mindless automaton. The process of education, on the other hand, makes the dog an enquiring and co-operative companion, with a mind of its own.

The first lesson, in most obedience schools, starts with instruction on the correct fitting of the choke chain and its application, together with

Ch Horst from Blackforest CDex seen exercising with his owner/breeder Mary Macphail. Worthwhile obstacles are good for both mind and body (Photo: courtesy Mary Macphail)

A Rottweiler at the Austrian Military School, Vienna. The school commandant is Herr Adolf Ringer who is internationally recognised as an expert in all aspects of the breed (Photo: courtesy Herr Ringer)

the lead, in various training motions. Commands are given in the harsh tones of a drill instructor, forgetting that a dog's hearing ability is far more sensitive than ours. Commands and related action are repeated again and again, until response becomes a conditioned reflex. The command 'sit' is followed by pushing down on the dog's rump with one hand while the lead is jerked upwards with the other. Admittedly, this is the easiest and quickest method of getting a grown dog to sit, but much can be done to establish a working relationship before any physical response is sought. The choke chain itself is a useful adjunct in communication, but only when used as a signal wire and not as an anchor chain. The dog depends on other means than commands and these, in contrast to the same senses in man, are much more sensitive. Compared to man, the dog is far more aware of messages conveyed by body movements, facial expression and scent. Senses deteriorate through lack of use, just as they improve with exercise.

The marking out of territory by animals is a well-established fact. This is equivalent to a notice of 'Private Property' or 'Trespassers Prosecuted'. The scent used, apart from the obvious method, is also left by scent glands between the toes. I have seen many wild animals inspecting these scratch marks and smelling the area with the greatest deliberation. My dogs scratch the turf vigorously before setting off on the morning walk, or when they sight a strange dog. They do not inspect such marks, however, and I suspect that domestication has robbed this action of its significance. Visiting cards play a major role in the wild. The urinating action of a bitch, for example, does have a purpose. A bitch in season will leave her scent every few yards; the obvious reason being to advertise her condition.

By far the most important method of communication, in the context of our relationship with dogs, is postural signalling. This covers a wide range of behaviour – facial expression, licking, mouthing, hackle raising, tail positioning, submissive rolling over, etc, and the dog may resort to two or more of these postures simultaneously. These gestures will start to appear in a litter just after weaning – the most obvious being the establishment of a pattern of dominance: the mother may be a passive onlooker or she may interfere. Gesturing, within the pattern of play, and mock fighting will continue as the pups grow and meet other dogs. This is a vital aspect of development and an orphaned pup, or one deprived of this phase of education, may not relate to other dogs later in life.

Dogs communicate fear, suspicion, submission, anxiety, gaiety, good humour, etc, and the trainer must understand this complex of

A Rottweiler goes through a hoop at the Austrian Military School (Photo: courtesy Herr Ringer)

behaviours and respond. Konrad Lorenz, with his experienced eye and his empathy with dogs, has been able to explain what each facial expression means. Eberhard Trumler reproduced the sense of these expressions in pictorial form. The degrees of intensity indicating fear, fight, and so on, may be seen in his series of nine sketches of dingo heads, each depicting a particular frame of mind. Rudolph Schenkel – *Expressive Studies of Wolves* – made a study of these expressions of mood in wolves. Each mood is indicated by a range of facial expressions. I agree with Trumler that facial expression in dogs, while providing a useful adjunct in expressing mood, does not, however, compare with the body which is a more used and useful tool in the manifestation of mood and emotion.

The science of ethology – interpreting behaviour by studying the anatomy of gesture – introduces a refreshingly new understanding of behaviour and, interpreted by Lorenz, the father of the movement, it brings the subject within the bounds of a layman's comprehension.

The first lesson a pup learns is to come to the sound of our voices, thus a close relationship between the litter and ourselves is established

Training a Rottweiler in attack work must *be done by experts as is demonstrated by Bill Hoffman with Atlas. The pet companion has no need for such training – it will defend by instinct wthout risk of an attack in error* (Photo: courtesy Greg Hope)

even before the pups leave the whelping box. When they are about three weeks old, the pups are picked up, stroked gently and taught to associate this pleasant treatment with the sound of our voices. Within two or three days they learn to anticipate the sound of voices with this pleasant contact. At about five weeks, the pups are placed outside in the puppy yard and a call from the gate will bring them to us immediately, each pup looking to be picked up and fondled. This is the foundation on which a training programme can be built. Tone of voice and feel of hands can impart a very definite message, whether it is to reassure a nervous pup or restrain a boisterous one.

The same semi-hypnotic suggestion can be used to quieten a pup that is restive, or even get one to stay. Call the pup to you, place one hand on its chest, sit it down, and, with your other hand, stroke gently down its back saying 'stay, stay'. The pup, conscious of the voice and the mesmeric quality of the hand, will focus its attention on you and remain sitting. The same technique can be used when training a pup for the show ring. Stand the pup in the required stance, repeat the word 'stay' and, at the same time, run the hand gently along the flank.

When the pups are five weeks old, we take them for walks. 'Come' can be practised from various distances, the important action being the fuss that greets them when they come. Each pup is taken out individually. The stay and come can be practised from varying distances. If the pup comes happily to you at this stage, the recall, at a much later stage, will be learnt without difficulty. This phase of training does not involve the use of a lead and is only play learning.

The other aid to establishing a good working relationship is conversation. When out walking with pups and dogs, I talk to them continually, drawing their attention to birds, animals and even flowers. On my call 'look at this', they will come immediately to look. This is training by tone of voice. My voice will be slightly raised and attention-getting in its excited urgency. Curiosity to see what all the fuss is about will bring the pup running. Action or interest, in relation to dogs, must be genuine. They are quick to detect any action that is simulated.

The use of food as a training aid has been debated by experts, but I have not seen conclusive evidence to support either view. Bribery, no matter what form it takes, is repugnant, but it is better than beating! Praise is a subtle form of bribery and dogs – as well as human beings – are receptive to praise and attention, especially if augmented by fulsome and overt manifestation. Reward and punishment, the carrot and the stick, have been used in various guises ever since man first organised others to work for him.

A start can be made in some of the obedience exercises by using a piece of cooked liver or cheese. It can be overdone, however, and

Swed Ch Tell v Hackerbrücke seen with opera star Per Grunden when they appeared in a film. Tell was imported into Sweden by Mrs Hyden and lived until he was fourteen (Photo: courtesy Mrs Hyden)

become a case of payment by result. It should be offered to get the message across rather than as a reward for doing something. Baiting in the ring, unless done with subtlety, can be counter-productive. A judge, wishing to assess expression, sometimes sees only the side of the head as the dog searches avidly for the titbit!

A facet of training that has received some attention recently is the use of such training aids as spiked collars, electronic collars, transistorised prods and similar items. Although I have seen these aids I have not used them; nor do I intend to try. They are, in some countries, such as the UK, banned in any case. These aids are for extreme cases. Circumstances may arise to warrant this treatment. When they do, treatment should be applied carefully by an experienced specialist. In my view, the necessity for this extreme measure should never occur with a dog reared with affection and respect. The Hush Dawg is an electronic collar advertised widely in some countries as a sure-fire cure for inveterate barkers. Its use merely treats the effect, and does not cure the problem.

Michael Tucker, a most experienced trainer, and a man who has thought deeply on the subject, told me about experiences he has had with regard to these aids. One concerned a German shepherd in his class, who had a reputation for killing cats. He was fitted out with an electronic collar which 'hit' him at precisely the right moment. The dog was cured after one lesson, the cure being permanent. News of this miracle got about and another German shepherd, with the same problem, was produced. He was also subjected to the cure and it appeared to be satisfactory. However, the owner found, on removal of the collar, that the habit had not been eliminated. The dog killed another cat. More experiments followed and the conclusion reached was that the dog behaved when he wore the collar, but misbehaved when wearing an ordinary one. A smart trainer like Michael soon had the answer. He made up a collar that looked like the electronic one, the only difference being that it was not live. No one could tell the difference, no one that is except the dog who could distinguish easily between the real collar and the mock-up: some dogs are smarter than others!

A question that is frequently asked is, 'How can we stop this or that bad habit?' The short, simple and obvious answer is, 'Do not let it develop.' This is of no immediate use, of course, but the answer may be remembered in the future. An appreciation of this subject will be helped by reference to Marais's two simple phrases, phyletic memory and causal memory. Behaviour induced by phyletic memory is unconscious and difficult to influence. The Rottweiler that barks at passing strangers fulfils a natural function and is not conscious of giving offence. It is better, in these cases, to remove the cause rather than treat the effect.

Behaviour evoked by causal memory, on the other hand, can be influenced. The dog that jumps up at the dining table expecting a piece of food has learned this behaviour; it was probably encouraged as a pup. Its action is conscious and can be stopped. Moreover, the means to do this can be firm, extending to harshness if necessary, although it would be quite unfair to use extreme means in the first instance.

Another question is, 'How do I train my pup?' My first dog, Chab, developed with little guidance from me. This was partly because I did not know enough about the subject and partly because I did not want to mould him into a shape considered suitable by me. I encouraged him to express himself, watched his development with interest and gave him my affection and confidence. Chab, on reflection, taught me more about dogs and gave me more satisfaction than any dog I have ever owned.

Intelligence, if my definition is accepted, is a prerequisite in the selection of a working dog. Curiosity also rates very highly on my list, and I find that these two qualities usually appear together. Mental and physical energy also come within this group of important characteristics. Aggressive energy, and I use the word aggressive in its fullest sense, is another important quality, and it is usually linked with that of alpha. Alpha is easy to recognise, but its definition is too simplistic. It is not a static or permanent quality. It is assumed by different dogs and bitches in the kennel at various times and in certain circumstances; it is affected by age, physique, pregnancy and parenthood. No one animal is permanently alpha, and the wearing of the mantle is by mutual consent; it is rarely contested except, perhaps, when a new animal arrives on the scene.

The final requirement in the selection of a dog, is the relationship reflecting confidence, trust and communication, that flows both ways. The astute reader may exclaim that these qualities cannot be evaluated in a pup. It is more a matter, however, of being the right person, rather than a question of selection, and the breeder, having studied the litter, is in a position to match the prospective purchaser with the right pup. There are few bad dogs, but many careless and unthinking trainers.

Before learning a little about dogs from my association with Rottweilers, my treatment of the species *Canis familiaris* left much to be desired. My conversation with dogs was entirely one-sided and confined to commands; gesture was limited to the occasional pat. I was fond of my dogs but my treatment, though kindly, was paternal and patronising. Rottweilers have provided a new dimension in my understanding. Late in life, like Silas Marner, my miserly approach to communion has given way to an inverse generosity. The friends of my youth, eavesdropping on my conversation with dogs, would entertain serious misgivings about my sanity. However, greater men than I were unashamed of this conversation and my defence would rest on a quotation from Kipling.

> There was never a king like Solomon,
> Not since the world began,
> Yet Solomon talked to a butterfly
> As a man would talk to a man.

Aus Ch Auslese Beaujolais was the first Australian BIS all breeds Rottweiler. The trophy donor's wife had just died and Beau, sensitive to the atmosphere, offered his condolences – he had never before reacted to someone in this way and it illustrates just what sensitivity the breed has (Photo: Max Neilson)

Glossary of German Terms

Breeding Terms

Besitzer	Owner
Gekört	Qualified for breeding for two years
Gekört EzA	Qualified for the rest of breeding life
Körung	Breeding qualification test. Dogs that pass are approved for two years and the pedigree endorsed
Zucht	Breeding
Zuchtbuch	Stud book
Zuchter	Breeder
Zuchttauglich	Suitable for breeding
Zuchttauglichkeitsprüfung (ZTP)	Breed test of suitability. All dogs must pass before breeding approval is given

Breed Categories

Kör-und Leistungszucht	The highest category where parents are qualified and all grandparents have working degrees (pink pedigree)
Körzucht	Both parents are qualified (pink pedigree)
Leistungszucht	Both parents and all four grandparents have working degrees (pink pedigree)
Gebrauchshundzucht	Both parents have a working degree (white pedigree)
Einfache Zucht	Simple breeding. Only one parent has a working degree (white pedigree)

HD Categories

HD–	Normal hips. *Körfähig*

HD+/−	Minor changes. *Körfähig*
HD+	HD present but mild. Breeding is restricted to certain partners and dogs with this grading are not eligible for the *Körung* *Zuchttauglich*
HD++	HD present. Breeding forbidden. *Zuchtverbot*
HD+++	HD severe. Breeding forbidden. *Zuchtverbot*
CACIB	*Certificat d'aptitude au Championat Internationale de Beauté.* Dog/bitch winning a beauty show where CACIBs are awarded. Working qualifications are not necessary

Working Degrees:*Schutzhundprüfung*

SchH 1, 11, 111	Awarded when a dog qualifies in the trial. A dog need pass only once in each class
IPO 1, 11, 111	*Internationale Prüfungsordung.* Equivalent title to SchH awarded by the FCI
FH	*Fahrtenhund.* Tracking degree
PDH	*Polizeidiensthund.* Police service dog degree
MIL DH	*Militärdiensthund.* Military Service dog degree
AD	*Ausdauer Prüfung.* Endurance Test. Dogs offering for the *Körung* must pass this test
BLH	*Blindenführhund.* Guide dog for the blind

Titles

Sieger/Siegerin	Best male/female of show
Bundessieger/Bundessiegerin	National champions. Contested annually in October

Klubsieger/Klubsiegerin	Champions at ADRK annual show
	Contested in August/September
Europa Sieger/Siegerin	European title conducted in April
Weltsieger	World titles held generally in March
Leistungssieger/siegerin	Working trial winner conducted by the ADRK in conjunction with the club show
Leistungssiegerprüfung	Working trials championship
CD	Companion dog. The first obedience degree
CDX	Companion dog excellent. The second degree
UD	Utility dog. The third degree
TD	Tracking dog
TDX	Tracking dog excellent. The titles are awarded to dogs that pass each test three times under different judges

Show Classes

Jüngstenklasse	Nine-twelve months
Jugendklasse	Twelve-eighteen months
Junghundklasse	Eighteen-twenty-four months
Offene Klasse	Over two years without working qualifications
Gebrauchshundklasse	Open to dogs with working qualifications, the *Sieger* and *Siegerin* come from this class
Siegerklasse	Open only to *Siegers*, recently introduced
Zuchtgruppen	Progeny group from one kennel

Show Gradings

Gut (G)	Good. No serious form faults and no working faults
Sehr Gut (SG)	Very good. No working faults. Dogs that correspond to the standard with only minor variations

Vorzüglich   Excellent. The highest grading
given to animals that conform to
the standard, move well and show
true Rottweiler character and
temperament

Rottweiler Clubs Worldwide

UK: Elizabeth Harrap, Pangora, Crays Pond, Goring Heath, nr Reading

USA: Jolain Engel, 10800 SW 67 Court Miami, Florida, 33457

Germany: Herr Klaus Altpeter, Geisberg 14, 6601 Bischmisheim

Italy: Dr Lensi, Via Griffini 28, Pavia 2700

Finland: J. A. U. Yrjölä, Pajamaentie 70 33, 00360 Helsinki 36

Sweden: Gerd Hyden, Vinterbrinksvagen 17, 13300 Saltsjobaden

Denmark: Aage Christensen, St. Merlose E, Bjarne Olsen Hundslundveg 7, 2770 Kastrup

Norway: Tenja Johansen, Postboks 6732, St. Olavsplass Oslo 1

Australia: Jenny Woodman, 149 Bastings Street, Northcote 3072 (Victoria)

Rottweiler Registrations

Year	Germany*	UK*	USA*	Australia*	South Africa*
1935	797	–	18	–	–
1975	955	211	952	313	–
1976	1,396	332	1,406	488	–
1977	1,325	608	1,878	683	–
1978	1,213	921	2,439	744	–
1979	1,546	1,033	3,286	902	2,429
1980	1,559	1,298	4,701	962	3,313
1981	1,679	1,641	6,524	1,285	3,068
1982	1,768	2,466	9,269	1,594	4,269
1983	1,995	3,526	13,265	2,073	4,740
1984	2,067	4,690	17,193	2,751	3,993

*Extracted from stud books. Total number registered 1935–84 14547

*Kindly made available by the AKC Library NY.

*From secretaries of State Clubs. Each State registers its own pups.

*From kennel Union Gazette NB Year opens 1 September ends 31 August

Bibliography

ADRK *The Rottweiler in Word and Picture* (Stuttgart, 1926)

  The Regulations Regarding Breeding Matters for the Rottweiler Dog Paul Dorny˙ (Essen, 1970)

  Forty Years of Stud Book Recorded (Stuttgart, 1947) Translated by Thomas K. Aalund, New York. 100 copies printed in English by the Colonial Rottweiler Club, 1968

  Special Publication for the Fiftieth Anniversary of the Allgemeiner Deutscher Rottweiler Klub (Stuttgart, 1957) Published in English by the Colonial Rottweiler Club (1969), translated by Mr and Mrs Frederick Zopp

Battaglia, Dr Carmello L. *Dog Genetics* TFH Publications Inc (New Jersey, 1978)

Bresson, H. *Rottweiler* J. FR. Clausens (Copenhagen, 1972) Translated by A. Pederson for the Rottweiler Club, England (Powderhorn Press, 1975)

Fox, Michael W. *Understanding Your Dog* Coward McCann and Geoghegan (New York, 1972), Blond and Briggs (London, 1974)

Frankling, Eleanor *Practical Dog Breeding and Genetics* Popular Dogs Publishing Co (London, 1961)

Freeman, Muriel *The Complete Rottweiler* Howell (New York, 1984)

Gould, Jean *All About Dog Breeding for Quality and Soundness* Pelham Books (London, 1978)

Harmar, Hilary *Dogs and How to Breed Them* John Gifford (London, 1968)

Hass, Hans *The Human Animal* Translated from the German by J. Maxwell Brownjohn. Hodder and Stoughton (London, 1970)

Hauser, Gayelord *Look Younger, Live Longer* Faber and Faber (London, 1951)

Korn, Hans *Der Rottweiler ADRK 1939* Translated from the German by John MacPhail. The Colonial Rottweiler Club (1968)

Levy, Juliette De Bairacli *The Complete Herbal Book for the Dog* Faber and Faber (London, 1955)

Lorenz, Konrad *Man Meets Dog* Translated by Marjorie Kerr Wilson Methuen (London, 1954)

Marais, Eugene *The Soul of the White Ant* Anthony Blond (London, 1969)

— *The Soul of the Ape* Jonathon Cape and Anthony Blond (London, 1971)

Mowat, Farley *Never Cry Wolf* Dell Publishing Co (New York, 1963)

Page Elliot, Rachel *Dog Steps* Howell (New York, 1973)

Pfaffenberger, Clarence *The New Knowledge of Dog Behaviour* Howell (New York, 1963)

Schänzle, Manfred *Studies in the Breed History of the Rottweiler* (Stuttgart, 1967) Translated by John MacPhail. The Colonial Rottweiler Club/ the Medallion Rottweiler Club (1969)

Sluckin, W. *Early Learning in Man and Animal*, (Allen and Unwin) (London, 1970)

Smythe, R. H. *The Breeding and Rearing of Dogs* Popular Dogs (London, 1969)

Trumler, Eberhard *Understanding Your Dog* Translated by Richard Barry. Faber and Faber (London, 1973)

Acknowledgements

I have always had the greatest respect for the breeding principles and practices of the ADRK and I have been privileged to be guided by two people who, in the last twenty years, have had the greatest influence both on the breed and the ADRK. The late Friederich Berger, and particularly Marieanne Bruns, who has corresponded for fifteen years, sent me hundreds of photographs and articles and helped so patiently with all my queries. I shall always be in their debt. I am grateful to Joan Wheatcroft, who has such a keen appreciation of the breed, for her help, and to Isobel Morrison, who recognised a Rottweiler in England fifteen years before the first one was registered, also Mary Macphail who sent me pedigrees of some of the early English imports. My thanks to Muriel Freeman, Barbara Hoard, Marthajo Rademacker and Dorothea Gruenerwald for information on the American scene, to Carla Lensi for many hours of fruitful discussion; to Dolf Ringer for explaining so much and to Rotraut Michels for her help over the years. I appreciate the kindness of my 'personal' translator, Geoff Allport, who was available for translation at all times in spite of his duties as a school principal. My thanks go to Gerd and Sven Hyden for Scandinavian details; Dr Regula Frei-Stolba of Bern University for details of the Alpine passes; Dr Hecht, archivist of Rottweil, for his help on the history of the city; to the secretaries of the canine associations in Australia for their help with registrations; and particularly to Roberta Vesley, AKC Library Director, who gave me two days of her valuable time. My grateful thanks to the breeders and judges around the world who have helped me to gain knowledge of the breed. My thanks to all the people who sent photographs, and a special thank you to Dennis Kelsey-Wood who commissioned me to write the book in 1979 and who helped with his advice in editing the copy down to its present length.

Finally I must thank my wife who has played a major role helping with typing, drawings, corrections, advice and criticism and especially for her support and encouragement without which the book could not have been written.

Index

LLS